Ways of Knowing in Science Series
RICHARD DUSCHL, SERIES EDITOR

ADVISORY BOARD: Charles W. Anderson, Nancy Brickhouse, Rosalind Driver,
Eleanor Duckworth, Peter Fensham, William Kyle,
Roy Pea, Edward Silver, Russell Yeany

Reforming Science Education:
Social Perspectives and Personal Reflections
Rodger W. Bybee

STS Education: International Perspectives on Reform
Joan Solomon and Glen Aikenhead, Editors

What Children Bring to Light:
A Constructivist Perspective on Children's Learning in Science
Bonnie Shapiro

What Children Bring to Light

A Constructivist Perspective
on Children's Learning in Science

Bonnie L. Shapiro

Teachers College, Columbia University
New York and London

Published by Teachers College Press, 1234 Amsterdam Avenue New York, NY 10027

Library of Congress Cataloging-in-Publication Data

Shapiro, Bonnie L.
    What children bring to light : a constructivist perspective on children's learning in science / Bonnie L. Shapiro.
        p.   cm.—(Ways of knowing in science series)
    Includes bibliographical references and index.
    ISBN 0-8077-3376-8 (cloth : acid-free paper).—
    ISBN 0-8077-3375-X (pbk. : acid-free paper)
    1. Science—Study and teaching (Elementary)—United States.   2. Constructivism (Education)—United States.   I. Title.   II. Series.
LB1585.3.S53   1994
372.3'5'044—dc20   94-20208

ISBN   0-8077-3375-X (paper)
ISBN   0-8077-3376-8 (cloth)

Printed on acid-free paper

Manufactured in the United States of Ameirca

01   00   99   98   97   96   95   94   8   7   6   5   4   3   2   1

To those devoted to the love of learning,
who delight in knowledge,
and who value the
process of coming to real understanding.

Contents

Acknowledgments   xi

Introduction   **xiii**
Personal Meaning and Public Knowledge: A New View
of Knowledge Acquisition in Science Learning
A New View of Knowledge and Knowledge Acquisition   xiv
The Importance of Understanding Children's
   Thoughts and Feelings About Science Learning   xvi
The Organization of the Book   xvii
The Selection of Light as a Topic of Study   xviii
Listening as the Organizing Structure of the Study   xix

PART I—CONSTRUCTIVISM AND SCIENCE LEARNING:
A GUIDE TO SENSITIVE LISTENING

Chapter 1   **3**
Beginning a Study of Children's
Knowledge Construction in Science
The Meaning and Challenge of the Constructivist Perspective   3
Constructivism and Evolving Ideas About Human Knowledge   4
Constructivism and Conceptual Change: Torn Between Two Positions   8
Constructivist Ideas in Educational Thought   10
Finding Personal Construct Theory   10
With Children in Classrooms: Toward a Study of Learning   11
The Need for a Study Focusing on Children's Learning in Action   12
The Need for an Alternative Research Approach   17

Chapter 2   **19**
The Learner Constructs Meaning:
Research on Children's Learning in Science
Examining the Alternative Frameworks Literature   19
Research on Children's Ideas About the Nature of Light   22
The Impact of Alternative Frameworks Research
  on Educational Practice   31
In Summary: The Need for a New Research Approach
  and Insights into the Processes of Learning   32

Chapter 3   **33**
The Importance of a Perspective on Language in
Science Learning
Language and the Construction of Meaning   33
Personal Construct Theory: A Guide to Careful Listening   36
Becoming Acquainted with the Children   38
Another Type of Conversation:
    The Use of Repertory Grid Conversations   40
An Introduction to Part II: The Case Reports   43

PART II—THE CASE REPORTS: CHANGING THE
WAYS WE LISTEN TO ONE ANOTHER

Chapter 4   **47**
Donnie: The Communicator—A Deep
Personal Involvement in Learning
Thoughts and Feelings About Learning School Science   47
Donnie's Ideas About the Nature of Light Prior to the Light Unit   51
Organization of Donnie's Case Report
    Using Personal Construct Themes   57

Chapter 5   **76**
Mark: The Boy of Ideas—An Intellectual Orientation
to Science Learning
Thoughts and Feelings About Learning School Science   76
Mark's Ideas About the Nature of Light Prior to the Light Unit   79
Organization of Mark's Case Report
    Using Personal Construct Themes   82

Chapter 6   **93**
Martin: The Tinkerer—The Enjoyment of Physical
Involvement with Science Materials
Thoughts and Feelings About Learning School Science   93
Martin's Ideas About the Nature of Light Prior to the Light Unit   94
Organization of Martin's Case Report
    Using Personal Construct Themes   97

Chapter 7   **111**
Melody: The Social Butterfly—An Aesthetic-Social
Orientation to Science Learning
Thoughts and Feelings About Learning School Science   111
Melody's Ideas About the Nature of Light Prior to the Light Unit   114
Organization of Melody's Case Report Using Personal
    Construct Themes   116

Chapter 8   130
Yasmin: The Student—A Dedication to High Achievement
Thoughts and Feelings About Learning School Science   130
Yasmin's Ideas About the Nature of Light Prior to the Light Unit   132
Organization of Yasmin's Case Report
  Using Personal Construct Themes   135

Chapter 9   143
**Pierre: The Artist—Sheer Delight in the Details of
Natural History**
Thoughts and Feelings About Learning School Science   145
Pierre's Ideas About the Nature of Light Prior to the Light Unit   146
Organization of Pierre's Case Report
  Using Personal Construct Themes   148

PART III—IMPLICATIONS: THE DEEPER MEANING
OF LISTENING

Chapter 10   161
**Personal Orientation to Science Learning:
An Ecological Perspective on Knowledge Integration**
The Idea of a Personal Orientation to Science Learning   161
Revisiting the Case Studies with Personal Orientation Themes   162

Chapter 11   181
**Developing Teaching Approaches That Build
on Learners' Ideas and Actions in Science**
Key Assumptions of a Knowledge Construction
  Perspective on Science Learning   181
Learning to Use What We Know
  About Children and Science Learning   182
Opportunities for Communication and Reflection
  on the Learning Process   189

Epilogue   200
Toward Science Learning with the Psyche Left In
The Importance of the Personal   200

References   205
Index   213
About the Author   219

Acknowledgments

This book is about learning to listen in new and deeper ways to children. In many ways, I learned about listening by being so thoughtfully listened to as I undertook the journey of this research. I talked not only with the children in this project but with wonderful people whose work and thought inspired and encouraged me. When I was deeply involved in this study, I visited with scholars from all over the world whose works I had read, or whose wisdom I valued, to discuss some of the dilemmas and conundrums of engaging in this project. I was greatly rewarded in these conversations. I found that for many, nothing could be sweeter than to discuss new ways of thinking about science learning. I realize even more now how precious are the hours we spend in conversation with one another. The demands of academic life make such time very rare. I recall the generous gift of my colleagues' time whenever a bright student or a teacher pops into my office and asks for "just a few moments" to chat over an idea, just when I'm in the middle of a letter of recommendation or a report that is due. I realize how important it is to make the time to share ideas, but even more, how important it is to truly listen.

Though I could never begin to thank everyone, I'd like to acknowledge the generous discussion and encouragement of people who always took the time, time that none had—Glen Aikenhead, Joan Bliss, Bob Carlisle, David Dillon, Rosalind Driver, Gaalen Erickson, Peter Fensham, David Fisher, Jim Gallagher, Bob Gowin, David Kirby, Dick Konicek, John Leach, Margaret McNay, Joe Novak, Maureen Pope, Daiyo Sawada, Wilf Schmidt, Alan Shapiro, Clive Sutton, and Gordon Watson. I would like to give a special thank-you to the teacher in the study, Mr. Ryan, who allowed me to be a constant presence in his classroom during the project, and to Kendra Grabatin and Beth Vanner for their ever cheerful and invaluable help. I would like to express appreciation for the gift of time provided by a Killam Resident Fellowship granted by the University of Calgary and the research resources provided through a Canadian Social Sciences and Humanities Research Grant. I would also like to thank my own students for sharing their ideas and thoughts about this work. Most of all, I would like to thank the children in the study, whose thoughts and feelings about science learning constitute the heart of this book and who allowed me, a stranger, into their childhood and adolescent years of growth and thinking about light and science, life and learning. Donnie, Mark, Martin, Melody, Yasmin, and Pierre—I have learned the most from you.

INTRODUCTION

Personal Meaning and Public Knowledge: A New View of Knowledge Acquisition in Science Learning

When I heard the learn'd astronomer,
When the proofs, the figures were ranged in columns before me,
When I sitting, heard the astronomer where he lectured with much
    applause in the lecture room
How soon unaccountable I became tired and sick
Till rising and gliding out I wander'd off by myself,
In the mystical moist night-air, and from time to time,
Look'd up in perfect silence at the stars.
                    —Walt Whitman, *Leaves of Grass* (p. 86)

Walt Whitman's poem exemplifies a dilemma and a concern for science educators. Here is an individual who is attracted to a lecture that promises insight into the mysteries of the universe. Yet, when confronted with the instructor's systematic presentation of proofs and figures he becomes bored and leaves. And in so doing, we feel his profound sense of relief. What teacher would not be concerned about this individual's leave-taking? Whitman brings to our attention the fact that the ways that science is portrayed in learning settings can crush the initial joy and wonder that prompts the desire to learn about natural phenomena. However, if we are willing to listen carefully to this individual's experience, rather than condemn it as a weakness, it may increase our understanding of how it is that Whitman's experience turned him away from formal science study. When we teach science, we are asking learners to accept something more than scientifically verified ideas. We are asking them to accept initiation into a particular way of seeing and explaining the world and to step around their own meanings and personal understandings of phenomena into a world of publicly accepted ideas. In school science learning, the child develops not only an understanding of ideas about the natural world, but a conception of the nature of science knowledge. Furthermore, the child develops a conception of self as a science learner that ranges from a sense of great competence to one of despair or even total failure.

A NEW VIEW OF KNOWLEDGE AND KNOWLEDGE ACQUISITION

The primary purpose of this book is to help teachers develop new insight into the learner's experience of science learning in school settings. The majority of research studies in science learning focus on the identification of learners' ideas about phenomena, sometimes suggesting interventions to change learners' ideas to the ways that scientists view things. The focus is often limited to the cognitive. In this study, I begin with the personal experience of the learner, taking the position that we must understand learning not only as a cognitive experience but also as an emotional, personal, social, and cultural one. To construct new ideas means to take action based on beliefs about what one is doing when one is learning science. This book is written to give high status to these dimensions that are missing from the learning experience in science and that permeate all subject-matter learning.

The second major goal of this work is to explore what is meant by a constructivist perspective and to clarify its use in the context of this study. It is important to do so because of the many meanings attributed to constructivism in current educational literature. We begin this exploration by considering the historical and philosophical foundations of knowledge development. The constructivist perspective stands in contrast to the dominant paradigm in science education, the traditional or objectivist paradigm. Instead of a focus only on learner outcomes, its basic premise is that approaches to teaching and learning should begin by understanding what it is that learners *bring* to learning. The question, "How is meaning constructed?" permeates the constructivist position. In this effort, we need to identify the ideas students hold prior to the study of a particular topic, but in the context of personal, social, and cultural influences that impact the learning setting.

A constructivist perspective on teaching and learning departs from traditional views of many features of the teaching-learning dialogue: views of science, the role of the learner, learning, the role of the teacher, teaching, and the organization of curriculum materials. The constructivist perspective emphasizes the active agency of the learner, asserting that each learner builds or constructs his or her reality. It suggests how educators might enhance that agency. Because of its views on knowledge construction, it also is a way of challenging ideas about the nature of the knowledge we expect to be acquired by learners and the nature of the environment we create for learning.

The basic premises of constructivism used in this work are exemplified in the work of a wide range of educators and philosophers (Dewey, 1913; Gilbert & Watts, 1983; Magoon, 1977; Pope, 1982; von Glasersfeld, 1986), but of particular value is the personal construct psychology of George Kelly. Kelly argued that we might best understand how an individual views his or her experience by seeing the person not as a set of drives or responses acting upon the universe, but as a *person* who views the world in his or her own unique manner and whose view has individual integrity. The dynamic argument of this viewpoint for educational research and practice is that in planning for teaching, recognition and high priority should be given to students' ideas, language, beliefs, and expectations, as these personal meanings are the bases upon which students create meaning during instruction. Personal Construct Theory was invented by Kelly (1955) as an attempt to integrate a theory of personality with a theory of knowledge. Kelly considered each person to be an "intuitive scientist," formulating hypotheses about the world, collecting data that confirm or disconfirm these hypotheses, and then altering his or her conception of the world to include this new information. In this way, every person operates in a manner similar to the scientist.

The teacher who works with a constructivist perspective becomes a researcher in the classroom, a student of teaching and learning, asking such questions as: What do students know about this topic? How are students thinking about what I am presenting to them? How do they come to think this way? How can they learn to value new ways of thinking about things? How can I help them to grasp scientific ideas? Why do learners feel uncomfortable with science? These questions are of interest to a wide audience: curriculum writers, teachers, researchers, students, parents—anyone interested in thinking seriously about how to enhance students' ability to put ideas together and to be successful learners.

But is constructivism nothing more than good teaching? And what teacher is not interested in helping students learn in meaningful and positive ways? In the real world of classroom teaching, however, many dedicated teachers fail to achieve two important goals:

1. Effectively taking into account, the learner and his or her ideas and feelings about learning in organizing for teaching.
2. Inviting the personal participation of students in learning, thus engaging them in deep and involving learning experiences.

This book is intended to be a useful resource for those interested in rethinking their work with children to more effectively accomplish both of these goals. The title, "What Children Bring to Light," has several meanings. First, it is an attempt to refocus attention on the prior ideas, experiences, and habits of thinking—what it is that children bring with them to the school learning environment. The title also reveals that the book is a study of children learning about the topic, light. And finally, the title suggests the illuminating value of the insights to be gained through looking at learning from the child's perspective.

THE IMPORTANCE OF UNDERSTANDING CHILDREN'S THOUGHTS AND FEELINGS ABOUT SCIENCE LEARNING

Elementary School and the Initiation of Students to Science Learning

The elementary school years are a crucial time for the development of positive feelings about science learning. The ways that students think about learning science influence their interest in persisting in science study. Students' attitudes may contribute to feelings of pleasure and confidence or inadequacy, frustration, or even alienation from the experience. There is widespread consensus that the elementary grades are pivotal years for the development of an interest in science.

Perhaps one of the greatest problems in science teaching is that we ask far too much by asking learners to accept the collective efforts of the entire history of humankind to explain the world. Throughout the elementary school program, for example, we ask students to verify knowledge using the senses—seeing, hearing, tasting, touching, smelling. Suddenly, at around the age of 11 or 12, we ask learners to put aside their own ideas and ways of validating information. They must simply accept what they are told.

In addition, there is a crisis in science education. Students are turning away from science as a potential career choice, as an opportunity to gain insight into daily personal and political decisions, and as an area of study for the sheer intellectual adventure of trying to understand the mystery of the natural world. In the United States, fewer than 10% of precollege students profess a genuine interest in science, with only approximately a quarter of these students actually going on to pursue careers as professional scientists (National Center for Educational Statistics, cited by Hurd, 1984). Hurd (1984) concluded that high school students have generally not been empowered with the ability to identify and reasonably interpret a science- or technology-based personal or social problem. The National Assessment in Science Project (Hueftle, Rakow, & Welch, 1983) stated that by the time U. S. students leave tenth grade, half of them have already finished the major portion of their science education. Though not everyone will become a scientist, an understanding of the basic ideas of science is essential for anyone living in our world because we all make daily decisions that may enlighten or burden society, depending on our ability to use information effectively.

The Neglect of the Existential World of the Learner

For many children, the experience of learning science is filled with confusion and difficulty. Few research studies attempt to give insight into the meaning and value students attribute to science study. Little attention is given to such questions as, What do young learners find interesting in their studies? What keeps them from accepting some scientific explanations? What resources and strategies do they use for learning? Why is it that so many seem to reject some ideas in science, or science study altogether? Instead, it seems that in the name of improvement of science instruction, the complaint most often made is that students do not acquire a sufficient amount of content information. Interest in the number of specific facts students possess has often overshadowed concern for the child's interest in and understanding of the subject matter.

Pope (1982) writes, "Emphasis upon the person-as-meaning-maker is a dominant theme in educational theorizing, but in practice, the phenomenological world of the learner is often neglected" (p. 8). Echoing Pope, Brophy (1982) asserts that, "For the most part, educational researchers have considered students only as objects of teacher activity." He states further: "A complete account of classroom events will have to include, besides information about teacher behavior and its long-term effects, information about what students are doing in classrooms and how these activities affect their perceptions, knowledge and beliefs" (p. 519). Though much has been said of the value of collecting information of the latter type, little research in education has actually been undertaken to document and convey such insight. This book is an attempt to address this problem and fill this gap. It is a study of children learning science in the natural classroom setting.

It has likely been my own experience as a classroom teacher that led me to be concerned not just with the ideas learners hold about phenomena, but with their evolving views about what they believe they are doing as they learn science. The nature of this picture is organic—it is a complex of interweaving factors that contribute to the child's understanding of science and science learning. In order to discover and study the important factors involved in student learning in science, I developed an approach for study of and reflection on the children's developing ideas and approaches to science learning. In this book I share not only the results of my research, but also the ways in which I have constructed this work. I share my assumptions and the dilemmas that had to be resolved in the process of conducting the project.

THE ORGANIZATION OF THE BOOK

What Children Bring to Light is arranged in three parts. Part I, "Constructivism and Science Learning: A Guide to Sensitive Listening," spans three chapters. Chapter 1 introduces the idea of constructivism and its development and value as an alternative to traditional views of knowledge and learning, and sets the stage for rethinking learning through reflection on explorations in several classroom settings with the intention of looking in fresh ways at what goes on in classrooms. In Chapter 2, I have given order and organization to the enormous literature of children's learning in science and review research on children's ideas about light as a background to the study. Chapter 3 is an introduction to the case studies presented in Part II, and presents my research approach, and is an attempt to demystify the use of such research tools as repertory grid technique.

Part II, "The Case Reports: Changing the Ways We Listen to One Another," contains Chapters 4 through 9 and is the heart of the study. Each chapter is a snapshot portrayal of individual students in the same classroom setting as they learn about the topic, light, in the fifth-grade classroom. The children's experiences involve much more than simple interactions with materials. The case reports identify patterns that constitute each individual's efforts to make meaning in science learning.

Part III, "Implications: The Deeper Meaning of Listening," includes Chapters 10 and 11. The case reports identify patterns in the ways that each person anticipates and constructs events in the science classroom. Features of these patterns are presented in Chapter 10 to be studied as an ecology of interweaving classroom features, called *personal orientation to science learning*. Chapter 11 summarizes the picture of science learning presented in this constructivist analysis and suggests how understanding knowledge and learning affects the role of the teacher in the creation of learning environments and opportunities that build on students' natural approaches and efforts. In the Epilogue, I further discuss the importance of the personal in a consideration of science learning. As I continue on a regular basis to talk with the children, I share some of the details of their lives at this writing.

THE SELECTION OF LIGHT AS A TOPIC OF STUDY

The topic, light, was selected primarily because as a pervasive aspect of daily experience it is familiar, yet is also a wonderful mystery and source of fascination. As a typical topic of study in the science classroom, it is filled with conceptual dilemmas for learners and teachers alike. It is fruitful ground for exploring some of the greatest conundrums of science teaching and learning.

Ideas about light behavior are some of the most difficult for learners to grasp. It represents one of the first encounters in science learning when the ideas of science cannot be personally experienced. For example the idea of light reflecting from an object is counterintuitive. Many children comment that it simply does not make sense. Children are taught from an early age to confirm findings by using the senses—sight, hearing, touch, taste, smell.

Suddenly they are asked to suspend or ignore this information and simply accept as true what they cannot see for themselves. It is important for the teacher to understand the challenge this represents for students and realize that simply providing students with the scientific conception is not sufficient. The ideas must be considered by the children to be rational explanations. Students must be convinced that the scientific conception is the best explanation for the phenomena observed.

LISTENING AS THE ORGANIZING STRUCTURE OF THE STUDY

In this study, the emphasis on *listening* powerfully characterizes the approach taken in working with the children in developing the case reports and is used in the organization of the case reports. It is used as the organizing principle of the main sections of the book because the entire study is an exploration of what may result when we learn to listen differently to one another. Conversation has been the main form of data gathering in the study. An attitude of "sensitive listening" was the essence of the research attitude and my approach to working with the children has been one of friendship and caring. Because reflection was accomplished *with* the children, the nature and quality of our relationship was crucial to the success of the study. As I became deeply involved in listening to, conversing with, and sharing ideas with the children, I became interested in the deeper meaning of the act of listening in the research. I thought about listening itself, what it means in authentic human encounter, and what it means in teaching and in educational research. In the process, I discovered that when I truly listen to another human being, I listen with many aspects of myself. As I listened to the children and as they listened to me, I became more aware of the ways that I gave each one my attention and how my manner invited the sharing of ideas and feelings. Was I listening as a caring friend, the elementary school teacher that I had been for so many years, or as an educational researcher? Real listening is accomplished at many levels of response. Even though we may not be speaking as we listen, the act of listening conveys a message to the person speaking with us, who hears our words but also notices the ways we listen. We listen with our eyes. We see the ways the person speaks with us—his or her stance, changing facial expressions, shifting on the chair, and movements toward or away from us. We hear pauses, sighs, perhaps a laugh. When we sense that someone is giving us their full attention, that there is a sincere interest in what we have to say, there is a tendency to open up to the listener, to share more of our true selves.

As I listened to the children in the study with the intention of understanding personal ideas in science learning, I found not only that I was hearing the child's words, but that each child was sharing with me, through behavior and ideas, his or her own personal efforts to understand in school science. The *strong and consistent pattern* of individual efforts to learn became the basis of the personal orientation framework. Each child's effort to learn took on a powerful new dignity and meaning. What seemed at first glance to be "wasting time" or "goofing off" became, upon reflection, more purposeful, more clearly an expression of the person's approach to science learning. Every child attempts to make sense of the world, each in a unique and personal manner. We need to listen to these approaches with a view of teaching that values these unique approaches.

In this introduction, I have argued that a new emphasis is needed in science education—a focus on understanding what children *bring* to the experience of science learning. Nothing could be more valuable to a teacher than to understand what students know and how to teach to that level of knowledge, but in the fast pace of the modern school day, and with ever-increasing class sizes, the time needed to access student ideas is beyond the means of the typical classroom teacher. It has been my experience in sharing the ideas presented in this book with graduate students, researchers, and classroom teachers that this work is valued as a source of new insight and rejuvenation. This book is for those who want to explore and know more but are not sure where to begin. I have attempted to produce a resource that presents a basic introduction to an area of research that has much to offer in the understanding of teaching and learning. The enormous amount of work in this field can be daunting and somewhat perplexing. This book is intended to be a beginning guide for the perplexed, not a how-to book. This work does not translate directly into a specific technique, for it is a philosophical position. Rather, this is a resource to stimulate thinking about knowledge and learning in classrooms. This book is intended to be a guide for those who would like to begin an exploration of the literature in this field, and who would like to consider the implications for creating constructivist teaching approaches and constructivist learning environments.

It is my hope that this book will help those involved in the enterprise of learning and teaching to enhance the joy of learning in science that comes from deep and personal interest and involvement. I hope that the ideas in this book provide renewal to teachers and rejuvenation in their thinking about their work with children.

PART I

CONSTRUCTIVISM
AND SCIENCE LEARNING:
A GUIDE TO SENSITIVE LISTENING

CHAPTER 1

Beginning a Study of Children's Knowledge Construction in Science

This book is about children's knowledge in science. In this chapter, I explore the meaning of the term "constructivism" and how this perspective on learning has influenced the development of a study of children's knowledge construction in science.

THE MEANING AND CHALLENGE OF THE CONSTRUCTIVIST PERSPECTIVE

There is recent interest in the descriptive and explanatory power of a "new" perspective on human knowledge, which has actually been a part of Western thought for some time and can be traced to the ancient Greek Skeptics (Fisher, 1992). Their philosophy was embodied in the questions they asked, such as, "How do we know what we know?" and "How can people claim to know what they say they do?" The constructivist perspective asks us to consider how it is that we know anything at all, and it presents a challenge to established, institutionalized beliefs. Many interest groups claim possession of certain knowledge or absolute truth. Among these are politicians, religious leaders, and, often, those in charge of the administration of curriculum programs! The Skeptics challenged such claims. Constructivist challenges represent a healthy questioning of personal and public knowledge.

The constructivist perspective challenges the dominant view of knowledge acquisition, objectivism. The objectivist view is built on the idea that reality exists independently of the observer and can be "discovered" through the use of a series of systematic steps to achieve verifiable facts about the external "real" world. Objectivism gives rise to a behavioral view of teaching and learning. In contrast, the constructivist perspective views knowledge as a form of mental representation, a construction of the human mind. Constructivism has been overshadowed by objectivism in Western thought. This is largely because objectivism lends itself to the implementation of mechanical processes and is therefore efficient and functional.

The constructivist perspective is a powerful framework for understanding how individuals organize experience and what they believe to be reality.

3

In the field of counseling psychology, constructivist practitioners take the position that individuals adopt the behaviors they do because doing so is a means of coping with their unique problems and life circumstances. Understanding the beliefs that guide individuals' behavior helps the counselor to advise the individual who wishes to move away from inappropriate attitudes and actions. Vital to the use of this approach is the view that it is the person, not the counselor, who *makes the decision* to change. The counselor acts as a guide to help the individual recognize the choices that can be made. In a similar way, educators encourage learners to make choices between a range of new ideas. The teacher who employs a constructivist approach becomes a researcher in the classroom and asks the same questions as the Skeptics: What do students already know about the topic I am presenting? How are students thinking about the material? How have they come to think this way? Because the constructivist approach involves asking such questions, it is also a way of challenging the nature of the knowledge to be acquired by learners and the ways it is best acquired.

CONSTRUCTIVISM AND EVOLVING IDEAS ABOUT HUMAN KNOWLEDGE

The creation of new knowledge in science and the learning of science are very different activities, yet there are helpful parallels in our understanding of student knowledge development. Scientific knowledge builds on the publicly accepted constructions of ideas about events and phenomena. Ideas about what constitutes knowledge have changed over centuries of work in the field. The following are descriptions of three major trends in this thought that have shaped thinking about knowledge and science.

Idea 1: Knowledge Is "Out There" Waiting to Be Discovered

This idea permeates the earliest descriptions of the nature of scientific activity, which were written by Francis Bacon. Bacon presented science as a process of "induction." He argued that by making systematic observations, the scientist ultimately arrives at general causes, and, thereby, truth. According to the Baconian view, scientific truths are waiting to be disclosed. His picture of science is one of a dispassionate, impersonal, totally objective knowledge-gathering activity. Bacon is considered to be the father of the "Scientific Method." His conception of working to arrive at truth and explanation in science rested on a straightforward prescription: Begin with a set of observations. Gradually build toward general statements or hypotheses. Link these to the observations. Test the truth of the hypotheses. Use the hypotheses in further examinations. Finally, arrive at statements or rules about the functioning of the universe.

This view breaks down under scrutiny. Observation is not a mere collection of fact upon fact. We make observations selectively. Whether we are conscious of it or not, there is always some basis for selecting those observations we value and those we disregard. Scientific knowledge is created with understandings of phenomena that cannot be divorced from a set of beliefs and knowledge. Each observation is made from a perspective that embodies assumptions and beliefs.

Idea 2: Science Knowledge Is Not "Waiting" to Be Discovered— It Is We Who Create Meanings

Toulmin (1960) pointed out that the development of ideas in geometrical optics, which had been called a "scientific discovery," was, on closer view, a new way of construing facts that had been established previously. No new facts were "generated." What was new was the way that the facts were construed or organized. As Toulmin noted, the true achievement of Galileo was that he "ventured to describe the world in a way that we do not experience it" (p. 97). Indeed, scientific insight is often a wholly unique and personal view held by a single individual that has led us to consider "old data" in a new way or has prompted the total reconstruction of an entire way of looking at a field of knowledge.

Knowledge is a construction. Valuing the idea that knowledge is constructed by the learner guides educators in the development of resources and in the presentation of experiences for learning that take into account the learner's role in making knowledge his or her own. If it is recognized that students participate in the construction of knowledge in science, then we are careful to create experiences and opportunities that enhance the learner's participation in the process.

Knowledge is socially constructed. "Public science knowledge," a phrase coined by Ziman (1978), refers to knowledge that is accepted by a community of scientists. This type of knowledge is presented at conferences and is conveyed in science textbooks. In the classroom, the learner is made aware of the public knowledge of science that he or she is challenged to accept. Scientific information is presented to students through experiences that recognize students' interest in the ideas and understandings of others. "Others" refers to scientists and fellow students who are also struggling to grasp new ideas. By valuing the social construction of knowledge, we emphasize both the importance of working together to develop science knowledge and of comparing one's ideas with others in such experiences as group work and class discussions.

Idea 3: We Hold Commitments Not Only to Ideas But to Entire Schemes of Understanding

Kuhn's (1970) introduction of the term, *paradigm*, helps us to think about how a new perspective emerges, and why it is that when new views are presented they are sometimes so tenaciously resisted. The term, paradigm, comes from the Greek word *paradigma*, meaning "pattern, example, or model." It is a scheme for understanding and explaining aspects of reality. Kuhn used the phrase "paradigm shift" to describe what happens when a powerful new insight allows explanation of events that previously were only partially explained.

One example comes from changes in the description of movement in the universe. For over 200 years, scientists relied on Newton's description of predictable mechanical forces, which were based on a series of related concepts: trajectories, gravity, and force. Newton's physics was completely dependent on a set of logical certainties. But as work continued, scientists found that new data did not fit the scheme. For example, it did not explain movement at the level of atoms and electrons. At the height of the quandary, Einstein proposed a new scheme, a different model of events that offered a new way of thinking about motion. It became known as the Special Theory of Relativity and resolved the dilemma by explaining large scale motion with implications at the level of electrons and atoms. It was a superior idea, a more all-encompassing framework. Einstein had transformed the old knowledge *and* the old knowledge order. The new framework predicted events more accurately. It reconciled the apparent data contradictions, taking into account ambiguity and uncertainty.

Thinkers such as Bertalanffy (1975), Bateson (1972, 1979), Capra (1982), Jantsch (1980), Briggs and Peat (1984), and Varela (1979) have promoted the idea that human beings create the world they perceive, and that what we notice is in accordance with the sort of world we believe we live in. When we teach science, we in fact ask students to consider changing their beliefs about the world they live in. For a person to change what Bateson referred to as "one's epistemological premises," there must be awareness that what is perceived as reality may not necessarily be "real," and that it may be useful to consider the value of a new knowledge perspective, a new knowledge paradigm.

Changing Views and School Science Learning

In their school study of science ideas, learners are often asked to simply accept the ideas of scientists. Often these ideas cannot be verified through students' personal experiences and at first may make no sense at all. If recognized scientists have had such difficulties explaining their views to colleagues, then educators should not be surprised to find learners struggling to grasp and articulate ideas that are so removed from their own experiences with things and events. Many research projects in science education have demonstrated that learners embark on the study of natural phenomena with ideas already having been formed through their own backgrounds and experiences (Driver, Guesne, & Tiberghien, 1985; Osborne & Freyberg, 1985) such ideas are often inconsistent with currently held scientific ideas about the nature of phenomena. The research also shows that it is a natural tendency of the learner under such circumstances to cling to his or her own view of events. This seems reasonable from a commonsense point of view, for when confronted with a confusing new explanation for events and phenomena, one's own ideas may continue to make sense, whereas the new ideas do not. In order to take on a new viewpoint, one must decide to let go of an old one. There must be a reason to decide to make a shift in thinking. As Kuhn pointed out, this may be especially difficult because holding on to an old paradigm is often accompanied by a deep emotional commitment to it. Ideas about phenomena are not all that must change with new connections in learning. Learners also have ideas about what scientific knowledge is. They possess thoughts and feelings about what they are doing when they are learning science that also change when new meanings are grasped.

Some Features of a Constructivist Epistemological Perspective on Science Learning

In light of its importance in rethinking science education, it is useful to present some of the key epistemological features of a constructivist view of knowledge in science learning. The following categories are used to organize a discussion of features of the constructivist view: (1) Reality, (2) Knowledge, (3) The Purpose of Knowing, (4) The Role of the Learner, and (5) The Role of the Teacher.

1. *Reality*. Reality does not exist separately from the observer, "out there," needing only to be discovered. There are many forms of reality, each depending on the observer's frame of reference and interaction with the observed.

2. *Knowledge*. Knowledge consists not merely of the facts, principles, and theories deduced from observations of phenomena and events. Knowledge includes the ability to use information in meaningful ways and encompasses thoughts, feelings, and interpretations. Knowledge involves an ongoing interpretation of the meaning of events and phenomena.

3. *The Purpose of Knowing.* The purpose of knowing is not the discovery of reality. The purpose of knowing is adaptive. It serves to guide the organization of reality to successfully organize and cope with one's experience. The purpose of education is not simply the acquisition of information and skills. It includes the development of skills to organize and successfully cope with the world of experience.
4. *The Role of the Learner.* The role of the learner is not to passively receive information, but to actively participate in the construction of new meaning.
5. *The Role of the Teacher.* The role of the teacher is not to simply present new information, correct students' "misconceptions," and demonstrate skills. It is to guide the learner to consider new ways of thinking about phenomena and events. In order to do so, the teacher must have some understanding of what the learner brings to the learning experience, that is, his or her prior ideas, thoughts.

CONSTRUCTIVISM AND CONCEPTUAL CHANGE: TORN BETWEEN TWO POSITIONS

Even though many teachers see the importance of taking the learner's perspective into account in science teaching and learning, at times we may find ourselves torn, valuing both objectivist and constructivist positions. At one moment, we know the scientist's perspective and want students to simply accept it as true. At another moment, we see that understanding the student's way of organizing thinking about ideas is vitally important in our work to help the learner consider new ways of looking at things like the scientific perspective.

Part of the dilemma we are faced with is the efficiency of simply asserting the correctness of one viewpoint, usually the scientist's, and the wrongness of the other, usually the student's. The former approach uses the familiar "tabula rasa" metaphor—the idea that knowledge can be written on, transmitted to, or transplanted to a person's mind, as if the mind were a blank slate to be filled. In fact, we know that information memorized only for a test is poorly retained and is rarely regarded as useful or satisfying knowledge from the student's point of view. Despite the fact that the "blank slate" view of the learner is not well regarded, it is still the view underlying the practice seen most often in school settings. This does not mean that we should not, at times, tell students what it is that we want them to consider, but we must recognize that learners have ideas of their own that influence learning and are often used to integrate new knowledge.

Posner, Strike, Hewson, and Gertzog (1982), writing on conceptual change, presented the argument that learning is a wholly rational activity in which learners must make judgments, based on their interpretation of the available evidence, about the rationality and intelligibility of arguments presented to them. Although useful, several concerns make this view problematic. First, implicit in it is a conception of the human mind as an entity, separate from the person. As Nyberg (1971) noted, this is an old assumption that sees the mind as a special isolated datum that functions discretely and is to be approached directly, as one would aim at a target. In holding this view, we may ignore the importance of the impact of factors like the individual's feelings on the learning process, and the learner's image of science, of science knowledge, and of his/her social interactions in the classroom with other learners and the teacher. Any of these may positively affect the learner's persistence and delight in learning, or may serve to enhance the learner's feelings of inadequacy, frustration, or alienation from the experience.

Following the objectivist perspective, the learner comes to school to be "learning outcomed," that is, to eventually emerge from school with all or most of the predetermined objectives of the curriculum or of the teacher in mind. The "blank slate" metaphor is further maintained by evaluating the learner at the end of each "learning sequence." Here the learner is deemed to have either succeeded or failed to accomplish the stated objectives. Success in such a learning system means to exit with the correct answers to the questions posed by the curriculum or the teacher. This is usually the only outcome that is valued in an extreme application of this approach to learning. The learner who fails is systematically "recycled" back through the experience until success is achieved or until the learner drops out. It is not the experience of the learner that is paramount here—it is the success of the curriculum in quickly extinguishing the misconceptions of students that matters.

Constructivism offers a new set of assumptions about learning. It presents the argument that a complete explanation of how learning occurs in the classroom must include a consideration of the experience of the learner, the key participant in learning. Constructivist teaching approaches focus on learners' views and efforts to consider new ways of thinking about things, for it is *the learner* who must do the work of integrating new ideas into his or her thinking. To help learners do so, we must begin to explore the extent to which we involve them as active agents in their own learning. Little research in education, however, has actually been undertaken to document and convey such insights. This book is an attempt to provide such insight. It is a study of children learning science using a constructivist research perspective, and thus this is a primary goal of this book. Because of the many meanings attributed to constructivism in educational literature, let us begin by considering the historical basis for ideas about constructivism in educational thought.

CONSTRUCTIVIST IDEAS IN EDUCATIONAL THOUGHT

Current thinking about constructivism in education is rooted in Piagetian research studies, such as his foundational work, *The Child's Conception of the World*, first published in 1929. It builds on this foundational work in its concern with the *ideas* of the learner. But current work in constructivism also departs from Piagetian thought in that it is concerned with the ways that the construction of new knowledge by the learner is influenced by prior knowledge. Importance is placed on the learner's efforts to connect prior knowledge with new ideas. In this way, the learner essentially straddles the world of unfamiliar ideas and viewpoints with those that are familiar. Learning, therefore, reflects the way that prior ideas are changed, altered, or in some way modified by the learner (Britton, 1972a).

In an analysis of constructivist theories of learning, Swift (1984) argued that it is useful to consider a continuum of thought within the constructivist tradition. He analyzed differences in constructivist stances taken by researchers in terms of the *degree of individuals' active participation* in knowledge construction. In this analysis, the Piagetian perspective occupies a conservative position on a proposed conservative-active classification continuum. Those who place greater emphasis on the individual's active participation in knowledge construction are placed on the active end of the continuum. Constructivists who focus on the development of personal meanings are radically activist in orientation.

FINDING PERSONAL CONSTRUCT THEORY

In the search for a theoretical framework for studying children learning in classrooms, I discovered George Kelly's (1955) evolving "personal construct theory." Its primary emphasis is the importance of the individual's interpretation of the events of the world. Kelly advocated a research attitude and tools to engage the individuals under study in conversation regarding their interpretations of events. I used the tools he suggested and developed others to study how individual children's ideas change and grow as they interpret and construe the events in their classroom environment.

Personal Construct Theory and Personal Change

Kelly (1963, 1970) explicitly rejected a view of change in persons in terms of "push theories based on stimuli" or "pull theories based on needs." He envisioned change in persons not as a result of external forces bearing upon the person, but as a result of the ways the person reconstrues situations.

Kelly's approach not only takes the individual into account but *asks* the individual about his or her ideas concerning the meaning of experience. If one is to change, Kelly suggested, one must first become aware of the ways one is construing the world. Then, one must decide that it is worthwhile to make the effort to change.

The Importance of Conversation

The research approach advocated by Kelly is a framework for conversing with the individual. This conversation can serve to help the person to clarify his or her way of construing reality. The caring guide makes an effort to understand the person's perspective. This is a collaborative effort. The subject is not *told* what he or she believes or how he or she is construing events, but an effort is made by both parties to understand, through conversation, how the individual is making sense of circumstances and thus preserve the integrity of his or her experience.

WITH CHILDREN IN CLASSROOMS: TOWARD A STUDY OF LEARNING

As a current catchword in education, constructivism has been used in such a wide variety of ways that there is much confusion regarding its meaning and domain of interest. It has been referred to as a philosophical position, an epistemology, a form of research, a learning theory, and even a model of learning. The term itself contains an important root metaphor, which is at the heart of the constructivist viewpoint: Knowledge is *constructed*. It is constructed by individuals and groups. The constructivist paradigm departs from traditional approaches in its view of such ideas as the nature of reality and knowledge, the purpose of knowing, the role of the learner and of learning, the role of the teacher and of teaching, and the organization of the classroom and of the curriculum and its evaluation. Because it does so, it also is a way of challenging the nature of the knowledge to be acquired by learners and the ways in which it is best acquired.

To begin a study of children constructing ideas in science, I started by thinking freshly about my own knowledge of children and learning. The first step involved visiting elementary school classrooms to talk with and observe children and their teachers. Being close to the experiences of children allowed me to reflect on the goals of the project, to form useful questions, and to begin to test out what might be the best approach for recording and conveying children's experience. During this exploratory period, I made regular visits to a wide range of grade levels and settings.

In the beginning, I framed several questions about the nature of children's opportunities for participation in the science program, in particular, opportunities that allowed children to talk about their ideas. I was concerned with the lack of participation of so many children in science and planned a study of the learning process. I wondered to what extent the children would be able to talk with me about their own learning. It was during this initial period of observation that I was able to speak with children about their understandings of the various tasks they had been assigned. It became clear through sitting and talking with children that, in many cases, when it had appeared to the teacher that the class as a whole understood an idea or direction, many individuals, in fact, did not. In these cases, the teacher's conclusion about the students' grasp of ideas appeared to be based on one or two individuals' correct responses to a question that had been directed to the entire class. Because one or two children were able to respond correctly, the teacher assumed that the majority of class members also understood the idea.

THE NEED FOR A STUDY FOCUSING ON
CHILDREN'S LEARNING IN ACTION

As I worked with individual students, I became more aware of the difficulties in understanding that children have that go unnoticed in the classroom setting. Though observable, tangible results are considered to be highly desirable in school systems, these results are more often measures of success or failure than of understanding. Educators who encourage learners to work through difficult problems for themselves must spend a great deal more time with students, helping them to work through challenges. Oldham (1982) explored the dilemma through the experience of "difficulty" in the high school biology program. She argued that, in our culture, we give little value to the experience of difficulty and attempt to eliminate it as quickly as possible. Children learn to be ashamed of having difficulty with schoolwork. But it is by working through difficulty that we learn and grow. If we show children that we value this experience, that it is important in a person's growth, then perhaps there will be less shame and more encouragement to succeed for those who encounter difficulty.

It was through such reflection on experiences in the classroom and further reading that I realized, even more strongly, the need to provide information on the process of learning that goes beyond the usual focus on outcomes and outward appearance or success at grasping the scientists' views of the nature of phenomena. So little information appeared to be available to teachers on the child's processes of learning, his or her experiences and approaches in trying to understand what was being taught. I believed that providing this perspective could offer insight for teachers, student teachers, researchers, and, potentially, learners themselves. This information would help educators to understand how they might more meaningfully assist students in their efforts to grow and develop in science. The best approach to documenting and conveying this information seemed to be to work closely with individual children, as they learned about a specific science topic, asking them to help me make sense of the material and activities presented to them.

As observations and reading progressed, I envisaged a study describing the ongoing experiences of several children as they learned about a specific topic in the science program. I selected the topic, light, as a focus for out-of-class interviews with small groups of children. Light is a topic typically presented in the elementary program, and I wanted to uncover some of the ideas children held about light because of its many conceptual challenges and its constant source of wonder and delight for children. I discovered that very little research had been conducted to understand children's ideas about the topic.

Pilot Interviews and Explorations: Talking With Children About Light

To begin the exploration of student ideas regarding the nature of light, two sets of interviews were conducted. The first set involved children aged 6 to 10. The second involved students aged 11 to 13. My first question to all of the children interviewed was simply, "What is light?" Here, I used no reference or prop materials other than those already present in the room where our interviews took place. I wanted to know about the children's prior experiences with light phenomena and to understand how they described and talked about light. Later I provided activities involving numerous objects producing intriguing light phenomena: a flashlight; a mirror and card with letters; transparent, translucent, and opaque objects; waterglasses and pencils; a glass prism; a "jupiterscope" (a "space-age," jellylike clear disc containing hundreds of prisms); two types of magnifiers; several moving object cards; and a fiber optics flashlight. I asked individual children to try several activities with me using one of the objects, then invited each one to describe what they had observed and why the light behaved in the way that it did. Finally, I asked the children to tell me how they knew that what they were saying about light was true.

I used pictures and books to prompt discussion about understandings of previous experiences with, and interest in light. I encouraged the children to share with me any experiences with light phenomena they might have recalled previously or any interest relating to light phenomena they might recall now. Students frequently referred to toys they played with that either reflected light or created some special light effect. Students reported other experiences with light, for example:

- Don referred to his electricity set when telling me how light functions.
- Inge asked me questions about the wires she noticed under the switchplate in her room when her father was changing the wiring.
- Ching spoke about an activity with a teacher in a previous grade that she said proved to her that "light gives off heat."

During these discussions I became aware that the individual children with whom I was working were approaching the tasks I had presented in very different and personal ways. Some examples from my notes follow:

Leon becomes very physically involved with the materials we are using. His response to my questions are terse and to the point. He uses little language to respond to my queries, but uses abundant language to spontaneously describe the experience *he* is having with the materials as he is working with them. He continually encourages me to become involved in the exploratory directions he is taking.

Belinda appears very concerned with giving the correct answer to my queries. She wants to know the answers to my questions, but prefers not to speculate on them herself. She seems to want to be sure that she is right before she puts an idea forward. Once, when I asked, "Why do you think that light is behaving that way?" she paused and said, "I don't know. I'll bet you do. Tell me. Why *does* it behave that way?" She is reluctant to suggest her own reason as to why it does so. Yet frequently during our conversation, Belinda uses similes to describe her observations. When we held a flashlight up to a translucent plastic surface, she looked at the reflection on the wall and spontaneously remarked, "That looks just like a spider's web!"

Penny began the investigations with a description of her own theory of light, which involved positive particles always in motion. In each subsequent task I gave her, she made a conscious effort to provide an explanation consistent with her own original theory. When I asked her the source of her theory, she said that it was based partly on her reading and partly on her imagination. "I like to add my own ideas to what I learn about. It makes it more fun."

Noting the existence of patterns in student approaches to the materials and ideas led to the most important findings in the initial stages of this research. These approaches seemed key to understanding how students conceived of, anticipated, and reacted to the ideas and experiences being presented to them as they were learning. The attempt to understand and characterize individual approaches to science learning became central to my interest.

Another purpose of the pilot work was to test out the effects of using audio- and videotaping equipment with the children. I was concerned that the children might feel inhibited or intimidated by such recording equipment. These initial studies provided the opportunity to assess student ease in being recorded by the equipment and to determine if this was appropriate technology for recording and reflecting upon ideas. After an initial nervous self-consciousness, the children seemed to ignore the presence of the camera and spoke with me in a candid and relaxed manner. It became clear that one of the goals of the research project would be to understand children's ideas about light and how these differed from the scientists' ideas. A second goal would be to determine the best ways that these ideas were constructed by the children in the classroom.

Foreshadowings and Emerging Insights

The exploratory studies yielded some important observations that guided further development of the study. First, I found that in general the children who were interviewed and videotaped had very little understanding of current scientific ideas about the nature of light. Even sixth-grade students, who had been involved in formal study of the topic less than a year prior to our interviews, showed little or no understanding of the most basic and current scientific ideas about the nature of light. Students' explanations of light behavior were often based on spontaneous and commonsense reasoning.

Another finding emerged when students were encouraged to pose their own questions about light. These questions focused on topics typically not found in their curriculum programs, but were also of real and current interest to the students interviewed. Some examples of the questions asked were:

> What is a black light? How does it work?
> What's inside a light bulb, like the ones in the classroom?
> How do you get the light from the sun to make an engine go?
> What is a laser, exactly? Could I make one?
> How does a firefly make light? Why does he do it?
> How come it's better to wear white than black on a really hot day?
> What makes my shoelaces glow in the dark?

But the individual approaches students took as they explored ideas and materials were even more clearly emerging as a crucial focus for the study. I found that each child demonstrated a very different *approach* to the tasks I presented. In some instances, the approach was a very spontaneous, creative, and imaginative effort by the child to make sense of the problem posed.

Some students seemed less willing to speculate on the nature of light or were reluctant to propose explanations or even ask questions about the topic. The general way each child approached the phenomenon seemed to be reflected in the entire manner the individual became absorbed in, interested in, and attentive to the materials and ideas I presented. There also seemed to be a relationship between the approach taken in the tasks and the student's interest in knowing more about the subject. Even though each learner's ideas about natural phenomena seemed to be unique and personal, there were still similarities between students apparent in the elements of their approaches to materials.

A final set of discoveries was made during the effort to encourage the children to externalize their ongoing thoughts as they considered some of the problems I posed for them. This revealed that students held different perceptions of their own abilities to "do science." These different conceptions of self as learner emerged through the ways that children spoke about their previous science experiences both in and out of school. These findings led to an extensive investigation into the literature pertaining to student "learning styles." I was seeking to understand the significance of the individual approaches to science learning I had observed in the tasks given students.

Through exploratory studies it became clear that the structure of personal and individual approaches to science learning were interwoven in complex ways with learners' ideas about phenomena. How could such complexity be studied and portrayed? I read, thought, and studied further. The "learning styles" literature, specifically the pioneering work of Gregorc (1982) and Gregorc and Butler (1983), provided an explanatory framework and theoretical constructs for categorizing learners' modes of perceiving and organizing information. But because the learning-style categories were conceived as previously existing entities to be imposed on learners in the classroom, they were not useful in the kind of study I intended to undertake. Although this work offered some interesting explanations of student approaches to learning, the study I planned differed in that I wanted to capture significant themes depicting the personal orientations of the students themselves rather than impose preconceived categories on the individuals in my study. This required a research approach that would allow such patterns to emerge over a lengthy period. Personal Construct Theory, in its emphasis on the uniqueness of each person's thoughts and actions, suggested approaches for the study and emergence of such themes. I intended, through the documentation of individual children's experience, to provide greater understanding of the interplay between (1) Children's ideas about the nature of light (2) The presentation of scientists' ideas by the teacher and the curriculum material, and (3) The structure of individuals' unique and personal approach to learning during science lessons.

The examination of personal orientations to subject matter would emphasize the uniqueness and integrity of the individuals whose approaches were being discussed rather than viewing and describing the children through predetermined categories or stages.

Reflection on Matthews' (1980, 1984) work reemphasized the crucial argument that, in an examination of children's philosophical development, there is no progression through fixed or standard stages at different age levels, as was suggested by Piaget. Because my study would ask students about ideas that are essentially philosophic viewpoints about science, learning, and light, Matthews's comments seemed particularly appropriate. The normative studies of Piaget and his co-workers have given us some of the first and most detailed understandings of children's intuitive ideas about the physical world. The emphasis of his later work shifted to the assumption of the priority of logical-mathematical structures of knowledge and the age-related stages of intellectual development based on the acquisition of these structures. "Physical knowledge," knowledge about the physical properties of objects, was distinguished from logical-mathematical knowledge, which was considered to be a set of internalized systems of action. Although these two types of knowledge were distinguished from one another, they were also considered to be interdependent developments. Much of the criticism of Piaget's later work is directed at its overemphasis on context-free, logical aspects of knowledge and stage development (Brown & Desforges, 1979; Donaldson, 1978; Matthews, 1980, 1984; Novak, 1987; Vygotsky, 1962.)

THE NEED FOR AN ALTERNATIVE RESEARCH APPROACH

As I became more familiar with the research on students' ideas in science, I found that the great body of empirical studies acknowledge and delineate the preformed ideas children tend to bring to their learning experiences. It seemed important and useful to develop an *interactive* study to complement this work in order to provide an understanding of children's approaches to learning about natural phenomena in classrooms. This work would provide implications for the adult's role in guiding and directing the child's formal experience in school science and would allow insight into the experiences of students who deviate from the general population.

Wilson (1977) argued that the "social scientist cannot understand human behavior without understanding the framework within which the subjects interpret their thoughts, feelings and actions" (p. 249). Guided by this thinking, I planned to conduct the study in the "naturalistic setting" of a fifth-grade classroom using a case study approach. The case study approach has long been known as the research procedure of anthropologists and other behavioral scientists but it does not have a long history in the field of education (Eisner, 1981). Goode and Hat (1976) describe the case study "not as a specific technique, but as a way of organizing social data so as to preserve the unitary character of the social object being studied" (p. 114). I planned to use several techniques to clarify and preserve the unitary character of each child's story. Information for the case study reports would be gathered through formal and informal conversation; through the use of repertory grid conversations, through videotape and audiotape recordings; through the collection and discussion of student work, notes, stories, drawings; and written work; and through my own participation and observation in the classroom. The patterns or unities I would then perceive would be grounded in direct experience and long-term involvement with the children in the class. The next step was to thoroughly examine the literature on the selected science topic and the research approaches in studies of children learning science.

CHAPTER 2

The Learner Constructs Meaning: Research on Children's Learning in Science

A review of the research literature in science education showed the study of children's ideas about science phenomena at the forefront of interest. This vast body of literature examines many different content areas in science and researchers employ a variety of approaches to understanding the experience of children's learning. Piaget (1929, 1974a, 1974b) was one of the first researchers to systematically study children's ideas about the nature of the world. Piaget's work is the foundation for current thinking in research in science education, but has come under recent scrutiny. It is subject to a variety of interpretations, and a wide variety of opinions exists concerning the purposes and eventual uses of the research on children's ideas in science. There are many views regarding the appropriate and most useful terminology in these studies and the best methodological approaches to explain and guide research on children's ideas in science.

How are we to make sense of the enormous literature in this field? A review of the research is presented in this chapter to introduce this literature and its value in understanding children's meaning construction. The first section, entitled "Examining the Alternative Frameworks Literature," provides a general overview of the terminologies and research paradigms used in the studies conducted. The second section, "Research on Children's Ideas About the Nature of Light," reviews the findings and orientations of research studies that have attempted to describe students' ideas about the nature of light. There are two main thrusts evident in the studies on light: (1) Studies focusing on pervasive misconceptions, and (2) Studies emphasizing the child's interpretive framework.

EXAMINING THE ALTERNATIVE FRAMEWORKS LITERATURE

Several major conferences have been devoted to the alternative frameworks research in science education. Of note have been the research seminar, *Investigating Children's Ideas About Science* (Sutton & West, 1982) and the series of conferences, *International Seminars on Misconceptions in Science and Mathematics*, held at Cornell University in 1983, 1987, and 1994 (Helm & Novak, 1983; Novak, 1987, 1994). The primary purpose of these conferences has been to promote dialogue among scholars concerned with the "highly robust" (Posner et al., 1982) influence students' prior conceptual frameworks have on shaping the meaning of new learning (Helm & Novak, 1983). Each conference has resulted in sets of proceedings containing extensive reference materials.

Current Studies: Terminology

Studies have been conducted dealing with a variety of topics, including such topics as paths of acceleration (Viennot, 1979), energy (Wheeler, 1983), dynamics (Osborne, 1980), geologic time (Ault, 1980), and growth (Schaefer, 1979). Terms have been used to describe student ideas about these topics. For example, ideas formed prior to instruction have been termed *prior knowledge* (Wittrock, 1974). Incorrectly formed ideas have been referred to as *misconceptions*, and ideas that may diverge less drastically from "scientifically correct" explanations of natural phenomena have been called *alternative conceptions*.

Children's views about the nature of phenomena have also been variously labeled using such terms as *ideas* (Osborne, 1981), *beliefs* (Kargbo, Hobbs, & Erickson, 1980), *understandings* (Nussbaum, 1976), *preconceptions* (Anderson & Smith, 1983a), *viewpoints* (Erickson, 1975; 1980), *prior knowledge* (Sutton, 1980), *alternate conceptions* (Minstrel, 1983), *alternative frameworks* (Watts, 1984), *conceptual ecologies* (Posner, et al., 1982), *conceptual frameworks* (Driver, 1983), *cosmographies* (Sneider & Pulos, 1983), *mixed conceptions* (Ault, 1984), *personal constructs* (Kelly, 1970), *gut science* (Claxton, 1982), and *children's science* (Gilbert, Osborne, & Fensham, 1982; Zylbersztajn & Watts, 1982). In this book, I propose yet another phrase by considering constellations of meaning about science and science learning that contribute to children's scientific ideas. As mentioned in chapter 2, I call this set of epistemological features *personal orientation to science learning* (Shapiro, 1989). These features are described in chapter 11, following the case studies of children learning science.

An examination of the literature shows that many different conceptual approaches have driven the various projects. Gilbert & Watts (1983) noted that the pace of research in content- and context-dependent science rapidly increased since the early 1970s. Yet, despite so much activity in this area, there has been little agreement on the aims of the inquiries or on the terminologies to be used in discussing student views. Several researchers indicated a preference not to use the term "misconception" to describe learner ideas (Gilbert & Pope, 1982; Wheeler, 1983) because use of the term emphasizes the incorrectness of student ideas, promoting a behavioristic view of learning. The assumption behind the language is that the student's process of understanding is less important than the product or endpoint of learning. Placement of high value on the learner's meaning making is conveyed in other such terms as *alternate*, or *alternative, frameworks*. Most of the research in alternative frameworks has attempted to determine the patterns of ideas students hold and cling to even after instruction. However, documentation of the processes of how many other factors affect the individual child's creation of meaning and interpretation of science learning has not yet been adequately conveyed.

Some researchers ask, "What are the *barriers* to science learning?" (Appelman, Colton, Flexer, & Hawkins, 1982; Ault, 1980). Those with a concern for understanding the child's interpretive framework would ask the question differently: "In what ways do the children's past experiences, understandings, and expectations influence the learning of science?" Again, a difference exists between the two questions. The former question seeks to define the hindrances to learning science. The "solution" for these researchers would lie, then, in discovering how educators might direct their energies to "break down" these barriers. In contrast, the interpretive framework orientation sees the student's present knowledge not as a barrier to understanding but as a framework through which ideas are interpreted (West, 1982). The attempt to understand the learner's thinking causes us to view the learner not as someone who is simply "wrong," but as someone who may be "intelligently wrong" (Ault, 1984). The emphasis is on attempting to understand the ways in which the child is thinking about a problem, to value the child's thought, and to help the child become aware of and participate in the development of his or her own ideas.

Current Studies: Research Paradigms

It has been clearly established in several studies (Driver & Erickson, 1983; Driver & Oldham, 1985; Fensham, 1983; Osborne & Freyberg, 1985) that children embark on the study of natural phenomena with ideas already formed from their backgrounds and experience. It is evident that children's ideas about phenomena grow and change as they are taught science in school settings, though not always in ways that are intended by teachers or even by curriculum makers who are aware of the research findings. It is also apparent that studies are guided by one of two basic research philosophies, which determine the ways in which information is collected and ultimately used. Studies guided by the first approach are called "nomothetic" studies (Driver & Easley, 1978) and seek to determine specific ideas that are in conflict with the scientific presentation of ideas in the classroom. Students' understandings are assessed in nomothetic studies in terms of the congruence of their responses with "accepted" scientific ideas. As described previously, suggestions are then made concerning ways to "extinguish" incorrect ideas and bring students to the correct responses on posttests (Anderson & Smith, 1983b). Studies guided by the second research philosophy are called "ideographic" and emphasize the interaction of student ideas with those presented by the teacher or with curriculum materials in the science classroom. In these studies, the child's ideas are used as an interpretive framework. This framework is used to gain an understanding of how the student is thinking about the phenomena and how these ideas affect the development of new ideas. Parlett and Simons (1979) refer to these studies as illuminative. The methodology used in these studies is referred to by Power (1976) as "the anthropological paradigm." Such studies do not attempt to predict student behavior, but, in the tradition of ethnomethodology (Cicourel, 1974; Garfinkle, 1967; Lincoln & Guba, 1981, 1985; Stake & Easley, 1978; Wilson, 1977) seek to *understand* participants' viewpoints.

Taking an ideographic approach, Brook, Briggs, and Driver (1984) examined student ideas about the particulate nature of matter. Some incorrect answers occurred because students misunderstood the questions given on a written test of subject matter understandings. Some of these students responded at higher conceptual levels during the interviews than on written tests. The methods we use to assess student understanding greatly affect our findings.

In another set of studies using an ideographic approach, Solomon (1984) showed how children's knowledge of the everyday meanings of terms such as "work" or "force" may be one reason why students have difficulty understanding and using scientific definitions of the same terms during science class. She suggests that children are asked to operate in two different knowledge domains as they learn in school, namely, the domain of their own living experience and the domain of knowledge generated by science. The confusion of switching from one domain to the other makes the experience of learning difficult because the student is unsure of the boundaries of the knowledge domains or when words have one meaning and when another.

RESEARCH ON CHILDREN'S IDEAS ABOUT THE NATURE OF LIGHT

Light in the Science Curriculum

The topic, light, is typically presented early in the elementary school curriculum. "Light and Shadow" is a topic commonly studied when children are 7 to 8 years old. The mechanism of vision is often presented when children are age 9 to 10, during the study of human body systems. Such topics as light movement in straight lines, the nature of light reflection, refraction, light travel through various media, the light spectrum, and color mixing are typically studied in limited detail by children in Grade 5 or 6 (ages 10 to 12). Light is studied in greater depth in the secondary school physics program, but not all students will select physics as a topic of study. To assist the reader in a review of some of some of the most basic scientific ideas about light, a concept map is provided in Figure 2.1.

Despite this fairly extensive emphasis on the topic throughout years of school science learning, many of the scientific ideas about the nature of light have traditionally been very difficult for students to grasp. In a review of the literature examining student ideas about light, we can see in science, I have delineated two basic research emphases: (1) Studies focusing on students' pervasive misconceptions, and (2) Studies that stress contextual features of the child's interpretive framework.

Studies That Focus On Pervasive Misconceptions

Light transmission and vision. Piaget (1974a, 1974b) studied children's ideas of causality in operations with specific phenomena. He noted certain "lags" in students' general understandings of ideas regarding the transmission of heat. He then turned to light to add further to his understanding of children's ideas of causality. In almost every individual questioned about the nature of an image in a mirror or the light cast by a lamp, Piaget noted the understanding of vision as a passage from the eye to the object, rather than the reverse (p. 103). When a flashlight is shone in the dark, there was acknowledgement by some individuals that the light is shining on the eye. However, most children continued to describe the direction of vision as passing from eye to object.

When a light was shone on a screen located at varying distances from the person, no idea of light transmission or travel was mentioned up to Piaget's level IIB, but some type of "action" was described as taking place at a distance. When this distance was changed and the size of the circles of light were seen to increase and decrease, children in level IB suggested that the larger circle was being created by a greater amount of light, yet, the majority claimed that there was nothing between the light sources and the screen. In Piaget's level IIA, this same point was made by children, though at this stage students appeared to sense a contradiction. At level IIB, individuals began to make statements such as, the light "leaves" or "comes straight forward." Piaget hypothesized that for these individuals the cause of light was attributed to the fact of its *being turned on*, for example, by using a light switch, and ideas about the transmission of light were not understood. Piaget (1974a,

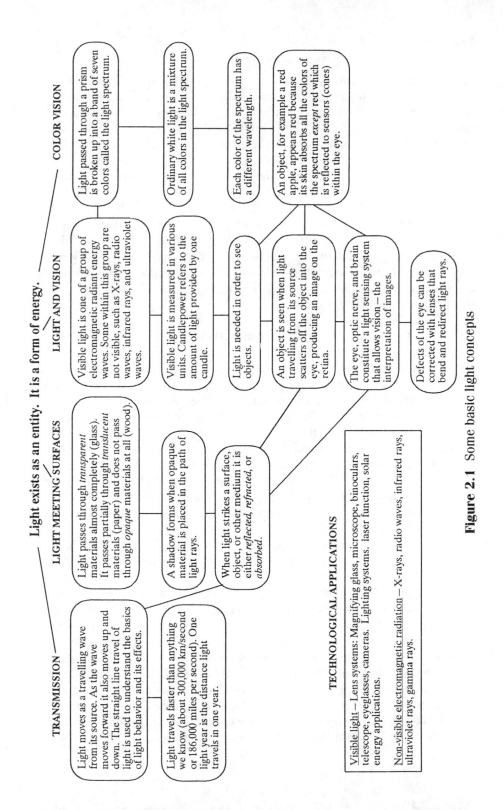

Figure 2.1 Some basic light concepts

1974b) was the first to note that children at early stages made no connection between the object and the eye. At later stages children considered vision in terms of a passage from the eye to the object.

Guesne (1978, 1985) conducted interviews on the nature of light and vision with twenty 14-year-old students. Given an object, the students were first asked, "What is it that makes you see this object?" They were then encouraged to explain how both primary and secondary sources of light are seen. Guesne reported that most of the students expressed the belief that objects are seen *because they are bright or because light falls on them*. However, most of the students interviewed did not mention that the eye detects light reflected from an object. Most of the students reported that objects are seen by the action of looking at them, that is, that vision can be traced in a direction from the human eye to the object. Guesne argued that everyday language describing vision tends to support this view and that it is therefore very similar to Platonic and Pythagorean theories, which assumed that vision could be best described as a ray emanating from the eye of the subject to the object seen. A diagram showing the most prominent views about vision delineated by Piaget and Guesne is presented in Figure 2.2.

Crookes and Goldby (1984) found that some older children hold the view that light comes to the eye from a light source, then goes to the object viewed. Most studies agree with Guesne (1985), however, that the majority of students do not grasp the scientific view that objects that are not light sources may reflect light (Feher, 1990; Feher & Rice, 1988). La Rosa, Mayer, Patrizi, and Vincenti (1984) suggest that students who do believe that light moves from source to object may employ an analogy that includes some means of connection from the source to the object, like a wire or road. Fetherstonhaugh & Treagust (1990) noted that three quarters of the students in their survey sample held the idea that visible rays of light are reflected not from the source object to the eye but through *the person's act of looking* at the object. Watts (1984, 1985) noted that most children view light as necessary to illuminate objects, and that light remains around objects whether the observer is present or not.

Fetherstonhaugh and Treagust (1990, 1992) suggest a number of teaching approaches to address common difficulties in understanding the nature of light. The topic areas addressed are: (1) How does light travel? (2) How do we see? (3) How is light reflected? (4) How do lenses work? In posttest studies, several of the suggested approaches were found to be helpful in moving some students towards the selected scientific ideas. The topic of greatest difficulty appeared to be the understanding that a whole lens is necessary to form an image.

Ramadas and Driver (1989) found that children held distinct views about the nature of light rays. Many children considered them to be unreal,

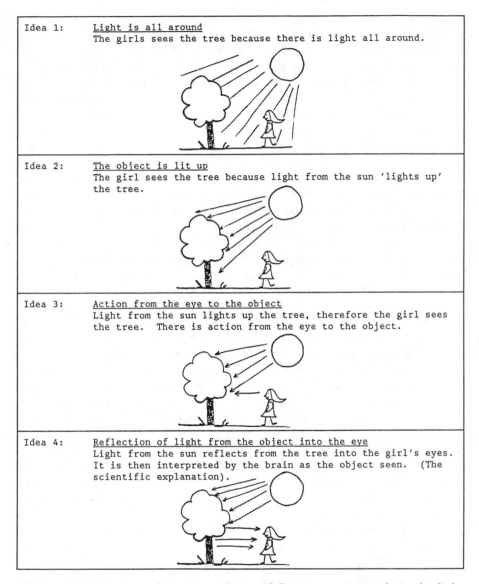

Figure 2.2 How does the girl see the tree? Prominent views about the light source, object, and vision connection

only associated with science fiction stories. Osborne, Black, Smith, and Meadows (1990) explored children's drawings depicting light sources such as the sun, lightbulbs, and fire. Almost all of the children represented light as being close to the light source by using sets of very short lines. Very few students indicated a link between the light source and the object being viewed by using lines in their drawings. These authors also noted that younger children's views were far more similar to one another than were the views of older students. As children grew older, their drawings were more varied, relating to specific contexts.

Shadows and darkness. Ramadas and Driver (1989) noted that children emphasized darkness as an important feature in understanding the nature of light. Many students made reference to light as an absence of darkness. Fetherstonhaugh and Treagust (1990) noted the popular idea that cats and people can see in the dark. What is meant by darkness is, of course, crucial to determine and was not clarified in the study. City dwellers did hold this idea more prominently than people in rural areas, presumably because most city children have never experienced total darkness. The experience of city versus country darkness thus appears to have an important influence on this view.

Color. Feher and Meyer (1992) described the pervasive idea that darkness is an ingredient of color, suggesting that this might be accounted for by a confusion between physical and perceptual phenomena. Many children report, for example, that "yellow light is less dark than red light" (p. 503), or that colored light "has dark in it" whereas white light is bright. When shown red light coming from a slide projector, Zylbersztajn and Watts (1982) found that even after direct instruction about the transmission of light frequencies, nearly half of the children believed that it was white light from the projector that had some substance added to it. Most of the children in a study conducted by Anderson and Smith (1983b) stated that color was a property of the object viewed and that what we see is the actual color of the object rather than the color of the light reflected from the object.

Light meeting surfaces. Children's ideas about the interaction of light and surfaces has raised some fundamental questions about children's grasp of ideas about light reflection and bending. I found that a large percentage of students believe that when light coming from a flashlight strikes a rock it stops on the surface rather than reflecting from the rock. Many students stated that light reflects from mirrors and shiny or metallic objects, but not from other types of objects, such as rocks or clothing.

Mirrors are typically used in curriculum units on light to demonstrate characteristics of light reflection. Several studies have shown that students have difficulty understanding image formation on a plane mirror (Anderson & Smith, 1983b; Feher & Meyer, 1992; Fetherstonhaugh & Treagust, 1992; Goldberg & McDermott, 1986; Guesne, 1985; Jung, 1981; Ramadas & Driver, 1989; and Watts, 1985). Most students believe that the image exists on the mirror surface or is just behind it.

Jung (1981) provided 12-year-old boys and girls with a mirror and reported that in 90% of cases students spoke of seeing their images on the "surface" of the mirror, rather than "from behind" the mirror. Many students suggested that because light is reflected from the surface of the mirror, that it is the place where the image is formed. Although the topic, ray reflection, had been taught extensively prior to the research, no student provided an adequate explanation by drawing on this prior instruction. In another example, students said that a light beam directed onto a mirror in a darkened room could be seen both reflected from the mirror and on the mirror because it was actually lying on the surface of the mirror.

Emphasis II: Studies That Stress Contextual Features of the Child's Interpretive Framework

Several early studies explore the process of the development of scientific concepts in children. In some of these projects, embryonic ideas are presented that have directed future work. One example is the emphasis on children's questions, as found in the appendix of Susan Isaacs' (1960) study *Intellectual Growth in Young Children*. The appendix, "Children's Why Questions," offers insight into the ways that children puzzle over events and phenomena in their environment. Such an approach informs us of the types of questions the young child thinks are important and reasonable to ask about the world. For example, one 4-year-old asks, before going to bed, "Why does it get lighter outside when you put the light out?" In a commentary on the questions, Nathan Isaacs (1974) stressed the importance of considering the child's question not with an emphasis on the incorrect idea in the question, but as a resource for understanding the child's ideas about the phenomenon and how to come to grips with what is perplexing him or her. For the child asking this question, it appears as though it *has* become lighter outside. It is perhaps less an "error" in thinking than it is that the child focuses on himself or herself as the central and only observer in the situation. Isaacs (1974) suggested that the *way* the child learns is a framework through which the child meets and interprets the world. In this view, understanding the child's working model of the world prior to his or her puzzlement will guide us in helping the child work through difficult problems.

Navarra's study (1955) of a preschool child, his own son, spanned a period of 2 years. He also believed that it was important to look beyond the

child's "incorrect" ideas and to the ways in which the child considered a
problem. An example is given through his records of a conversation with the
4-year-old subject of the study, L. B. The light from the moon is being discussed:

> L. B., his mother, and his father were taking a walk. Mother casually remarked
> as she pointed toward the moon, "Only half the moon is *lit*. Isn't it pretty?" L. B.
> very seriously interjected, "Would it burn your hands?" His question was not
> answered directly. Rather, his mother prompted, "What do you mean—would it
> burn your hands?" L. B. wrinkled his brow as he thoughtfully replied, "If it's lit
> up, it could burn your hands." (p. 99)

Navarra showed how the child's immediate and direct experiences with
moonlight are limited. He cannot touch and handle the moon, but information supplied by his mother did contain some meaning in terms of L. B.'s
experience. He had seen and touched lightbulbs that were hot enough to
"burn your hands" and, was thus making a logical deduction on the basis of
this past experience. This experience was a reference point for the integration and organization of further information pertaining to the moon. "Thus an
erroneous assumption within L. B.'s experience became a potentially useful
guide in his conceptual development" (p. 99). Navarra states that the most
significant inference from the records of his study was the persistent growth
and refinement of L. B.'s experience. The child's understanding appeared to
derive from a procedure that was directional and systematic. The process,
whereby L. B. coped with his dilemmas, grew out of his interaction with the
environment. The understanding of this process was possible due to the
long-term nature of the research project that enabled Navarra to consider
L. B. as a whole person and to see how both ideas and emotions affected the
development of his concepts.

Jung (1981) studied children 12 to 15 years of age and showed how ideas
about light could be understood through "meaning frames" of perception as
well as of cognition. He gave as an example the "commonsense frame" of
seeing light and color. Following the philosophical argument describing perception as a phenomenon, he noted "that which is perceived is given itself,
as something that exists in its own right, irrespective of the fact of being
perceived." Thus, color is seen as something the object possesses as a real
quality. What we do not see is light itself. It is regarded primarily as the
condition for seeing. Light is not commonly known as the mechanism by
which the color of an object arrives at the eyes. As light is not recognized as
the mechanism of sight, but at various times as radiation, streaming of colors,
or brightness, there is a confusion of perceptual and cognitive frames. Jung
suggests that the teaching solution is not a matter of simply giving students

the correct information, but of showing them the differences in context, thus making one "meaning frame" more appropriate than another.

The only study found that explored the ongoing development of ideas during instruction was that of Appelman and colleagues (1982), *A Report of Research on Critical Barriers to the Learning and Understanding of Elementary Science*. This National Science Foundation Project culminated 2 years of research on the experiences of elementary school teachers who were learning about science topics in which they had little or no previous instruction. The teachers attended evening classes at a local university to learn more about selected science topics. The authors of the project sought to understand the difficulties the teachers experienced in the study of science and mathematics and to begin to develop what they refer to as a "pre-theoretical" set of categories describing these difficulties.

Appelman and colleagues called the pre-theoretical categories presented in the study "barrier phenomena," that is, phenomena that apparently inhibit learning. The ethnographic character of the study allowed the authors to describe these phenomena in the ecological contexts of learning events. An effort was made also to seek clues from the history of science to understand the intellectual origins of "barrier phenomena." Examples of barriers include:

1. *Pervasive barriers:* Problems with scientific reasoning, confusing two concepts that apply to the same situation, confusing reality with its representations, making inappropriate associations, and retrieving misinformation.
2. *Barriers recognized in narrower contexts:* Invisibles and impalpables, conservation laws, transformations and cycles, wholes and their parts, constructs and their measures, and scale and relativity.

Other published research reports repeat and support the points made in Appelman and colleagues' (1982) groundbreaking study. La Rosa and associates (1984) reiterate the distinction between the ideas inherent in the ancient terms, *lux* and *lumen*, making an argument similar to that previously stated by Guesne (1978, 1985), Appelman and colleagues (1982), Andersson and Karrqvist (1982, 1983), and Solomon (1984). This argument states that the meanings of everyday terms are quite different when these terms are used in the science learning context and that this may be a source of confusion for the learner.

Stead and Osborne (1979, 1980) used an "interview-about-instances" procedure to obtain records of the ideas that students between ages 9 and 16 hold about light. Three main aspects of the nature of light were delineated for study: (1) Transmission of light, (2) Sources and reflectors of light, and (3) Vision. The results of two different approaches to data collection were compared in this study. Students were shown a set of pictures depicting light phenomena and were asked to make statements about the light in the pictures. The test results showed that students who had received recent instruction on the topic held views very similar to those who had received no instruction. The authors commented that a weakness in the findings on the multiple-choice test was that *students' reasons* for selecting particular answers on such a test cannot be known with any certainty. The authors concluded that the reason teaching appeared to be unsuccessful in moving students to the scientific conception was that no teaching was deliberately directed to confront the "erroneous" ideas that students held. Similar points are made in a study of Swedish students, aged 12 to 15, published by Karrqvist (1983) and Andersson and Karrqvist (1983). In this study, only a few of the students interviewed indicated they understood the nature of light as a physical entity existing in space and separate from its source and effects—the scientists' viewpoint.

THE IMPACT OF ALTERNATIVE FRAMEWORKS RESEARCH ON EDUCATIONAL PRACTICE

Fensham (1983) suggested that two main aspects of the findings of alternative frameworks research have begun to have an impact on curriculum development and classroom practice. First, teachers may not be aware that students bring their own conceptual structure to the classroom, and second, even after direct instruction designed to change learner ideas, students often hold to their previously held conceptions. Minstrel (1983), writing about his experiences as a high school teacher, noted that teachers do not address the ideas students bring to science class, but "try to superimpose new information onto a student's way of organizing the world." Science class then becomes "a foreign culture, rather than a place to discuss, to investigate, and organize the phenomena of the world" (p. 53).

However, once the most pervasive alternative orientations towards phenomena are identified, the next logical step may not be only to ask, "What can we do differently in classrooms to correct these wrong ideas?" Phrasing the problem in this manner suggests that we can already clearly identify and understand the mechanisms by which children come to be right or wrong about an idea. Such a question focuses on the beginning (entry) and the endpoint (exit) of learning rather than the processes of learning. If we focus our attention only on the entering and exiting points, without developing an understanding of the processes of children coming to understand, we may fail in our attempts to assist children in making conceptual reorientations.

IN SUMMARY: THE NEED FOR A NEW RESEARCH APPROACH AND INSIGHTS INTO THE PROCESSES OF LEARNING

The research paradigm of the majority of studies in the alternative frameworks literature has been based on the assumptions and procedures of a clinical interview methodology. The information gathered has not always taken into account children's learning processes and interaction in the class-room. In most studies, an attempt has been made to generalize regarding the normative pattern of ideas or the trend occurring in the population. Many of the studies have sought to identify specific and pervasive "misconceptions" students hold and then to suggest ways to correct these "wrong" ideas. Power (1976) notes that the underlying assumption of this approach is that of the "scientific paradigm," or the objectivist paradigm, which suggests that gener-alizations across populations, classrooms, and classroom phenomena are both possible and useful (p. 18). Although this approach has provided us with some important details of certain aspects of student understanding, little in-formation has been provided about the physical, social, and temporal con-texts of events that help to give them meaning. In this book I propose consid-eration of some of the elements of a research approach used to develop case studies of science learning. The cases are developed to provide insight into the wider range of interweaving features that influence the grasp of concepts and the learner's experience of science in school. Because of its crucial role in the development of understandings in science, we begin in the next chap-ter, with a perspective on language in science learning.

CHAPTER 3

The Importance of a Perspective on Language in Science Learning

Language is a primary means by which meaning is constructed. Because of its central importance in the design and creation of the case studies, a discussion of the vital role of language in the research is presented in this chapter. This view of language guided interviews with the children and was the basis for the interpretation and development of the individual case studies. In the last part of the chapter, the first steps in becoming acquainted with the children in the study are presented, as are details concerning one of the conversational tools used in the study, the repertory grid. The repertory grid conversations provided interpretive framework for revisiting the case study reports. The grid procedures are of great interest to many teacher/researchers, and I attempt to clarify and, I hope, demystify the use of this technique as a powerful resource for sensitive listening.

LANGUAGE AND THE CONSTRUCTION OF MEANING

Language is not only a *medium* for conveying new ideas, it is also a *means* whereby new meanings are constructed. Freire (1982) goes further. In his view, words are more than instruments making dialogue possible. They also contain the two dimensions of *reflection* and *action*. To use a new word is to transform one's world. For Freire, "to exist humanly is to name the world, to change it. Once named, the world in its turn reappears to the namers as a problem and requires of them a new naming" (p. 76). Although scientists frequently create new language to reconceptualize and rename the world, rarely are students shown the creative nature of this process. In the science classroom, students are more often asked to simply memorize the terms scientists have used to conceptualize problems. The student's task is to accept and understand the scientists' ideas. As students progress through the school program, science learning becomes less and less a personal experience. Most of the ideas resulting from scientists' reconceptualizations of facts cannot be experienced but must be simply accepted by students. This often leaves students with the task of memorizing scientists' language and ideas without understanding the processes of thinking that have brought these ideas into existence.

Cassirer (1944) considered language use to be an activity shaping all other human activities. He believed that language gives us the power to shape our own experience, and thereby to actively create our world. In addition to the language used by the individual to create and define the world, language is also used by others in the person's environment to define, control, or regulate experience. Language can be used to create social, psychological, or political distances between people (Freire, 1982). Although valuable in shaping human activity, language can be used to dominate, control, or restrict human understanding.

In educational settings, language can be used to free and enhance communication. By insisting that students remain silent, we restrict involvement in language use. Restricting involvement appears to inhibit student interest in learning, yet the teacher's responsibility for managing a learning environment demands a balance between freedom and restriction. Douglas Barnes (1975) describes this contradiction:

> At the heart of teaching as we know it in our culture lies this dilemma: every child learns best when he is finding out about something that interests him; children are compelled by law to attend school, and are in the charge of teachers who are employees responsible for large numbers of them. There is an implicit conflict between the teacher's responsibility for control and his responsibility for learning: One treats pupils as receivers and the other treats them as makers. (p. 176)

When language is used to shape and control unwanted behavior, the teacher may completely dominate classroom talk. Implicit in this approach is the view that it is the teacher who is responsible for making the student learn. Wade & Wood (1980) argue that the teacher who encourages students to use language can often detect difficulties that might otherwise have remained hidden. This is a first step towards helping learners take responsibility for their own meaning construction.

Children's Language and the Personal Construction of Meaning in Science

To be interested in the child's interpretation of the world is to be interested in the ways that children use language to make sense of their world. Britton (1972a) wrote about the importance of talk in making meaning every day:

We habitually use talk as a means of coming to grips with current or recurrent experience. The newspaper accounts of important events will be talked about in every train and office and on every street corner. As people talk, each is relating the event to his own personal experience, his own world: creating his own personal context for it. (p. 30)

Kelly (1955) suggested that each individual makes use of very personal categories to organize and understand the world. Kelly (1963) believed that these linguistic categories, called personal constructs, are used as a kind of template that allows us to "straddle the familiar with the unfamiliar" (p. 18). He used the metaphor, the person as a form of motion, to emphasize the dynamic, changing nature of the person's use of language constructs.

The idea of motion is central to a consideration of the tentative nature of new thinking. Kelly (1963) referred to the tentative use of language in the construction of ideas as the "language of hypothesis." He suggested that the child's tentative and changing representation of the world is his or her personal construct system. The modification or "bringing up-to-date" (p. 19) of this representation of experience is accomplished by means of talk. We habitually use talk to go back over events, interpret them, and make sense of them in a way that we are unable to do while they are taking place. Bruner (1956) commented that the thrust of Kelly's work suggests that it is not from experiencing that we learn but from the *reconstruing* of experience, that is, from the ways in which we reflect on experience. Reconstruing is an active process undertaken by the individual to cope with the contradictions and dilemmas of everyday experience.

Spontaneous and Nonspontaneous Ideas

Vygotsky (1962) made important contributions to our thinking about the development of scientific ideas and the child's construction of meaning. He contrasted the formal presentation of scientific ideas in school with the child's approach to ideas about phenomena. He referred to the formal introduction of scientists' views about phenomena as the presentation of *nonspontaneous* ideas. The child's ideas, rooted in his or her experience of the world were referred to as *spontaneous* ideas. Vygotsky regarded the development of children's thought as the interaction of spontaneous ideas, rooted in the child's life experience, with nonspontaneous concepts, requiring a process of active and strenuous mental activity on the part of the child. He believed that the child's own efforts to integrate the two must be the basis of the adult's efforts to assist in the learning process. Vygotsky criticized Piaget who he said, "assumes that development and instruction are entirely separate, incommensurate processes, that the function of instruction is merely to introduce adult ways of thinking, which conflict with the child's own, and eventually supplant them" (pp. 116–117).

Vygotsky's work emphasizes the importance of understanding learning from the child's perspective. If we are to incorporate the child's ideas into the teaching/learning dialogue, we must learn to listen more carefully to the child's language and views about the experiences that we present.

PERSONAL CONSTRUCT THEORY: A GUIDE TO CAREFUL LISTENING

George Kelly (1955) portrayed his entire theory, and its various corollaries and related techniques, as "a guide to careful listening designed to discover the full import of the person's thinking, that is, why one construes what one does as the right thing to do" (pp. 71–72). Kelly suggested several research techniques that facilitated the attainment of this knowledge. Some of these were used in the study and others consistent with his philosophy were developed. The use of videotaping and participant-observation techniques were also used to allow a search for patterns in the children's experiences. I have documented the use of such approaches in several research studies (Shapiro, 1989, 1991a, 1991b, 1994).

"Kelly's First Principle": Self-Characterization

Kelly remarked that, if he were to be remembered at all, he would prefer it to be not for the invention of Personal Construct Theory, but for what he called "Kelly's first principle, self-characterization." Self-characterization results from inviting the person we are attempting to understand to speak directly about himself or herself. He summarized the first principle in the following statement: "If you want to know what is concerning a person, ask him, he just *may* tell you" (1963, p. 68). This approach was unlike the psychometric evaluation procedures of his time, which involved questionnaires with oblique questions designed so that what was being measured was completely hidden from the individual. Kelly felt that what the person had to say about himself or herself provided more significant information. In the process of discussion with a caring guide, he believed that both parties could achieve an understanding of the individual's view of the situation he or she was attempting to cope with. Repertory grid technique was a less casual and more systematic form of conversation in the study, but one that guided me to help the students use their own language and forms of expression to describe various aspects of the school learning situation.

The Importance of Trust

If the "tools for sensitive listening" were to enable understanding of the person, as suggested by Kelly, an attitude of caring and trust was absolutely essential. It was particularly useful to consider the work of thinkers who propose that we think carefully about engaging in dialogue in research. Maslow (1966) described the type of relationship required in such an encounter:

> In such relationships it is characteristic that the knower is *involved* with what he knows. He is not distant; he is close. He is not cool about it, he is warm. He is not unemotional; he is emotional. He has empathy, intuition for the object of knowledge. He feels identified with it. He cares. (p. 113)

Gadamer (1975) wrote that research based on interpersonal interaction demands that we reconsider our approach to listening, that we listen caringly, carefully, and openly to the child. Such listening does not merely survey or assess the child. The approach to listening reveals something about the child and reveals something about the researcher as well. Buber (1955) conceived of dialogue between two persons as a mutual unveiling whereby each person is experienced and confirmed by the other. In order for participants to share their thoughts and feelings with one another, they must trust one another.

Erikson (1975) called a basic sense of trust the fundamental prerequisite of mental vitality. By trust he wrote that he meant an essential trustfulness of others as well as a fundamental sense of one's own trustworthiness. During the study, I strove to establish trust by taking time to allow the children to become acquainted with me and to help them understand my purposes and interests in conducting the study. Our initial time together was filled with casual conversation.

Conversation: "The Heart of the Process"

Conversation has been fundamental in the attempt to understand the children's experiences in the development of the case study reports. I adopted what Kelly referred to as an "attitude of credibility," an acceptance that what a person says is true, that it is worth listening to, and that it will contribute significantly to understanding that person's thought and behavior.

Varela (1979) and Pask (1976) stress the importance of seeing a conversation in its totality. The text of a conversation is an "alloy" of participants' contributions, the contribution of each party cannot be neatly delineated. A conversation stems from the perspective and linguistic tradition or culture of its participants. A conversation between two individuals is usually open to presentation of new ideas, to question or to revision. Varela (1979) writes that every statement a person makes reflects a history of interactions that, in fact, make language possible. But the very act of listening also creates a history and brings forward new ideas at the same time.

In both our structured and informal discussions, I attempted to create the kind of conversational environment that would allow students to feel comfortable in questioning, challenging, or disagreeing with ideas rather than simply responding to questions as might be expected in a typical learning situation. It was important that the children relate to me not as another teacher in the classroom, but as someone interested in what they thought their ideas about their own learning. As Gadamer (1960) noted, the attempt to establish openness to change and to challenging ideas is not a failure or weakness of conversation, but is at the very "heart of the process."

BECOMING ACQUAINTED WITH THE CHILDREN

Once the decision was made to conduct a study of individual idea development during the process of learning, the next step was to select a classroom and begin working with the children. I was fortunate to quickly find a teacher who would be working with the topic, light, and who was interested in having a visitor in the classroom. Over a period of 6 months I became a member of Mr. Ryan's fifth-grade class. Although I came to know all of the children in the class well, I spoke in depth with six—three boys and three girls, about their thoughts and feelings while engaged in the study of the topic, light. Donnie, Mark, Melody, Martin, Yasmin, and Pierre shared their thoughts with me. They understood that I was studying the ways that children thought and felt about their learning, confided in me, and did all that they could to assist in the research process. At this writing, I continue to regularly talk with all of the children about science learning.

How did I select these individuals? Prior to the study, I developed several criteria. The first was student comfort level. I looked for individuals who appeared comfortable in speaking with me—not simply those who were outgoing, but students who approached me openly and shared their perceptions with me easily. The second criteria was sample heterogeneity. An equal number of boys and girls were invited to participate. I selected children from a range of academic and cultural backgrounds. Two of the children were experiencing serious learning problems in the regular school program. Two were achieving at an average level and two were considered high-achieving students.

I spent the first 2 weeks in Mr. John Ryan's fifth-grade classroom simply observing, talking with, and becoming acquainted with the children, their teacher, and the program. At times, I sat with students, at other times, I set up and used videotape equipment, or helped Mr. Ryan. Whenever possible, I participated in activities with the children.

I had hoped that the children would begin to communicate with me freely and would come to know me well before I worked with them in the light unit. Many of the children spontaneously approached me, knowing that I wanted to know about their science interests. Some typical comments the children made during this period were the following:

> Martin: Hi, Miss, you're really good in science aren't you? I love science! Can you teach us about rockets and outer space?
>
> Denise: Oh, you're here *again* today! Oh, good, good, then we're going to have science more now? Are you coming all the time now?
>
> Raini: I really like science a lot. Last year me and Julie did an experiment on the different types of cola drinks there are and everybody thought it was the very best. This year we're going to do one on gerbils. Can you come to the science fair and see it?

The children and their teachers made me feel welcome in the classroom immediately. I spoke with the class casually about the purposes and goals of my work in their classroom, and they asked many questions about my personal background and about science topics. Several children made a point of discussing their science interests and projects with me. Raoul and Lou had an idea about an engine they had decided to build. They stopped by after class to ask for suggestions about its design and connecting the solar cell.

During the second week of my stay, I spent time testing the video recording equipment I would be using to record the science lessons. I hoped to accustom the children to having the camera in the room. One afternoon, as I was peering through the camera, Donnie tugged at my elbow. "Ms. Shapiro," he said, pointing to the camera system, "can you tell me how this stuff all works?"

I told Donnie that I had a great deal to learn about the camera system myself, but that if it was acceptable to Mr. Ryan, she could come with me during her free time on Friday and I would show her all that I had been able to find out about how the camera worked. She was thrilled by this possibility. When the Friday session came she asked permission to bring two equally inquisitive friends. I reviewed basic principles of sound and image recording on videotape with the girls and they were invited to touch various parts of the equipment, ask questions, and become camerawomen. Donnie would often approach me with a special question that had been sparked by a lesson or had emerged from her own experience. The children identified me as someone interested in their ideas and questions in science. The most frequent topic I was approached to discuss centered around planning for the upcoming school science fair. The discussions were usually about past projects and what was being planned for the current year's project. The children thoroughly enjoyed sharing their science fair experiences and I encouraged them to speak with me whenever there was an appropriate moment during our getting acquainted time. To facilitate this, I went out for recess with students and remained in the classroom after school, a time when students seemed to particularly enjoy talking about science.

ANOTHER TYPE OF CONVERSATION:
THE USE OF REPERTORY GRID CONVERSATIONS

Repertory grid technique is a powerful tool used to search for patterns in thinking by facilitating understanding of the individual's use of language to organize his or her world of experience. I have reported use of adapted forms of the technique in several research projects (Shapiro, 1994, 1993, 1991a, 1991b, 1989). In this section, I hope to demystify and clarify its use by describing how it was an important aspect of conversation and information collection with the children. The central aim of the "rep grid" is to reveal the construct patterning or the "unique psychological space" (Bannister & Fransella, 1971) of the individual.

Repertory grids have been applied in many research contexts. Beveridge and Brierley (1982) explored third-grade students' constructs about their ideas about the meaning of classroom settings using repertory grid technique. Repertory grid technique allows collaboration between "researcher" and "subject." The approach not only places the researcher in the same role as the subject to an extent, but it makes researcher and subject partners in the business of interpreting meanings. In the present study, individual meaning as it related to approaches to science learning was of central concern in the study. The children's own ways of describing events emerged during the many conversations conducted with the children throughout the study. It was particularly significant when children's phrases and expressions were used both in regular conversation and in the repertory grid conversations.

The elicitation and organization of constructs using the repertory grid took place in three sessions with the children during the final weeks of the light unit. At that time, I had been in the classroom over a period of 6 months.

Session 1

At the end of the science unit, I met with the six children as a group. We used a round table in "the discussion room," a pleasant, quiet setting in the school, to talk about the types of activities and experiences that had taken place during the unit. Each group member was encouraged to contribute to the list and care was taken to ensure that the statements were recorded in the student's own words. In all, 45 statements were listed. We reviewed the list for any repetitious or unclear statements and produced a final list of 37 statements of activities (Figure 3.1).

Session 2

Each activity or experience was written on a separate index card. In private meetings, each individual was given a set of 37 activity cards and was asked to become familiar with the cards by sorting and organizing them into groups. Together, we looked at each group and discussed the categories each child selected for organizing the cards. I wanted the children to become comfortable with the list and the idea of sorting the cards by category. The cards were shuffled, then three were picked at random. I asked the student, "How would you say that two of the cards are similar and different from the third?" This response became the first construct pole. For example, in Donnie's first experience with the procedure, statement 29 was selected, "We experiment with Ms. Shapiro's light meter," along with statement 13, "I hear the other kids give their ideas about light." The third card was statement 14, "I don't understand what I'm supposed to do." In Donnie's view, the first two statements were similar because, *"Here, people are helping you to understand."* This phrase became one pole of Donnie's first construct. She contrasted this idea with the third card, stating that in that case, *"No one is helping you at all."* This response then became the second pole of the construct. Fifteen construct sets were elicited with each participant using the same procedure.

Session 3

The next step was to ask the children to rate each of the activities using their own constructs as rating criteria. For example, when Donnie rated the activity, "I think up something to try on my own," using her first set of constructs, she indicated that the activity was more like the experience of her construct, "no one is helping you at all." A sheet for each of the 15 constructs was prepared for each student. At the top of each sheet one of the activities, was listed.

The students met with me in groups of three for two 45-minute periods each. During these sessions, they placed an "x" on the position along the line between or close to the poles of the construct indicating their rating of each of the activities or experiences. I was initially concerned that the students would find the tasks tedious, but this was not the case. The children

1. Mr. Ryan *tells* us about light.
2. We draw diagrams.
3. Mr. Ryan asks me to answer a question.
4. Mr. Ryan tells us what we are supposed to do.
5. We experiment with prisms.
6. We experiment with light sources and magnifiers.
7. We experiment with colored light.
8. We experiment with light sources and beakers.
9. We experiment with mirrors.
10. Mr. Ryan tells me what I am supposed to do.
11. I ask a question in class.
12. I read the worksheet to find out what to do.
13. I hear the other kids give their ideas about light.
14. I don't understand what I'm supposed to do.
15. Kids are goofing around during the activity.
16. I ask the teacher what I'm supposed to do.
17. I write the answers on the worksheet.
18. After the activity we talk about what we did
    and correct the worksheet.
19. I think up something to try on my own.
20. I talk with the other kids in my group.
21. Mr. Ryan tells us the meaning of words like
    reflection, refraction, and convergence.
22. We copy down what Mr. Ryan writes on the overhead.
23. I get the right answer to the questions on the worksheet.
24. I ask somebody else for help.
25. I help somebody with their work.
26. I don't get finished with the worksheet.
27. I don't get the answers that I'm supposed to
    on the worksheet.
28. Mr. Ryan gives me a hint about the right answer.
29. We experiment with Ms. Shapiro's light meter.
30. I tell my ideas about light in class.
31. I experiment with other people and with Mr. Ryan.
32. Some people understand things that I don't.
33. I'm doodling while Mr. Ryan is talking.
34. I feel bored with what I am doing.
35. I'm really enjoying what I am doing.
36. I'm having trouble reading the worksheet.
37. I put ideas together to come up with the right answer.

Figure 3.1 Student statements of experiences
while learning about the topic, light

seemed to enjoy the unique and personal nature of the information they were giving and took note of how different the charts of other students were from their own, even though the 37 activities were a constant. The children also realized that their charts were a special way of sharing their personal perspectives with me. I ensured that the students were only absent from their regular classroom for brief periods, and I helped them with class material missed during any of our conversations. Both the students and the teacher appreciated this assistance.

One particularly gratifying aspect of the rating sessions was the lack of confusion students experienced concerning the nature of their task. Also, given that the two constructs the children had put forth were their own statements, there were no questions or confusions regarding the meanings of any of the terms on the sheets. When a student did become "stuck," it was a matter of helping him or her to decide which construct most closely described the experience. The help that I offered in these situations was to ask the student, "Which construct do you think best applies in this case? What would help you make a decision?" The children enjoyed these sorting activities. The results and our conversations about them are revisited in the construction of the case study reports presented in Part II.

AN INTRODUCTION TO PART II: THE CASE REPORTS

In Part II, six case reports of the children learning science are presented to show how individual personal orientation to science learning influences the experience of learning. Each child's learning experience has been constructed using themes to characterize each child's approach to science learning. The reports are based on repertory grid conversations, extensive informal conversations, and discussions during our review of videotapes of the class study of the topic. At the conclusion of the studies, personal orientation themes are used to discuss key cognitive and environmental features of the science learning experience.

Donnie's is the first case report presented. Because it is first, her study is described in greater detail to demonstrate the approach taken in gathering and organizing information in the development of the case reports.

The conversations took place prior to, during, and following the children's fifth-grade study of the unit, "Light." It was my intention to follow the progress of the students' idea development about the topic in the context of their study and to document the processes involved as each person worked in the classroom setting to understand the ideas presented by Mr. Ryan. Each science lesson was videotaped. During private conversations with the children, the tapes were played and the children were invited to comment on their experiences. These conversations and the repertory grid information were combined to create the case reports.

In the reports, dialogue and conversation that comes directly from the videotape is shown in italics in the case reports to distinguish it from conversations with the children *about* the videotapes.

PART II

THE CASE REPORTS: CHANGING THE WAYS WE LISTEN TO ONE ANOTHER

CHAPTER 4

Donnie: The Communicator

A Deep Personal Involvement in Learning

Donnie was working with a small group of children in a reading/discussion center when I first entered the classroom. I sat near her group as they talked about their task—to write two evaluative questions about a story they had read. Donnie pleaded with various members of the group to help her understand what was meant by the phrase, "evaluative questions." She turned to me and asked if I would help her, and invited me to sit down and join her group. All of the children seemed eager to welcome and involve me, and I felt immediately comfortable sitting with them.

Throughout the initial observation period in the classroom, I noticed that Donnie demonstrated an exceptionally intense way of listening during large-group discussion. She tried to become as involved as possible in the lessons, often physically miming the teacher as he demonstrated a point. Donnie was particularly enthusiastic about responding to questions in class and was visibly disappointed when she was not chosen to answer. Her teacher, Mr. Ryan, told me that he regarded Donnie as an above-average student, and he could foresee no difficulties if I were to engage in conversation with her over a long-term period during the study. Donnie was not only approachable but also readily shared her thoughts with me, an important criterion in the selection of study participants. She became the first member of the study group.

THOUGHTS AND FEELINGS ABOUT LEARNING SCHOOL SCIENCE

An initial survey was administered to all of the children in the class (Figure 4.1). Donnie revealed, in our first conversation, a remarkable contradiction regarding her feelings about learning science. At first, she gave the impression of an attitude of disinterest, with a somewhat sullen, "Science is okay, I guess." She then added, "I never liked science. It's fun, though."

I was interested in the apparent contradiction in her feelings about science. In our first interview, I asked Donnie to explain. She commented:

47

GETTING TO KNOW YOU!

Name _____

I'd like you to fill in these two pages to help me to understand more about what you think and know about science. Remember, though, this is not a test, and if you have any trouble answering the questions, please ask for help to write in your answers. Please answer all of the questions as best you are able to! I'm interested in your ideas.

1.   What is science? _____
      Science to me is fun with
      experament and diagrams.

2.   How do you feel about learning science?   Mark an "x" under the response which suits you best.

( )	( )	( )	( )	( )
I really like it!	I like it.	It's ok.	I don't like it very much.	I really don't like it.
_____	_____	_____	_____	_____

      Why do you feel this way? _I never really liked_
      science, though it's fun

3.   Is science in school the same as science out of school?
      Not yet.
      If you say yes, how is it the same? _____
      _____

      If you say no, how is it different? _Because out of school_
      you learn about rocket going out to space.

4.   Do you study science only in school?   _Yes_

5.   Do you study science at home or on your own? _Sometimes_

Figure 4.1 Survey: Getting to know you! Donnie's responses

6. If yes, please tell where and tell what you do _Only when_
   I do things for the science fair

7. What do you like most about studying science? _The experuments_
   and drawing diagroms

8. What do you like least about studying science? _I don't_
   like it when it's hard

9. Finish this sentence. Studying science is like _a fair, you_
   have lots of fun.

10. When you study science either at home or in school, what do you like to
    do best? For the activities you like the very best, mark A. For the
    activities that you think are just "ok" mark B, and for the activities
    that you don't like, mark C.

_C_	Read the textbook
_A_	Watch demonstrations by my teacher
_C_	Write reports - science topics
_B_	Do experiments on my own
_C_	Do science worksheets
_A_	Do experiments with other kids
_C_	Read library books on science topics
_A_	Talk about science ideas with other people
_A_	Go on fieldtrips
_A_	Make science diagrams and drawings
_A_	Do science fair projects

11. Are there other activities that you like to do in science either at
    home or in school? If so, please list them _____

12. Mark one answer below which finishes the sentence,

    For me, learning science is _____ very easy
    _____ fairly easy
    I redly don't Know, _____ fairly difficult
    _____ very difficult
    sometime its easy, sometms it hard.

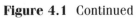

Figure 4.1 Continued

I really like science, and I usually get good marks in it. Sometimes it's difficult though. Some science projects I've been on were quite easy in the smaller grades, and I really *enjoyed* it. This year it's getting a little bit difficult, but I still like it. When I was younger, I always knew what the teacher wanted, but this year, I don't really understand some things. Before you came, we were doing the electricity unit, you know, where you light the bulb with the little bulbs and wires and batteries, but I still didn't get how the light went on. I know there's electricity going through, but I still didn't get it. I thought that it was fun to make the diagrams and experiment with them, but I just didn't understand how it lit. I just never really got it.

Donnie repeated her feelings about the unit "Batteries and Bulbs," and commented that she felt that she often did not understand in science class. I asked for some further clarification:

Ms. Shapiro: Do you feel that the concepts were explained and that you really didn't understand? It sounds like you are saying that it was never explained.
Donnie: Well. It *was* explained, but I never really understood. I never really did get it. It made me feel like the other kids knew what he was talking about, and I didn't really understand it. It just didn't make sense to me.
Ms. Shapiro: Do you ask for help when that happens?
Donnie: Oh, sometimes, but I think they might think that I'm pretty strange [laughs]. Usually I ask, but I sometimes feel sorta dumb, you know, I think I should *get it* and not have to ask.

Throughout our conversations, this conflict between interest and delight and feelings of inadequacy emerged again and again. Throughout the study, I endeavored to explore how Donnie's views about science learning were intertwined with concept development, asking how these ideas affected her efforts to learn—what she paid attention to and considered important in science learning.

Donnie's Ideas About Ways of Learning Science

In the initial survey, the children were asked to rate activities in response to the question, "When you study science either at home or in school, what do you like to do best?" Donnie's ratings were:

A. "Activities you like the very best"
   Watch demonstrations given by my teacher

> Do experiments with other kids
> Talk about science ideas with other people
> Go on field trips
> Make science diagrams and drawings
> Do Science Fair projects
> B. "Activities you think are just okay"
>   Do experiments on my own
> C. "Activities you don't like"
>   Read the textbook
>   Write reports on science topics
>   Do science worksheets
>   Read library books on science topics

When we discussed the groupings, Donnie emphasized that of all of the activities, she most enjoyed drawing and making diagrams. She also spoke of the enjoyment of having the opportunity to speak up in class. The special value that Donnie attributed to these experiences became increasingly apparent as the term progressed.

DONNIE'S IDEAS ABOUT THE NATURE OF LIGHT PRIOR TO THE LIGHT UNIT

Even among scientists there have been differing views about the nature of light, but several ideas are generally accepted and are presented in curriculum materials. Scientists describe light as an entity that propagates in space from its source. In homogeneous space, light moves along straight lines. It interacts with objects in its path and various effects are then perceived, such as warmth, rainbow colors (as when light passes through a prism), and shadows (when light hits opaque objects). Light travels at a specific, predictable speed. Light reflects from objects that are not made of a light-absorbing medium. Human vision is possible because the eye is designed to collect light reflecting from objects, placing light rays on the retina for eventual interpretation by the nervous system.

Prior to their science unit, all of the children in the class were asked questions concerning their ideas about light. The questions focused on the four concept areas presented during the light unit: (1) The nature of light, (2) How we are able to see objects, (3) The nature of light beam reflection, and (4) The nature of color.

What is Light?

The first question sought an understanding of the children's ideas about the nature of light before they began the unit on light. I asked Donnie, "What is light?"

Light. It's something that shines and is bright and comes from lightbulbs and things. When it comes from the sun it's quite warm sometimes. And it comes from light bulbs as I've said. It's something that lets us see.

Where is the Light?

In a continued attempt to understand ideas about the nature of light, I asked, "Where is the light in this room?" Donnie remarked:

Well, light is all around. It's in the lightbulbs overhead, and we made it just before you came with batteries, bulbs, and wires. There's also sunlight and rayses. There's light in this room in the tubes [points up to fluorescent lights]. And you need light so that you can see.

In these early conversations, Donnie showed that she identified light both with its source *and* with its effects. Paralleling the everyday use of the term light, she stated that light was both "everywhere" in the room and was also "in the tubes." She described light as both an entity and a condition necessary for vision. During our conversations and throughout the light unit, Donnie shifted from one meaning to the other, referring to light as an effect at one time and as a source at other times.

Association of Light Phenomena with Everyday Objects

The children were given a list of objects and asked to check those that they felt had anything to do with light or were related to light in any way. It was interesting to note that none of the six children in the study group checked "telescope" as being associated with light phenomena. Of the children who checked "camera" and "x-ray machine," all stated that the reason they did so was because they recalled seeing a flash of light when they had either had a picture or an x-ray taken. In fact, no flash of light accompanies an x-ray, and very often there is no flash of light when a picture is taken with a camera. Pursuing this further, I asked, "If there were no flash in either case, would the camera and the x-ray machine still be associated with light?" All six students in the study group said no, suggesting that the children only

Figure 4.2 How does sunlight allow the boy
to see the house? Donnie's response

associated these devices with light because they thought that flashes of light
were involved.

How Does Light Allow Us to See Objects?

Each member of the study group was asked to describe how sunlight in
the diagram enabled the child to see the house. Donnie drew in several lines
(Figure 4.2).

In her sketch, light rays emanating from the sun go to the house. Rays
of light are also shown coming from the house, then going to the boy. Her
diagram, like her response to this question during our discussion, was quite
different from the majority of students in her class. The most typical response in diagram form given by Donnie's classmates was to show a light ray
emanating from the sun, then striking the house. Donnie drew a second ray
reflecting to the boy. It also struck the house. Untypically, Donnie's response
was closer to the view put forward by scientists. I asked her to explain the
diagram to me:

> Donnie: Well, the boy sees the house because the . . . this is what I
> was *told*, that the rayses from the sun fall on the house and bounce
> off it to the boy.
> Ms. Shapiro: Oh, you say you were *told* this.
> Donnie: Well, yes, I think last year when we were opening a lightbulb,
> doing some things with light. Or maybe in third grade. I remember
> learning that. A teacher said that.

Donnie recalled that this idea came from a teacher, and she used this
authority, not her own opinion or personal judgment, to give credibility to

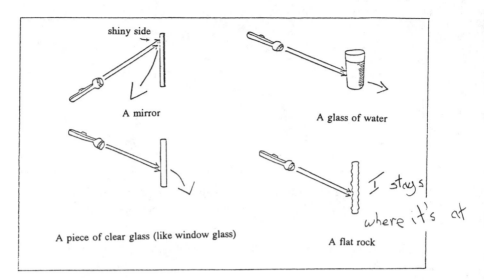

Figure 4.3 How do light beams interact with objects? Donnie's response

her answer. As will be seen later in the study, although Donnie provided the correct, scientific response in this example she did not fully understand what she had drawn.

Light Beam Interaction with Objects

This question presented a set of diagrams depicting flashlight beams visibly shining onto different objects. The children were asked to show what would happen to light beams when they came in contact with the objects. Donnie's responses are shown in Figure 4.3.

In the final example, Donnie wrote that "the light would stay where it is" when it struck the flat rock. I asked Donnie if the beams would interact differently if a person were standing near the object. I wondered if, with an observer present, she would see the light beam interaction in the same manner. Her response was "the same" in all instances except for the flat rock. In this case, she said: "Here, I'm not sure, but the beam would have to go to the person if the person were standing there."

Once Donnie had made this comment, she went back to her diagram of the light beam striking the glass of water and said that the beam in that case would have to bounce back to the person standing near it. She added, however, that in both cases this would occur only when a person was present. If a person were not present, then the "beams would stay right where they are."

From these examples, it was again clear that Donnie accepted the scientific explanation of the behavior of visible light rays and opaque objects only to a limited extent. She apparently based her thinking not only on the scientists' viewpoint, but also on her own memory of sensory experience. Unless a person were present in the last example, she apparently could not believe that the light rays would reflect from the rock. In Donnie's view, the event did not occur unless it was observed by a person. This idea is likely generalized by her to other physical phenomena, such as sound and motion. The discussion borders on the philosophical but, unfortunately, must also create confusion for Donnie in the grasp of concepts in science class.

How Do We See Color?

In this interview activity, each participant was shown four thick sheets of plastic, one red, one blue, one green, and one yellow. A flashlight was turned on to each piece of plastic. Visible beams of light appeared to pass through the plastic and were projected onto a white piece of paper on the table. I asked Donnie, in the case of the flashlight on the blue plastic, if she could tell me why she thought that we saw blue on the white piece of paper.

> Donnie: The plastic turns the light from the flashlight blue. It makes it blue.
> Ms. Shapiro: I wonder, how does this happen?
> Donnie: Well . . . I'd say that when the ray hits the blue plastic . . . that it makes it blue.
> Ms. Shapiro: Okay. I see.
> Donnie: The blue is in the way of the light and it colors the light.

Donnie's idea was typical of the viewpoint of her peers and is commonly held by children and adults. It was the accepted scientific viewpoint at the beginning of the 17th century (Ronchi, 1970). Light and color were believed to be separate entities. Color was thought to be a property of the surface of objects that was made visible when light was shone on an object. The scientists' explanation involves understanding that commonly observed light, white light, is made up of a combination of all of the colors of the visible spectrum. When light is passed through a filter, some of its colors are absorbed and others are transmitted. The color of the light we observe is the color that is transmitted.

Feelings and Experiences Associated with Light and the Study of Light

The children expressed many spontaneous feelings as they experimented during the light unit. The activity with prisms brought squeals of

"Cool" and "Oooooh, pretty!" Of course, feelings experienced during an actual participation with phenomena are expressed more readily than memories, but the children were able to recall the feelings they associated with light during our conversations. Donnie commented, "Sometimes it's sort of creepy at night, just before I go to bed, you know, like, you look at the door and you see that little line of light, so you know your mom and dad are still up, and you can hear their voices, and that's sometimes sort of creepy because the room is so dark, but you can still see the outlines of objects. I also think of cheerful, sort of friendly lights, like our Christmas lights. But when the light is really bright light that just makes your eyes go iiyaaah . . . like when someone pops a flash at you, and, oooooh, for about a half an hour you see this blue spot. I hate that, when it's too bright like that.

Donnie remembered studying light in the second and fourth grades. In the fourth grade, she recalled learning about light bouncing off objects. She recalled not quite understanding the ideas presented.

> In second grade we must have studied it because I remember the teacher doing all kinds of really cool things with the flashlight. And we made shadows with the overhead projector of stuff that we couldn't tell what it was at first. Then we had to guess, based on the shape, what it was. Last year we were looking at light bulbs one day and what was inside and all. Then the teacher drew an eye and a person . . . no, just the eye and some things the person was looking at, and told us about it. But, [laughs] you know, I really didn't get it. Well, I sort of did.

Views on Books About Light

I took each of the children in the study group into the school library to review the school's selection of books available on the topic light. Of the twelve books in the library on light, including related topics such as color, lasers, and photography, only four had been checked out more than four times. Donnie suggested that light was not a topic that she would study if she were on her own. "Unless I was working on a project on light, I wouldn't even go to this section of the library." The books that did interest her concerned topics relating to current technology—lasers, for example—and those containing experiments. It was also of interest that Donnie thought that the book on color was out of place on the shelf, even though it was correctly placed in the light section.

My impression of Donnie's overall feelings about studying light in the past seemed quite mixed. She expressed an interest in experimenting yet had had difficulty in understanding some of the ideas presented in past

1. People are helping you to understand.	1. No one is helping you at all.
2. Knowing just what to do.	2. Embarrassed, just about to get into trouble.
3. Doing what you're supposed to be doing.	3. Goofing around.
4. Going ahead and trying things.	4. Stuck.
5. Asking questions.	5. Writing things down and drawing diagrams.
6. Working on worksheets.	6. Working with an instrument (like a light source).
7. Working with Mr. Ryan.	7. Doing something on your own.
8. Getting the right answers.	8. Not understanding at all.
9. Talking about the learning with the other kids in class.	9. Talking about the learning with the kids in your group.
10. Understanding all of it.	10. Not quite getting it, but getting some of it.
11. Writing things down and drawing diagrams.	11. Just listening to the teacher talk and talk and talk.
12. Telling *your* feelings about it.	12. Listening, bored.
13. Easy stuff.	13. Hard stuff.
14. Putting the ideas together.	14. Being confused.
15. Knowing how to phrase an idea and say it.	15. Not being about to get the idea out, say it, not being able to quite phrase it.

Figure 4.4 Donnie's science learning constructs

classes. While she worked through the science unit with her classmates, we determined her personal constructs about science learning and I began to shape the case report further.

ORGANIZATION OF DONNIE'S CASE REPORT USING PERSONAL CONSTRUCT THEMES

Donnie's Personal Constructs

The procedures used to generate personal constructs are described in chapter 3. Donnie's personal constructs (Figure 4.4) regarding science learning allow us to see in her own words the ways in which she organized thinking about science learning. Each participant's personal constructs are presented to show the different ways that the children described science learning. The constructs were analyzed, along with interview and observational data, for the development of personal orientation themes that were used as a framework in the creation of each case report. The report was then used to revisit concept development and work in the classroom.

Theme 1. A Sense of Inadequacy as a Science Learner

Donnie's Self-Characterization: "I never seem to have all of the right answers, the complete answer. I know what the answer is, but I just don't get it. I can't seem to phrase it. I seem to have some of the information but not *all* of the information."

My Image/Impression: Donnie sees herself as an inadequate science learner, as not quite being able to grasp the concept presented, yet having a strong desire to participate fully.

Throughout the unit, Donnie spoke often of wishing for all of the information needed to respond during science class, but of feeling that she did not have all of the answers. Her statements in the construct groupings and the contrasting poles reflect these thoughts and feelings about involvement in the science unit. Her statements show that *understanding* has a special meaning for her. I recalled her concern in the remark, "When I was younger I always knew what the teacher wanted, but this year, I don't really understand some things."

In early science experiences, children are encouraged to develop *sense awareness*, to trust the senses as validating criteria for making observations and drawing conclusions. This focus on awareness and use of the senses was predominant in the early grades, but this year Donnie is being asked to simply accept on faith the insights and ideas that have been put forward as the result of centuries of accumulated and corroborated scientific endeavor. Such insights are very often counterintuitive or cannot be personally verified. Students may not believe scientific ideas when they cannot grasp the thinking behind them. They have not participated in the process of knowledge creation, therefore, they may not understand how ideas are verified or rejected in science. Waterman (1982) studied the epistemological bases of college students' understanding of science and found that at the university level, problems with grasping the concepts was often due to an inability to distinguish between personally verifiable knowledge and scientific knowledge, requiring simple acceptance.

Donnie readily reflected on her own thinking processes and was able to provide much insight during our reviews of the videotapes of the lessons on light. Dialogue and descriptive sequences directly from the videotapes are printed in italics in the following segments.

The introduction to the light unit. The class introduction to the light unit began with a question posed by Mr. Ryan: *"Who can tell me how we see things?"*

Leon: We see things upside down? Like we really see the things upside down but our brain turns them right up again.

Mr. Ryan: Okay, that's good. But how do we get the image in the first place?
Leslie: With our eyes.
Mr. Ryan: Good. Good. Any other ideas about how we see things?
Alana: Light.
Mr. Ryan: Light. How does that happen?
Alana: In the dark we can't see things. You need light to see where things are.
Mr. Ryan: In the dark we can't see things. You need light to see where things are.
*   Oh, good, good. Any other ideas?*
Diane: In the dark you need more light to see better.

Mr. Ryan summarized the points that the students made about how objects are seen. Prior to the lessons, he and I had informally discussed the research literature on alternative frameworks concerning the nature of light and the difficulty that students have in grasping concepts, such as the idea that light travels, that some objects reflect light rather than produce it, and that light must enter the eye to enable us to see. The teacher's edition of the materials Mr. Ryan was using suggested presenting the latter concept initially through discussion, by "eliciting from the student that the current way of explaining light and seeing suggests that light is something which travels from the thing we see to our eyes." Ryan could not elicit this difficult idea from the class.

Mr. Ryan: How many of you think that we see things because my eyes are send-
*   ing out to, say, the reason that I am seeing Martin is because something is be-*
*   ing sent out to Martin that is, my eyes are doing all of the work? [Silence. No*
*   hands are raised.] Nobody? Okay. That's good because a lot of people*
*   thought initially that that's how we saw things, that it was our eyes that were*
*   responsible for everything. It took a long time for people to figure out that*
*   light had a part in it and that it was the light that was coming from Martin*
*   into my eyes that allowed me to see him. Not something coming from my eyes*
*   to him, but light coming from him into my eyes—or whatever it is that you're*
*   looking at.*

Following our review of the videotape, Donnie expressed the confusion she had been unable to discuss in class:

Ms. Shapiro: So, you agreed with the statement that Mr. Ryan made, that the reason I see Martin is because light is coming from him into my eyes.

Donnie: No, uh. No. I didn't agree with that. It doesn't make sense.

Ms. Shapiro: You say it doesn't make sense.

Donnie: It doesn't make sense . . . because *people* don't make light. It's electricity that makes light and it's the sun that makes light.

Ms. Shapiro: Mmmhmm. Any other examples?

Donnie: Well, water helps to make electricity, so that, you could say that makes light.

Ms. Shapiro: So I understand that you are saying that it's not the light from me that you see. It's the light reflecting off of me.

Donnie: Well, the sun shines on you and I can see you because of the sun, it's not anything else. It's not *you*, it's the sun.

Ms. Shapiro: It's not *me*, it's the sun. So, is the sun reflecting off of me?

Donnie: No. No, the sun's not reflecting off of you, it's shining on you, but it's not reflecting off of you [her voice trails off to a whisper].

Donnie explained that she disagreed with the idea presented in class that light reflects from a person and is then reflected into the eyes of the observer. This was in conflict with the explanation shown in her diagram prior to the lesson. There she had given the correct scientific explanation for the interaction of vision, light, and objects. She stated that she remembered that in Grade 4 her teacher "said that." But following Mr. Ryan's discussion, she said that the idea "does not make sense." Donnie was not able to apply the idea.

Her confusion was also apparent in another video sequence in which class discussion centered on why we are able to see the moon from the earth.

Rena: Darkness must be a place where there isn't any light.

Donnie: Rena said that darkness must be a place where there isn't any light. I thought that was true. I was going to say the same thing.

Mr. Ryan: Yeah. I'd have to agree. Darkness is a place without light. Can anyone tell me what light is?

Marvin: The sun is light.

Kitty: Light is something that shines.

Melody: The lights around us are bright.

Donnie: The street lights are light at night.

Carey: You can get light from a campfire.

Mark: You can get light from stars.

Marvin: Light can come from electricity. Light can come from the moon. It shines at night.

Mr. Ryan: Oh, no. I see Michael shaking his head with that one.

*Michael: Like, the sun reflects its light to the moon—it comes from the sun. The
moon is like a mirror.*

*Mr. Ryan: Oh, good, good. Michael said the moon is like a mirror and it re-
flects the light that comes from the sun so that we can see it. Good point.*

Donnie: I agreed with Michael. He said that the moon is like a mirror.
Yeah. I saw that lots of times on, well [laughs], on Sesame Street.
Like it's really for babies, but I like to watch it [laughs]. That's probably where Michael saw it, too. The rayses [she uses her hands to
demonstrate on the table] from the sun reflect on the moon.

Ms. Shapiro: I see. He said that light travels from the thing to our eyes
and that's why we see it?

Donnie: Hmm [pauses]. Well, the light reflects on the thing and it
bounces off to us so we can see it, like he said.

Donnie applied the scientific idea supported by the Sesame Street lesson. Yet it was clear from our continuing discussion that she did not have a
firm grasp of the *presented* idea, as she was not able to consistently apply the
idea correctly. She *wanted* to give the correct idea in class, but could not deny
it when an idea truly did not make sense to her. This became much clearer
when Donnie expressed her views on the phenomenon *refraction*, which was
studied later in the unit by the class.

Mark's revolutionary idea. The next day, Mr. Ryan told me that he was
going to skip the program's activities that dealt with light passing through
liquids of different density, and would go directly to an activity that he found
the children enjoyed a great deal, which was intriguingly entitled, "So Deceiving." The lesson was comprised of two activities. In the first, students
put an empty saucer on a table, placed a coin in the saucer, then moved away
from the table and crouched just to the point where they could no longer see
the coin. Someone then slowly poured water into the saucer. When the saucer
was filled to a certain point, the coin suddenly appeared to the crouched
observers. The children were challenged to state why this was so. The second question was designed to help the students pull all of the ideas presented
in the unit together. The students observed a pencil placed in a beaker of
water and were asked to provide an explanation for the broken appearance
of the pencil. Donnie worked particularly hard during the lesson to respond
with the explanation. I asked her which activity she preferred.

Donnie: The saucer is the one I preferred. It was fun. You got to see
something that was really interesting happen. And then you open
your eyes and you think it's magic and . . . but it's not. It's just something that's really tricky and fun to find out. But I also liked that ac-

tivity a while back where we predicted which way the light would reflect. That was the *most* interesting and fun. I don't know, I might have found it interesting because I got them all right [laughs], but I thought that it was a lot of fun to make that decision, like about how the light would go. Here [watching video], this is where I'm going to start telling what the answer is. I was just going down to try to explain my idea there. What happened was that you took a saucer and you put a coin in it, and then you fill it up with water, and you have to be down on your knees . . . before you put the water in until you can't see anything but the edge of the saucer, and then when you fill it up with water, then you can see the coin. I tried to answer in the discussion, but my answer wasn't quite right.

Ms. Shapiro: You say your answer wasn't quite right here. I'm not sure what you mean.

Donnie: No. Sometimes I don't think that, well . . . I have some trouble with science. Mostly the last unit that we did. Like I told you what we had to do was take a tiny light bulb and we had wire and we had to figure out ways how to light this bulb, and we had different activities to do and actually it was quite fun, but in other ways it was hard to understand because I didn't know how they could take a little piece of wire and attach it to a battery and then put the light bulb on and the battery and make it light. That, that's hard to understand.

Ms. Shapiro: So you found it hard to *do?*

Donnie: No, it's kind of hard to *understand* how it all worked!

Ms. Shapiro: It seems as though you were finding the unit fun, but a bit difficult to understand.

Donnie: I'm finding it really interesting. Some of the activities are hard though. Sometimes I feel like I don't have it all, *all* of the information to tell what is happening.

Putting ideas together. As we reviewed the tape, Donnie related her frustrated effort to provide an explanation for the broken appearance of the pencil in the beaker. She described how she believed that listening to the other students in the class helped her to add to and develop her own ideas, to almost "get all of the information."

Donnie: That's Carey talking now.

Ms. Shapiro: She seems to be saying that there is only air in the top part of the glass and that the water in the bottom is what makes the pencil look bigger. Did you agree with that?

Donnie: Well, yeah, I took a little bit of *that* information too. I took some other people's information and put it into mine, but I still didn't quite get all of what I needed. This is where I'm going to answer.

Mr. Ryan: Can anyone think of an explanation using the words bending, light, and refraction?

Donnie: At that point I wasn't quite sure, how the . . . how it happened. Like, I didn't know that there was *light* in that part.

Ms. Shapiro: He asked, "Can anyone think of an explanation using the words light. . . .

Donnie: Bending and refraction.

Ms. Shapiro: That would have given a clue, I guess, about what was the right answer.

Donnie: Yeah, but it just didn't make any sense that there was *light* in there and that that's how it makes it bigger. I'm gonna say something here. . . .

Donnie said she felt that she had some of the right idea, but she believed that understanding the behavior of light was the key to the explanation and she was concerned that she had not thought about light at all as part of the explanation. She knew from listening to the discussion that an idea about light behavior was the key to the mystery, but she was not sure how it explained the pencil's broken appearance.

Mr. Ryan: What is the water doing to the pencil?

Ms. Shapiro: Right here it looks as if you were hit with a bolt of lightning. Right there. What happened there?

Donnie: I think that I just realized an answer that I wanted to give. Just, let's watch it a second, okay? Leanne is talking about the shadow that the pencil makes in the beaker, but that's not it, the answer.

Mr. Ryan: Do you see a shadow? When I took the pencil out, was it the same size as when it went in? Donnie?

Donnie: Well, the water and the glass makes it bend. . . .

Mr. Ryan: Makes it bend?

Donnie: Makes the pencil bend. Makes it look bigger.

Mr. Ryan: I'm not sure that I understand what you're saying. If I put the pencil in the water and I look at it, it looks like my pencil's broken. When I take it out it isn't broken any more. Did it bend and fix itself?

Class: No!

Mr. Ryan: [Emphatically] Okay, what made it look like it was broken?

Donnie: The water.

Mr. Ryan: Okay. [In a louder voice.] But what did the water do to make it look like it was broken?

Ms. Shapiro: You look very intense here. What was going on for you here?

Donnie: Well, I didn't know what the answer was. But I *wanted* to know. So I was just looking here to see what Mr. Ryan had on the overhead, so all I am doing here is copying down what he had up there. The right answer.

Natalie: I think that it is the roundness of the glass.

Ms. Shapiro: She is saying that it is the roundness of the glass?

Donnie: Yeah, later on, Jim says that it acts like a magnifying glass. I also took *his* information and put it into mine, and it made better what I had, what I was thinking, but I still didn't quite get all of it.

Ms. Shapiro: So it was Jim's information that you put together with yours?

Donnie: Only I had a little bit more than he had. I just took the magnifying glass part.

Ms. Shapiro: So you are saying that it acts like a magnifying glass?

Donnie: Yes.

Ms. Shapiro: So the magnifying glass makes it look bigger.

Donnie: Well, [pauses] a magnifying glass is like two glasses together. It makes things look bigger.

Ms. Shapiro: How do the glasses do that?

Donnie: [laughs] I don't know!

This conversation with Donnie took place one day after she had heard Mark's correct explanation and had heard Mr. Ryan reiterate it. In fact, Donnie and the other students in class were required to copy down the correct explanation as Mr. Ryan had written it and shown it to them using the overhead projector. Although Donnie had stated, on several previous occasions in discussion with me, that light is reflected from objects, in other conversations she stated that it is only reflected from *some* objects. Because she did not appear to have completely grasped the idea that light reflects from *all* objects, she did not use it in combination with the idea that light is bent when it passes through the beaker. The idea, that light is reflected from objects, had been presented repeatedly, and was the main concept on previous occasions in Donnie's discussions with me. However, in other conversations, she had stated that it is only reflected from some objects. Because she did not appear to have completely grasped the idea that light reflects from *all* objects, she did not use it in combination with the idea that light is bent when it passes through the beaker, even though the idea had been presented repeatedly and had been the main concept presented in the previous lesson, "Bend that Beam." In terms of a construct theory explanation, her thinking still reflected the idea that made the most sense to her. There was no reason to change.

Donnie's earnestness and persistence was evident in the lesson as she *repeatedly* tried to give her explanation in response to the question, "Why does the pencil appear to look larger?" *she continued to do so even while Mr. Ryan indicated to her that she was not giving the correct response.* Donnie persisted in the discussion, and at one point, Mr. Ryan told her that she had "some" of the idea, but not all of the idea. I asked her about this as we watched the videotape.

Ms. Shapiro: When Mr. Ryan told you that you had some of the idea, how did you feel about that, encouraged?

Donnie: No. Just as normal as I would feel if I got something *wrong*. He's saying that and I'm gonna say something after him, 'cause I'm still talking here, so I'm not quite finished.

Ms. Shapiro: He said that you had part of it. But I think you're saying that you somehow count that as being wrong.

Donnie: Well, you know, I'm sort of right and sort of wrong, but I wanted to *get* it [laughs]! My answers are never right in science.

Ms. Shapiro: You're always wrong in science?

Donnie: Well, it's usually that I'm halfway right, and in other ways I am sort of right.

Ms. Shapiro: So you know that you have some of the basic ideas?

Donnie: Yeah, but there are some that aren't there. There are some people who seem to always get it all of the time. Like Katy, Annie, and Carey, sometimes, or Mark. Last year I got most of the answers. This year it's just a little bit hard. I don't know why. My explanation for this one, I think it's this one here, Mr. Ryan said that I was on the right track here. He said that I had a really good answer for it, but here Mark had a better understanding of it. He got all of the information. I only got half of it.

Ms. Shapiro: What was it that Mark got that you didn't?

Donnie: Okay. I'm not good at explaining things, but [laughs] well, what happened is that *I* thought that the water *and* the glass did it.

Ms. Shapiro: The water and the glass is what you said before.

Donnie: Yeah! Because I didn't think of the *light*. I don't know why I didn't think of the *light* like Mark did [laughs]. I don't know why I didn't!

Ms. Shapiro: Hmm. Well, the glass is something that you can see through. . . .

Donnie: Yeah, you can see through it. Now I said that it acted like a *magnifying glass*. It was like this: I said that it acted like a magnifying glass, and it acted like a magnifying glass because the water, I said was a *liquid*, and I said that the glass is like a magnifying glass, and the beaker, well, the glass and the liquid together would probably make it look bigger, but I said *it*, the pencil, looked bent like this [bends her finger] or something, make it bend, like, but I didn't mean that it *was* bent, just that it *looked* bent.

Ms. Shapiro: I see. You know, it sounded to me like you meant that it did bend it, too.

Donnie: You know, that threw me *right off*. I had no idea, well, what was going on, what to say there.

Ms. Shapiro: What threw you right off?

Donnie: That it wasn't *just* the water. At this point I didn't have any idea that it had, that *light* was in it, was in the answer.

Ms. Shapiro: Hmm [pause].

Donnie: Because, well, I didn't know what was happening here because of the light. Because you can *see* light. I just didn't have any idea that light had something to do with it. I was really surprised. I don't know how I could've come up with that idea. But I know what happens now. The light, it goes through the water and it hits the pencil, and the water and the light makes it look broken and how it does that is that the light shines into the water, you know and you can see it, the water, and then it goes right in and then it hits the pencil and then you see on the water line, and the . . . you can make it go down, and it's supposed to be like that [shows me a straight finger and points to the beaker], but it goes like that [crooks her finger and points to the beaker and the pencil]. I didn't explain that very well.

Ms. Shapiro: No, that was fine. How did you get the idea that light is the key?

Donnie: From what Mark said in class . . . in the discussion.

Ms. Shapiro: So that gave you a clue to the idea. I see, so it makes sense to you now, that it's the light.

Donnie: No, not really. But Dean said that, and Mr. Ryan said that it was right.

Donnie was able to tell me that light was the key to understanding the problem. But despite the fact that she provided the scientific explanation for refraction, she realized that she did not fully understand the idea. She would be able to answer such a question correctly on a quiz, examination, or survey of ideas about light phenomena, but she herself stated that she did not have a real understanding of the refraction concept.

Learners' ideas and the design of curriculum materials. Donnie did not grasp this important light idea. She showed clearly that she believed light rays reflect off objects only when they can be actually seen to reflect. Indeed, in all of the lessons in the program, reference is made to visible beams of light that emanate from a light source box. It is understandable that Donnie would comment, "I had no idea that it was the light." No connection was made in the curriculum program materials between the behavior of the visible light beams the children observed and the pervasive light rays that are all around us.

The children were asked to accept an idea that did not "make sense." The idea could not be validated through experience, but simply required acceptance. In the early years and experiences of science learning, we teach children to become good observers, to trust in the senses—touch, taste, sight, smell, and hearing—to verify observations. As topics under study increase in complexity, we ask students to go beyond observation and accept the products of years of scientific investigation. We begin to explain events and phenomena not in terms of what students can see for themselves, but in terms of what others have found out through their observations, observations that are based on the use of very different equipment and ways of thinking than those available to the student. We provide further confusion in this situation by giving students hands-on activities in which an understanding of the behavior of visible light rays is shown in all activity examples and then the idea of the behavior of nonvisible light rays is introduced. Donnie did not make the mental leap of considering the visible rays of light as behaving like invisible rays of light. In fact, on several occasions she showed that she was not aware of the existence of nonvisible rays. She left the lesson very much aware that she was not able to master the concept.

Theme II. A Social-Aesthetic Orientation to Science Learning

> *Donnie's Self-Characterization:* "I like to talk in class and draw diagrams. Drawing diagrams is what I like to do the very best."
>
> *My Image/Impression:* Enjoyment in full participation in the experience of learning. Enjoyment of putting ideas together in a visual representation.

Donnie's second theme emerged as an interest in finding ways to communicate more fully in the science lessons. She enjoyed speaking up in class, but particularly enjoyed the use of drawings to keep track of her ideas. During the reviews of the videotape of this lesson, and in previous lessons, Donnie would often spontaneously ask me if she could make a diagram in my notes to demonstrate and discuss the particular point she was trying to make in our conversation.

The activity, "Drawing Beams and Shadows," asked students to use symbols in drawings on the worksheet in answering questions. I asked Donnie what she thought was the main purpose of the lesson. She said that she thought it was to learn to make the specialized signs used to describe the features of light. She enjoyed making the diagrams. I asked if she thought there were special reasons for learning to make the diagrams.

> Donnie: Well, it's easier to know what you're talking about because actually it's easier to do, like you don't have to write a whole bunch of words. You just have to draw a diagram of what you're talking about. It's quicker and it's more interesting.
>
> Ms. Shapiro: Do you think that scientists use symbols like this to talk about light?
>
> Donnie: Well, I'm not sure, but I know that if I was a scientist studying light, I would.
>
> Ms. Shapiro: Oh?
>
> Donnie: Yeah, for the same reasons that we do it. It takes a shorter period of time and you can just scan it and it tells what you're talking about. It makes it all easier to do. It's a little hard to remember the symbols, though, but it makes it easier to do. But they probably use it in different ways.
>
> Ms. Shapiro: Where do these worksheets come from do you think?
>
> Donnie: Oh, Mr. Ryan makes them up. He says that he's done this unit before with his other class.

Melody, Martin, and Pierre, three other students in the project, also thought that the worksheets were developed by Mr. Ryan. This could be one of the reasons why most of the children put forward the idea that their use of a conventional symbol system in the classroom was primarily to aid their teacher in correcting their worksheets. The real purpose was to help students learn to use symbols as scientists do in the communication of information. Only Mark and Donnie developed, on their own, the idea that scientists use convention in symbol presentation for communication with one another, and that learning these symbols was the main purpose of the lesson. Donnie noted the potential for a relationship between the symbolic representation that she used to communicate about light on her worksheets and the ways scientists communicate their findings, but she was not sure that she was correct about the connection.

Donnie often used drawings to clarify her ideas. She commented that her drawings of the color spectrum, for example, were useful as a guide to recall information for later use. And she expressed the pure enjoyment of drawing for its own sake as a way of fully participating. Clearly, drawing was a valuable study tool for Donnie. Although required by the teacher, interest in drawing originated within her, and it appeared to be an uplifting vehicle for deeper participation in her work, exactly what she was seeking.

Theme III. Enjoyment in Expression of Ideas to Others

Donnie's Self-Characterization: "I really like to speak up in class because then, well, I get a chance to listen and speak up and tell what I'm feeling."

My Image/Impression: The enjoyment of putting ideas together through participation in discussion in class. The sense of making a personal contribution.

Speaking up in class had special meaning for Donnie. She spoke about this for the first time during a video review session of the introduction to the light unit.

Mr. Ryan: We can take light and make it go in different directions. Okay. So, we've got two points of view now. We have Mark and Martin agreeing that light travels in straight lines and we have Sam thinking that light travels in circles, too, like a laser.

Donnie: I think it travels in a straight line because if you, like look at something, it isn't crooked or zigzaggy [mimes] like this, it's just straight *lines [she uses her whole body to demonstrate].*

Donnie: Here I got to talk a little. Well, first, I had also said that you can make light go in circles, but you can make it go different ways. You can make it go zigzag, though, but I see, no, you can't really make it go in circles. But you can have it come right over at you and then have one mirror up here and another mirror over here and then you turn them like towards each other [she draws me a diagram] like that and then the light would, something like this, it would cross. So really you can make light go in different ways.

Ms. Shapiro: So your talking here in class helped you to understand. . . .

Donnie: Helped me to get the idea out. Well, it helps me to understand, like if I'm wrong then I feel, well, by talking about it I can actually learn. It helps me learn. Like, if I get something wrong, if somebody tells me what the answer is, I'll remember it and learn something new.

Ms. Shapiro: So you're not afraid to be wrong.

Donnie: No [laughs]! Well, I'm not always right and I don't brag about it, that I'm always right and all like that, and I don't get surprised when I'm wrong either, 'cause I know sometimes I'm wrong and sometimes I'm right. But I like to say something that *I* think, that *I* feel.

Personal participation and the development of a sense of oneself as science learner. Donnie valued being able to add her own ideas to class discussion, to be able to draw on her own judgment and express her opinion on the nature of phenomena. She found talking useful to clarify her ideas, to find out if she is "right" or "wrong." Donnie's interest was in her active participation in the science lesson. Because she valued speaking up, she was aware of her own level of understanding. Donnie often expressed the idea that she *should* somehow be able to get the right answer, that she *should* be able to figure it out. She believed that it was more often than not the case that the other students were understanding what was being taught while she was not. She chided herself for not being able to piece together ideas as she believed others were doing. Although she saw others responding in class discussion with correct answers, she did not notice that they did not always understand the ideas fully. Mark showed an understanding of refraction because he grasped the idea that light reflects off all objects and used this information in a new situation. Even though Mark did not personally observe the bouncing of light rays, he was able to believe the idea or the possibility of its truth.

Between her joy in communication and her sense of not quite having all of the answer, Donnie was experiencing frustration as a science learner. She felt the responsibility to know and understand was hers completely. Because she felt that she was lacking in some way, she began to develop a sense of inadequacy in science. Donnie spoke as if she was beginning to believe that science simply wasn't for her.

"Weird words and funny language." Donnie was the first to mention difficulty in distinguishing the everyday use of terms from the specialized, scientific use of the terms in the light unit. Reference was made in one videotape we watched to the "bending of light rays."

> *Mr. Ryan: That's basically what happens. The water bends the light coming from the pencil. Okay? It is the bending of the light that makes the pencil appear as if it is in a different position in the water.*
> Ms. Shapiro: Can we stop here? Mark was explaining the bent appearance of the pencil here.
> Donnie: [Pause] Well, he said that the light *hit* the pencil and then would make it *bend*. It's the water *and* the light, mostly, I guess.
> Ms. Shapiro: It's the water and the light mostly? You were saying before that the glass is somehow involved. Do you still think so?

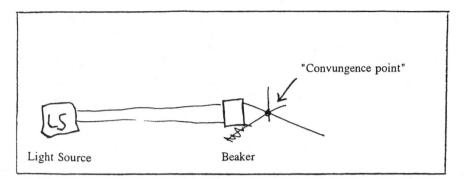

"Convungence point"

Light Source   Beaker

Figure 4.5 Donnie's drawing of light beam bending
and "Convungence Point"

Donnie: Yes. It has to have something to do with it I think. It *must*.
Mr. Ryan: *The water bends the light. The top part of the pencil was not in the water and did not appear to be broken. The top part with the air doesn't have anything to bend the light. The part of the pencil that was not in the water didn't have anything to bend the light. When the light is bent, it made the pencil appear to have moved position under the water. Good, good. So let's write that down.*
Ms. Shapiro: I see that at this point you are writing down your answer. Were you *understanding* here?
Donnie: Well, I didn't understand it, no. I didn't understand what was *needed*. I thought that it was weird.
Ms. Shapiro: Weird?
Donnie: Well, there are all of these weird things, you know, like light bends. Light bends? I don't know. Light bends? How does it do that? I thought I'd see, like, light bending in the light source. But it doesn't. Only when it reflects.
Ms. Shapiro: You mean that only when you see the light bounce from the mirror, hitting and striking an angle?
Donnie: Yeah.

I pursued Donnie's concern with the use of the word "bend" when describing light to try to understand what using the word meant for her and in what way she felt it was "weird." She explained by drawing for me a light source, then a beaker of water. The rays of light passed through the beaker of water and converged.

Donnie: [Pointing with a pencil to her drawing, Figure 4.5] Say you have a light source, here, okay? Not too straight, but who cares [laughs]? So you have a light source there. And you have the beams. Two small beams. Okay. What happens is, like, say the beaker of water or a magnifier, let's have the beaker of water. . .there's the beaker of water, and you have a mirror. Right here. The light rays would hit the glass of water. Well, they hit there and then bounce off somewhere else. But I don't think, well, what would happen would be that they would be going across like that, and then they would probably be going off like that over here. So there, they're sort of bending. They bend right here. These are what, convungence points? And then right there.

Ms. Shapiro: I see. So when it hits and goes off, that's where it bends?

Donnie: No. That's reflection. Actually, the only bending point is right there. At the convungence.

Donnie had not grasped the special meaning of "bend" in the way that it was used in the light unit, that is, the idea that rays of light shining through a beaker of water are angularly redirected. Instead, she was applying her understanding of the everyday use of the word, bend, to the effects of light. She did not realize that the term has a special meaning in the study of light. She commented during another lesson in which visible light rays were passed through a beaker of water:

Bend, he said the light rays bend. But they only do that when they bounce off, like, a mirror. Like, and go like this [she bends her finger]. Because you don't see the light bending. It has to bounce off something.

In other lessons, Donnie commented on her fascination with new words, yet at the same time on the confusion that they sometimes produced. During the review of the videotape of lesson 9, "Prisms and Spectra," Donnie stopped the tape.

Donnie: I read this over here, and I still didn't understand here 'cause they use funny language, sometimes weird words.

Ms. Shapiro: They use funny language. You mentioned that before.

Donnie: Well, the words "rotate" and then they say, "gradually observe" and "arrange" and things like that [reading from the worksheet]. Well, I know what they mean, it's just that some of the things, I just don't get what they're talking about. When they put them all together, like, it takes so long to figure things out.

Ms. Shapiro: What does it mean "to rotate the prism gradually"?

Donnie: Let's see, like, to move it around slowly, I guess. [She demonstrates by swinging the prism around as if drawing a full circle with

it.] To move it around like that. Move it around until you find a rainbow. I don't like all that language. And the words like arrange, procedure, rotate, gradually observe, spectra. Those are hard.

Ms. Shapiro: You know what a spectra is.

Donnie: No. And I just learned what the "prison" is. I never saw that
before. I like to learn all the words and stuff, like "converge." They
help me to learn. I like to use them all but sometimes it's just too
hard. But like "refraction," oh, I know he uses it all the time but I
just can't remember what it means.

Donnie's dilemma appeared to me to be the struggle of the authentic
learner. She took responsibility for her own learning and valued the technical
terminology introduced by her teacher. She struggled with it, though, and
became frustrated in her effort to make sense of it all. Her confusion may
have been inadvertently compounded by her teacher. His own high level of
understanding of the science content may have kept him from understanding
the struggle of his students to grasp ideas. Mr. Ryan may have been well
aware of the specialized use of terms, the two ways that the term "reflection"
was used, for example, but he did not share this insight explicitly with the
students.

Throughout the unit of study, Mr. Ryan used the term "reflection" at
times in a commonsense manner, referring to the visible beams of light and
visible images that the children actually saw in the classroom either bouncing
off a mirror or seen in a mirror. Reference to ambient light rays, nonvisible
rays of light that bounce off all objects in the environment, was frequently
made, for example, in an activity in which students viewed the reversal of
the word "light" written on a card as they moved the card farther and farther
away from them while viewing it through a beaker of water. In this example,
a very scientific understanding of "reflection" of light rays is required, and
yet, the teacher's explanation of the term "reflection" was almost always the
same, referring to mirror images.

*Mr. Ryan: We all know what reflection is. When you wake up in the morning
and look in the mirror, you see yourself, your image. That is reflection.*

When I asked Donnie to describe her understanding of light reflection
she spoke about beams of light *visibly* reflecting from an object.

Well, you take a light source and you know how when you take, see,
maybe two light beams coming out like this? [She draws a picture in
my notes.] And then you put a mirror here and it sort of bounces off
and it goes to something else. That's reflection.

Donnie's continuing description of reflection was that of "a" reflection, a physically perceptible image, showing that she was not making the connection between the idea of light rays that are visible and light rays that are not directly visible to the human eye that both bounce or reflect off objects. In fact, all of the children in the study group, with the exception of Mark, originally and vehemently denied this second meaning of "reflection," because, as Donnie repeatedly stated, "if it were reflecting off, you would be able to see it bounce somewhere else."

Ongoing Conversations with Students and the Teacher's Awareness of Student Errors.

Conducting regular conversations with Donnie, the students in the study group, and other students in the class was essential in developing an understanding of the extent of students' grasp of the ideas as they were presented during the unit. Others shared Donnie's confusion with the uses of terminology. This became apparent only during our discussions and not through the analysis of worksheet errors, because the children corrected their worksheets in class at the end of each activity, and turned in only the corrected forms. The teacher did not have an opportunity to note patterns in student ideas and the nature of difficulties with the unit.

Mr. Ryan's View of Donnie's Approach to Science Learning

I spoke to Mr. Ryan about his understanding of Donnie's approach to learning. I mentioned to him my ongoing perception of her continuing effort even in the face of often being incorrect.

> Donnie spends a lot of time "trying to make connections," as you say, in all areas. Like, she bounces a bit and she has trouble taking or making those connections, and putting them together, and she's a little bit frustrating because she doesn't concentrate on pulling them together either. They're just kind of there, let's pick from them here and there and if that doesn't work, well, you tell me. And I tell you, then why, and oh, okay, she makes the connections once you show her the path, but she hasn't yet gotten to the point where she can take some of those connections and put them together for herself yet. But you're right, she continues to try where others sometimes just don't bother.

Here Mr. Ryan expressed a view similar to Donnie's personal views about the way to achieve success in science learning, that is, that with the correct amount of effort, one should be able to figure things out, and thereby make the connections by one's own effort. Following the lesson, I showed Mr. Ryan the results of the questionnaire given to the entire class to assess their understanding of refraction. He was surprised by the results. He did not realize that the class as a whole did not grasp the notion of nonvisible light beams reflecting off all objects in the environment. Donnie, in fact, was one of the few children to speak up often. She consistently attempted to clarify what she did not understand, but Mr. Ryan had difficulty in taking notice of her comments and of her sometimes unsuccessful struggle to understand. Even though most of the students did not understand the concept, they showed was little effort to seek help.

Consistently attempting to understand what was being taught was one of the unique aspects of Donnie's orientation to science learning. She was aware when she did not understand and was troubled by her lack of understanding. Because Donnie was asking some of the most fundamental kinds of questions, the kind physicists have asked about the nature of light, her frustration was actually an indication that she was grappling with some very basic issues of learning science. It was my hope that rather than being overwhelmed, Donnie would learn to value and appreciate the qualities of persistence and honest questioning that I had observed in her learning.

The remaining chapters in Part II present the learning stories of the other five students in the study group. Their stories are similar in many ways to Donnie's, but each of the students brings a unique set of personal constructs and personal orientation themes to science learning.

CHAPTER 5

Mark: The Boy of Ideas

An Intellectual Orientation to Science Learning

Mr. Ryan described Mark as "an average to above-average student, a very cooperative person, but still quite young in some ways." In fact, Mark, at age 10, was the youngest person in his class, which was composed largely of 11- and 12-year-olds. I made some initial observations and reflections in my journal during the first 2 weeks:

> *In the classroom:* Mark listens intently to Mr. Ryan and other members of the class during the large group discussion. During a discussion on the development of "evaluative" questions in the reading period, Mark's eyes are almost constantly fixed on the teacher. He frequently tips back on his chair in a relaxed fashion, silently mouthing answers to questions posed by Mr. Ryan in a confident and firm manner. When Mark raises his hand to answer a question, he raises it high and waves exuberantly. He seems to be enjoying the discussion on the nature of light immensely.

> *On the playground:* Melody and Daphne are walking along with me, one holding each arm. I have been watching Mark play. He is crying after an incident in which he was unjustly accused by the playground supervisor (who doesn't know him) of deliberately sliding into another student, knocking her down. For 2 to 3 minutes he appears to be extremely embarrassed and frustrated by the ordeal. He looks my way but does not ask me to intervene. Then, suddenly, he stops crying and starts to play ice tag with three of his classmates. He seems to have forgotten all about the accusation. Although he is physically much smaller than the other children, Mark is quick, agile, and an effective competitor on the playground. By virtue of his speed and clever moves, he is a challenging and popular playmate.

THOUGHTS AND FEELINGS ABOUT LEARNING SCHOOL SCIENCE

Mark held a view of science and of himself as a science learner that was very different from the others:

> I find science pretty easy most of the time. I get things mostly that
> sometimes the other kids have, sort of, trouble with. I really like it be-
> cause I think it is challenging. I just really like finding out new things.

On several other occasions during my stay in the classroom, Mark reiterated
the sense of himself as a very successful science learner. He believed that he
possessed an ability to figure things out quickly, and that because of this
ability in Science class he often had more free time and the opportunity to
do extra science experiments on his own:

> In Science, me and Willis Simpson are always finished early, so we like
> to do experiments on our own . . . like, test out our own ideas and
> stuff, and try things that we want to.

The theme of enjoyment of working on his own was repeated throughout
our discussions.

Mark did not study science outside of school. He believed that science
outside of school "is not as important as the science we learn in school."

> I don't really study science at home, I have fun with it and things and
> mostly what I do in science at home is watch programs and read a few
> science books. But I don't really study it at all. I just sort of enjoy it at
> home and outside and things.

Mark's Ideas About Ways of Learning Science

Mark's classification of Typical Science Activities, grouped by preference, are as follows:

A. "Activities you like the very best"
   Do experiments on my own
   Do experiments with other kids
   Go on field trips
   Make science diagrams and drawings
   Do Science Fair projects
B. "Activities you think are just okay"
   Watch demonstrations by my teacher
   Do science worksheets
   Read library books on science topics
   Talk about science ideas with other people
C. "Activities you don't like"
   Read the textbook
   Write reports on science topics

I showed Mark the way that he grouped his activities. He pointed to the last group and remarked:

> Well, I do like reading and stuff. It's not that I don't like to read. But I really prefer to find things out by myself, like when I do the experiments about them myself. And yeah, well, science reports, yeah, I don't like them. Well, [I] like, sort of, when we get to pick the topic like that we want to. We did that last year. But usually we don't do that and it's really quite boring, so I guess that one's in the right place there because I like to do the experiments more.

Mark had defined science on the survey sheet as "mystery and fun." He described science metaphorically, saying, "Science is like going on a different kind of adventure. You're trying to solve a puzzle and you have all of these steps along the way." I asked Mark why he believed science is studied in elementary school. He answered without hesitating:

> So that people will be able to know about how things really are and how they work so that they can do things like go to the moon if they want to, or whatever, and so that they can understand about things like the beginnings of the world and how the world is, like, what it looks like from outer space and all.

Mark held two ideas about the benefits of learning science in school. One is embodied in the study of science for its own sake—the idea that science allows us to answer questions that are of interest. The other idea values the capacity of science to provide the technical knowledge needed to accomplish a task or goal.

Overall, Mark regarded learning school science very positively. In contrast to Donnie, he saw himself as a competent and successful learner of science and believed that science was a very easy subject to learn. He told me that he noticed that other students sometimes struggled with activities and ideas that he quickly grasped. Mark expressed confidence in his ability to perform in Science class. He also exuded obvious enjoyment when recalling past school experiences in Science. He regarded the activities of learning science in school as somewhat more important than the science activities that he participated in outside of school. Mark stated that outside of the classroom he participated in such activities as "watching television programs and reading books," and "wondering about my own questions." I asked for an example:

> Sometimes at night I look up at the stars and things. I wonder what made them, and what it's like on other planets. And I wonder if, like,

if there's an end to the universe and stuff. Or I try to figure out what makes a star sort of pulse like it does.

I asked Mark if his father or mother was interested in science and perhaps encouraged his scientific pursuits. He said "No, not really. I like to talk over my ideas about things with my dad." Mark's father, a carpet layer, and his mother, a career homemaker, had no special interest or expertise in science, but Mark stated that they encouraged him to talk about and pursue whatever he found interesting. He commented that they had bought him some National Geographic books on the universe for his birthday.

MARK'S IDEAS ABOUT THE NATURE OF LIGHT
PRIOR TO THE LIGHT UNIT

I asked Mark about his views on the nature of light.

What Is Light?

Light is, ah, well, I don't know what it is, like, but, it travels in outer space and from the sun to the earth. I guess it comes from the sun mostly. And we have electricity. That can be put in the form of light also.

Despite not having a straightforward definition, throughout our conversation Mark spoke with confidence in his ability to understand what was about to be presented to him. Some of the other students in the study seemed confused about what actually was meant by the question, as light is more commonly associated with the personal experience of lightness or darkness. For most of the students it seemed an odd question to ask, for to them light simply *is*, that is, it is an experience rather than an entity.

Where Is the Light?

Overhead in the lights. There's quite a lot coming in from the window, and some is coming in there from the hallway [the interview took place in a glass enclosed interview room with the hallway in full view].

Mark associated light both with its source ("the lights") and with beams that are visible.

Association of Light Phenomena with Everyday Objects

Given the same list of objects as Donnie, Mark was one of the few students in the class who checked the magnifying glass and plants as associated with light. He told me that he had personally directed sun light rays onto paper using a magnifier and that this is how he associated light beams with the magnifying glass. He stated also that he checked plants because he realized that plants require light in order to grow. Only one other student in the class made this association. Mark stated that he associated light with a telescope because it is used to observe light-emitting objects, like stars. He did not associate light with a microscope, however, and laughed, saying, "that's because you tend to look at dead things under a microscope, I guess. When I think of dead things, I think of the dark."

How Does Light Allow Us to See Objects?

Mark was given the same drawing as Donnie to use to answer this question (Figure 5.1). His comment in referring to the drawing was, "Light is falling onto the house shown by these rays here. The boy then can see the house." There was no indication in Mark's drawing nor in our discussion prior to instruction that Mark understood the scientists' conception that light beams reflect off the object into the eyes of the person standing nearby.

Light Beam Interaction with Objects

Mark was given the drawing of light beams shining on objects and responded with his own sketches (Figure 5.2). Mark told me that in the final example, when light beams struck the flat rock, they "stop because the rock stops them." When I asked him what a person standing by the rock would see, he answered, "Just the light stopping at the rock."

How Do We See Color?

I think that there are special things, like receptors in our eyes that let us see the colors in things. We studied the eye a lot last year. There are cones and rods and those are in the back of the eye.

Mark recalled studying the eye and vision in his fourth-grade health class.

Feelings and Experiences Associated with Light and the Study of Light

I asked Mark how he felt about studying light and how light made him feel:

Oh, I don't know. I look at the stars and I like to wonder sometimes about the universe and all. Sometimes I like to watch the light on

Figure 5.1 How does sunlight allow the boy to see the house? Mark's response

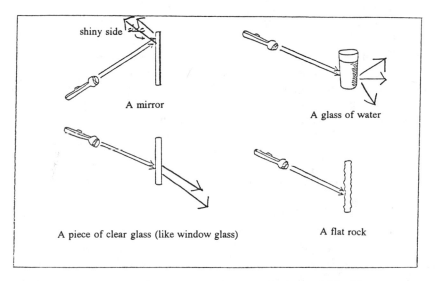

Figure 5.2 How do light beams interact with objects? Mark's response

water. The light on the snow out there is really pretty. But sometimes it's just too bright out there! I'm really interested in studying about light. We've been doing a lot with the "Batteries and Bulbs" unit and that's fun. And so, I'm looking forward to it. We did a little about light when I was, I think, in second grade. But I think we'll do a lot more with it with Mr. Ryan.

Mark appeared genuinely interested in the study of the subject, light itself. Only one other student in the study group, Martin, indicated that the topic was of real interest, something he was excited about pursuing.

ORGANIZATION OF MARK'S CASE REPORT USING PERSONAL CONSTRUCT THEMES

Mark's Personal Constructs

Mark's personal constructs regarding the experience of studying light during the unit are presented in Figure 5.3.

Theme 1. The Boy of Ideas: Enjoyment in Hearing the Story of Science

Mark's Self-Characterization: "I like to hear what *science* has to tell us."

My Image/Impression: Mark values science knowledge as tentative explanation.

Mark was the only person in the study group to make specific reference to his lessons and activities as activities and experiences by which we "find out what *science* tells us." In the elicitation of personal constructs, he contrasted "Hearing what *science* has to tell us" with "Telling what *we* think." He did not equate the two, yet he noted a connection between his own experience of "doing" science in the classroom and the experience of hearing the "story of science." Mark was open to the acceptance of an idea even though he might not be able to "see it with his own eyes."

Mark appeared to simultaneously hold two theories of science knowledge that seemed in contrast to one another. Both were useful to him in learning science. On the one hand, Mark was interested in learning the *story* of science, the ideas that have been conveyed by scientists to this point in time. He was also interested in knowing *how* the ideas have come into being. This view casts science in the role of "telling us what is out there," and suggests a view of truth as waiting "out there" and needing only to be found. This was repeatedly emphasized in our conversations and video recall sessions. Mark referred to doing science in the following way: "It's like you're putting together the pieces of a mystery." In fact, Mark was a very serious reader of mysteries. All of the students had made a record of books read throughout the year. Mark classified 14 of the 25 books he had read as mysteries. He also spoke of doing science as an effort to find out "about the way things really are." Therefore, at the same time that he likened learning science to a puzzle to be put together to discover an answer, suggesting that "most things in science are right," he also held the view of science as knowledge that is tentative and changing. I asked if he had some insight into how it might be that he was so able to grasp ideas that others seemed to have so much trouble with.

1. Doing things that you really like to do, really enjoy.	1. Somebody tells you what to do.
2. Doing things for yourself.	2. Somebody else tells you what should happen.
3. Hearing about things that make you wonder.	3. Hearing things, but you aren't really listening.
4. Experimenting with other people.	4. Doing it on your own, reading more.
5. Doing what you're supposed to, working to find an answer to a question.	5. Not doing what you're supposed to, so you won't be able to answer.
6. Getting help to find the right answer.	6. Not getting the idea.
7. Sure of yourself.	7. Confused.
8. Just telling and talking about ideas in class.	8. Ideas are being corrected as right or wrong.
9. Helping someone come up with something different from what is on the overhead.	9. Helping someone get exactly what is there.
10. Work on my own.	10. Needing help/asking for help.
11. Experimenting with things.	11. Just listening to what Mr. Ryan says.
12. Copying down exactly what's there on the overhead.	12. Coming up with something different.
13. Talking about things.	13. Just jotting down the information.
14. Knowing what's going on.	14. Don't know what's going on.
15. Find out what *science* tells us.	15. Telling what we think.

Figure 5.3 Mark's science learning constructs

Mark: Well, most science things are right.

Ms. Shapiro: Most science things are right?

Mark: Yeah.

Ms. Shapiro: Can you tell me what you mean by right?

Mark: Mmmm. Well, when you say, like, people used to say that the earth was flat, and it's really round. So science is the right ideas about things. Some of the ideas in the future might change though.

Ms. Shapiro: I see. . . .

Mark: And like Mr. Ryan said, people used to think that there was something that came from your eye to the object and that let you see the object. But the right idea is that the light reflects on the object and goes into your eye, like I said before. So that helps.

Ms. Shapiro: How do you know that that is true?

Mark: Because Mr. Ryan said so [laughs].

Ms. Shapiro: How do you know that Mr. Ryan's answer is the correct one?

Mark: Well, he's taken light in college and all and he tells us what he knows from that.

Yet, in addition to accepting the current ideas conveyed by scientists, Mark appreciated the tentative, changing nature of the processes by which ideas are acquired in science. Mark said that he regarded Mr. Ryan as his most valuable source of help and direction in the study of science and, particularly, in studying the topic, light. Valuing the tentative nature of science knowledge also implied for Mark a special relationship with Mr. Ryan, whom he saw as his primary source of special insights. However, acceptance of Mr. Ryan's authority did not keep him from questioning an idea presented in class or one that deviated from his own experience or sense perceptions. As an example, during our review of the videotaped lesson on color, Mark commented on his understanding of Mr. Ryan's discussion about how it is that we are able to see color.

> Mark: It was always known that color was, like, seen by light and all. Mr. Ryan is saying that people used to think something different. They used to think that it was in stuff, like in the thing. But Mr. Ryan was saying that it's reflected off of things and we see the colors by the way it reflects off.
> Ms. Shapiro: Do you think that is true?
> Mark: Yeah. Oh, yeah. Except here. I didn't get it here, with the colored light and all that we were doing. There's color here that we were seeing. I'm not sure what that was supposed to be. You know, when we were looking here, and we couldn't figure out what it was and we asked you and you even said that it was sort of pinkish too?
> Ms. Shapiro: Yes, the mixing of colored light.

During this activity, each group produced colored light by directing light beams through colored plastic. The resulting colored beams were directed and redirected using mirrors so that they were mixed with one another. The children were asked to describe the newly formed color. Having some differences of opinion, several groups had asked if I would come over and say what I saw as the new color. Each group had plastic of slightly differing shades of color, therefore, each group produced a slightly different result. In each case, however, the color resulting, when combined on the white screen used, was a pale rose or pink. The "correct" answer, Mr. Ryan informed them, was not rose or pink, but white. Every group had difficulty accepting this answer. No one had seen a true white in the combination, yet "white" was the only answer accepted as the correct response to the question.

Although every group showed confusion over this problem during the activity period, when the time came to discuss their results in the large group, no child protested, challenged, or even expressed puzzlement about the contradiction between what they had seen for themselves in their groups and what they were told that they were supposed to have seen. Most students quietly corrected their worksheets, but many had confused and puzzled looks on their faces. I was astonished by this response from the class. During the video recall sessions on this activity, I inquired about the incident. All of the students in the study group expressed frustration with the experience in private conversation and questioned me about the light, which they saw as one color and were asked to accept as another color. I asked Mark what he thought of the suggestion by Mr. Ryan that students should be seeing one color when, so many, in fact, saw something else.

> Mark: Well, I didn't see white, either. You didn't either did you?
> Ms. Shapiro: No.
> Mark: So, I thought maybe Mr. Ryan made a mistake at first. But he said he saw white and that that's what it's supposed to be. So I guess I thought maybe that's what it's supposed to be even though it doesn't look that way, that's what it should be, because maybe the light here isn't the best. But I don't know, because it, if you looked at it a certain way, I could see how somebody might say it was white.

Here again, Mark's orientation to being open to "what science has to tell us" allowed him to consider the possible truth of what he could not verify with his own eyes. Still, he did not deny that he had difficulty seeing what he was told he should have seen.

Mark's interest in the ways that we learn from science was unique among the children of the study group. In contrast to Donnic, Mark did not believe it was necessary to take complete responsibility for working out the correct answers himself. Mark was open to changing his viewpoint without a need for direct personal evidence. He was very interested in knowing about the trials and errors of past researchers. Mark appeared to have a sense of the history of science. He recalled, for example, how "people used to think . . ." when referring to the nature of light and color. In this way, Mark placed himself in intellectual partnership with the past, learning from the work of others while at the same time constantly seeking personal autonomy. Mark liked to test ideas out for himself, and to confirm others' findings, yet he was still able to listen to and comment on the story of science.

Grasping the Idea of Reflected Light

Mark's approach to learning science during the unit showed areas of significant contrast with the other students' experience, both in terms of his grasp of ideas and his characterization of himself as science learner. Notably, Mark was the only student in the study group able to quickly grasp the single concept that was basic to further development of ideas in the light unit. This idea was that light rays reflect off objects. Many ideas appearing later in the unit were built on an understanding of how reflected light enables vision, a concept that students of all ages have difficulty grasping. Light rays, continually reflecting from the objects around us, enable us to see objects. Not only was Mark able to grasp this idea early in the presentation of the unit, he was able to use this fact to explain other types of light phenomena in subsequent lessons.

Mark's personal orientation to science learning appeared to be based on an interest in and openness to acceptance of new ideas. Even though new information presented in Science class was in conflict with his own ideas, Mark was able to believe and to completely accept new ideas because they were established in science and were conveyed via the authority of Mr. Ryan.

Mark's personal orientation to learning science not only included an openness to new ideas, but also an interest in making connections between his own experience and the ideas the teacher was presenting during the unit. During a classroom visit, I recorded an example of Mark's skill in making connections between his own experience and the ideas presented during the refraction or "bent pencil" activity that was described in Donnie's case report, as it had an important impact on her experience of science learning as well. This incident provided an example that demonstrates all three of the themes of Mark's personal orientation to science learning. We can see that Mark is working much of the time on his own. Mark's second theme shows a rather remarkable, unshakable confidence in his science learning ability.

Theme 2. The Self-Sufficient Learner: The Enjoyment of Thinking and Learning on His Own

> *Mark's Self-Characterization:* "I really like to do experiments and things, things that I'm doing for myself. I really enjoy doing things myself and coming up with ideas that are different than just what's on the overhead projector."
>
> *My Image/Impression:* Self-motivated. He enjoys finding things out for himself and the possibility of coming up with original insight.

In our conversations and reflections on the lessons, Mark spoke often about the enjoyment of experimenting with ideas and materials on his own. On several occasions, I observed Mark working creatively on his own with materials. During these times he was in charge and autonomous. Other students either followed his example or asked Mark to help them to understand the material. But Mark saw himself as receiving real help only from his teacher. He commented that Mr. Ryan was his most valuable resource in building new ideas and insights in Science class. He accepted Mr. Ryan's statements not only because they came from a trustworthy authority, but also because the teacher spoke about phenomena and events that were truly of interest to him. Mark said during one of our conversations, "Sometimes he really makes you wonder." Mark had provided, as one of his personal constructs, a distinction between hearing about "things that make you wonder" and those that you do not really listen to:

3. Hearing about things   3. Hearing things, but
   that make you wonder.   you aren't really listening.

He explained that when he really listened in class it was to the "stuff that's really interesting, that I want to know about. The other stuff I just usually don't pay attention to." Mark made it clear that he preferred to gain insight through actually doing science activities himself. Yet he reiterated that he also valued information coming from the teacher, his most important source of information.

Theme 3. The Confident Science Learner

Mark's Self-Characterization: "I'm really getting all of it and I feel sure of myself and what I'm learning. And I'm really enjoying myself."
My Image/Impression: Mark has a long history of success and confidence in science learning. He feels strong in his memory and in his ability to understand ideas in science.

Lesson 9, "So Deceiving," proved to be one of the most enjoyable, but one of the most difficult lessons of the unit for the class. The lesson was helpful in the characterization of many of the students' personal orientation themes, and it had a strong impact on all of the students in the classroom. This lesson began with the coin-in-the-saucer activity that was previously described in Donnie's case report. The "nonvisible" coin suddenly became visible to the crouching observers. Why? In the second activity, the pencil-in-the-beaker activity, students observed the pencil in the beaker, then explained why the pencil appeared to be broken when viewed from the side.

I sat near Mark's group during these activities. In the first example, I watched as he observed the coin slowly appearing. Suddenly he jumped up, excitedly telling the others:

I know! I know what's making it do that! It's the light rays. The water's bending them!

The other group members at first appeared perplexed by Mark's statement. They ignored him and continued to look at the beaker from different angles. Still excited about his insight, Mark tried to reexplain his idea to the group. This time, his activity group listened, but once again, did not appear to understand his explanation. They returned to talk among themselves about what they thought was happening to make the coin appear to float to the surface. Mark walked over to Donnie and Carey's table, pointed to their saucer, and proclaimed to Carey, "I know why it's doing that!" Carey did not ask Mark for his explanation. She seemed intent on finding a solution of her own. Undaunted, Mark emptied his saucer into the nearby sink, then literally hopped and skipped back around the room to his desk.

Mark's Revolutionary Idea

In this sequence, Mark had made some very important connections among the ideas and experiences presented to the class to this point. He connected ideas and information presented weeks before to explain the changes in the appearance of the objects in this lesson. Because of the extraordinary insight he demonstrated, I asked Mark if he would mind staying after school with me to discuss the science lesson. Mr. Ryan had informed Mark at the end of the lesson that his explanation was correct, and he was still quite excited about his insight. He seemed pleased to discuss it further.

> Ms. Shapiro: I'm very interested in your telling me more about the activities that you have been involved with today. You know from our video sessions that I'm trying to understand how kids are learning ideas like the ones presented here. I was with your group when you were looking at the saucer of water today. I was watching when you saw the coin. I heard you say, all of a sudden, as you were looking at the coin, "It's the reflected light!" I wondered if that was an idea that just came to you all of a sudden or, can you tell me what it was like, what happened for you there?
>
> Mark: Well, hmmm. I guess it's that I just like science a whole lot, and I just think that it was because of being, well, of remembering from before.
>
> Ms. Shapiro: I see. You know, it looked like the ideas just seemed to come together for you all of a sudden. But you say you remembered from before.
>
> Mark: Well, yes, it was sort of all of a sudden. Well, I knew that, pretty much the ideas that were going on before, because, he had told us. Mr. Ryan had told us lots of things, and then we did a few experiments and that made things a lot clearer.

Ms. Shapiro: Oh, I see. Can you tell me what you remember and which experiments you found helpful?

Mark: Well, I guess mostly when he told us about the light, how people used to see things, like they thought they saw things coming from your eye to it, or thought it was coming from your eye. But we know it doesn't now. And the one, well I guess, with the beaker and the light bending through the water, that one was the one that helped me the most. That showed me how the light bends and all when it goes through the beaker and water, you know, from the light source?

Ms. Shapiro: Yes, I remember that. When you started to tell the others in your group that it was the light that was reflecting off, how did they react?

Mark: Oh, yeah. They acted sort of surprised and stuff. At first they didn't understand it, but then I told them again. They thought that the penny floated up to the top or something. I told them that the light was doing it. It was the reflected light. A lot of people didn't listen.

Ms. Shapiro: Yes, when the class discussion took place later, and when Mr. Ryan was asking, "What was happening, why do we see the penny, why do you see the coin there, and why does the pencil look like that?" Everyone gave different answers.

Mark: Yeah, some people thought it was the water, some people thought it was the glass. . .and some the curve in the glass.

Ms. Shapiro: I wondered why in the class discussion you waited until the end of the discussion to give your answer.

Mark: Well, I was, sort of trying to figure out if I was right.

Ms. Shapiro: So, you weren't quite certain whether or not you were right.

Mark: No. Well, I guess. But I just waited.

Ms. Shapiro: So you waited. But then when you finally did give your answer, were you sure you were right then?

Mark: No [laughs]. Not really at all. But see, I was going a way back in the beginning and putting things I learned together, and I didn't, I thought I was right, but, I coulda been wrong, too. I guess, it just seemed to fit all together.

Ms. Shapiro: Was there a particular part of this activity that you found made it most clear to you?

Mark: Well, like I said, when I was little, and even now, really, I used to always have a really good memory and stuff, so that helps me a lot to remember things.

> Ms. Shapiro: Were there parts of the lesson itself that seemed to help you to make the connection to this important idea, that explained things for you?
>
> Mark: Well, not here, because we were just putting together here all the things we learned from before.

Although several children in the group spoke about previous or current science learning experiences as being difficult or frustrating, Mark consistently spoke of past and present science learning in very positive ways. He seemed very happy in the lessons. He commented:

> I've always liked science. Always a lot. And I usually . . . I find it very easy. In the last thing we did with batteries and bulbs, I got things all finished early, because all you had to do was light the bulb. And that was easy, so I went on to do some other things. And sometimes I can help the other kids with what they're doing.

These comments were unusual. All of the other students in the study group complained about the difficulty of the previous unit, "Batteries and Bulbs." But Mark remarked on how interesting the unit was and told me how he had done some extra activities on his own.

The Impact of Mark's Ideas on the Rest of the Class

Through a clarification of Mark's personal orientation to science learning, we can see how Mark's approach to science learning served him in the understanding of ideas in Science class. But Mark had a great effect on the larger classroom system also. By simply possessing and expressing his ideas, he incited a small flurry of interest and discussion in the classroom. Several of the children reported that they listened much more carefully to Mark's comments during large group discussions because they found them unusual, improbable, or puzzling. All of the children in the study group commented that the teacher's manner toward Mark indicated that he had achieved the correct answer to the pencil-and-beaker question. All of the study group participants suggested that the teacher's act of writing Mark's statement on the overhead projector indicated beyond doubt that the answer he had given was the correct one. But not one of the other five students in the study group understood Mark's idea. Several members of the class commented that hearing and contemplating what Mark had to say about the phenomenon was something that changed their thinking about light behavior. The interest the children had in one another's ideas was an effective catalyst, providing an opportunity for changing thinking in the class. Following the lesson, Mr. Ryan believed that he had been successful in guiding the class to the new understanding Mark had voiced. Because Mark had given the correct answer, Mr. Ryan was left with the impression that the class grasped the idea of refraction. Unfortunately, the idea was well beyond almost every student in the classroom. It was true, though, that many members of the class were beginning to think differently about the phenomena. Other students, though slower to change their thought, might have done so with just a bit of further encouragement and reinforcement. It was a wonderful opportunity to maximize the benefits of the disruptive impact of Mark's "radical" idea.

The kinds of changes that occur when a new idea is introduced in an interactive system like Mark's classroom have been the subject of study by researchers Prigogine and Stengers (1984). They created the term *dissipative structure* to refer to the fluctuations and disorganization that eventually lead to reorganization and change within a system. "Dissipative structure" is a useful metaphor for understanding how interactions occur within human groups to bring about change in individual and group thought. The subsequent effect on the class of Mark's insight is an excellent example of a dissipative structure. At the beginning of the class discussion, no one in the group understood why the pencil appeared broken in the beaker of water. Mark's new and unusual ideas generated intense interest and interaction in the class. The children became very attentive to this portion of the discussion. This critical period provided an opportunity for students to discuss and consider Mark's new ideas. Under conditions like these, a single individual can prompt such discussion to cause the knowledge structure of the larger group to very suddenly change or "dissipate," into a new knowledge structure.

Another aspect of Mark's impact on the rest of the class was seen throughout the study in the ways special friends depended on one another as caring listeners who were working ideas out together. When I first became acquainted with Mark, for instance, I noticed that he would often go over to Donnie's table to talk with her work partner, Carey. Mark frequently went to Carey to share an idea or to see how she was progressing on a task. His classmates teased Mark about "having a crush" on Carey, but their special friendship allowed the sharing of ideas and insights that had an important influence on their enthusiasm for their science work and on the development of ideas in other subject areas, particularly mathematics. Both Mark and Carey were respected and admired by their classmates for their academic abilities. Carey and Mark's influence on one another was a significant feature in the story of Mark's science learning development.

Mark was often ahead of other students in his insights and thinking in science. His ideas were often so advanced that they were not heard or accepted when he attempted to share them with other students. Although this did not seem to discourage his continuing insights, he commented that he often preferred to work on his own to come up with "something different" from what the rest of the students were working on. Having a special friend in the classroom with whom he could share his insights and findings appeared to serve as an important vehicle that allowed him to discuss and develop his ideas even more joyfully.

CHAPTER 6

Martin: The Tinkerer

The Enjoyment of Physical Involvement with Science Materials

Martin was one of two students in the study group who, in addition to regular classroom activities, received remedial instruction in reading and mathematics given by Mrs. Lauren, a resource teacher who visited the classroom three afternoons a week. Martin had unusual difficulty with reading. District testing showed that he read at second-grade level.

Early in our conversations, Martin told me that for the previous 5 years he and his brother attended a private religious school. His parents were unhappy with his progress there, and enrolled him in a public school hoping for more adequate preparation for junior high school. Martin described his public school experience:

> Martin: At the beginning of the year they put me in sixth grade, they found that I had a little difficulty, they found that I couldn't manage it. They saw that I was having a little trouble, so they put me back in fifth grade. Like, that wasn't too great, you know, at first. Like, how would you feel if that happened to you?
>
> Ms. Shapiro: Well, I guess I'd wonder what was happening to me and how the other kids would respond to me.
>
> Martin: Yeah. Right. Right. So I just let it play, let it play, so I could see what would happen, right? And just let it play, let it play. But the very first day some kids were trying to bug me. I grabbed them and just, you know, started to whale on them [laughs]. After that, you know, a lot of people stayed away. Now, I don't care if they call me names. I mean, they're only joking *now* [pause]. See, like, you saw on the video, Steve is writing on my paper, "Martin the Great." See, like, I'm the big shot of the class now. Like, most kids, they play with me, right? Like, now, they're sort of scared of me.

THOUGHTS AND FEELINGS ABOUT LEARNING SCHOOL SCIENCE

The themes of Martin's personal orientation to science study interweave and interplay to such an extent that they were difficult to separate. This may have been partly due to the dominating theme of difficulty with academic work, to Martin's initial humiliation at being placed back a year in his new school, and to his apparent need to "prove himself" to the other children and to his teacher.

Science class was one of the few arenas where Martin experienced success. Here he was able to relax and, as he said, "to really enjoy myself." In Science class he was able to demonstrate some positive behaviors to the other children and to Mr. Ryan.

Martin's Ideas About Ways of Learning Science

Martin gave a very positive response to the question, "How do you feel about learning science?" He said, "I feel I learn things and I like to experiment a lot." He enthusiastically responded that there was nothing that he did *not* like about science study. He finished the sentence "Studying science is like . . ." in the following way: "with have fun and Lring [learning] will [while] you are haveing fun." Martin told me that "science is one of my best subjects. I like it as much as gym." After seeing Martin in Science class, it was obvious that he derived enormous pleasure from the physical manipulation of objects. He was always motivated to find out how things worked and told me many stories of his adventures in taking objects apart and putting them back together.

MARTIN'S IDEAS ABOUT THE NATURE OF LIGHT
PRIOR TO THE LIGHT UNIT

What is Light?

Light is, well, made by electricity. So whatever is in or goes into electricity is what it must be made of. It comes from the sun and stuff, and flashlights.

Where is the Light?

The light in this room? It's everywhere. It's all around. Especially by the light bulbs, and, well, in this room it's mainly there (points to the lights in the ceiling). The lights in the ceiling are different than the light bulbs like the kind that we have at home, like the kind we opened up last year. So there are all different kinds of lights.

Association of Light Phenomena with Everyday Objects

Like many other students, Martin associated cameras with light because of the flash of light he recalled seeing when pictures were taken. He associated the microscope with light because he recalled using a microscope with a small light source attachment. Both Mark and Martin told me they liked to set paper on fire by directing rays of light through a magnifier, and that is why they associated light with the magnifier. I watched groups of children performing this "experiment" on the playground at recess.

How Does Light Allow Us to See Objects?

In response to this question (Figure 6.1), Martin stated, "Light shines down on the boy and so he uses it to see the house." He did not comment on the light reflecting from the house, but his idea that the boy was somehow *using* the light might later be useful in leading him to a clearer understanding of the scientific idea that light reflection is interpreted in the eye-brain interaction.

Light Beam Interaction with Objects

In his response to this question (Figure 6.2), Martin noted that light passes through the translucent piece of window glass, but did not believe that this also occurred with the glass of water. He said that light did not pass through the rock, but told me he had no idea what happened to the light rays after they struck the rock.

How Do We See Color?

Well, if something's got like a red dye in it or some other sort of dye in it, that's what we see. And if there's not enough, it could look like a different shade. Or if it's a little dark, say, then it would be a little different shade.

Figure 6.1 How does sunlight allow the boy to see the house? Martin's response

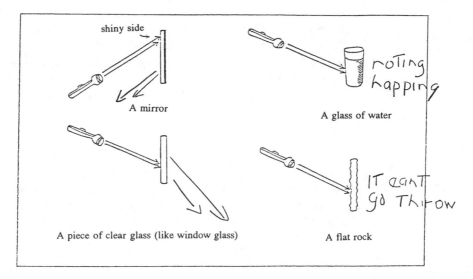

Figure 6.2 How do light beams interact with objects? Martin's response

Again, like his classmates, Martin suggested that color vision is a function of the color being *in* the object observed rather than making reference to reflected light.

Feelings and Experiences Associated with Light and the Study of Light

Martin already had quite a bit of experience in tinkering with electricity, light bulbs, and many other objects in his home environment. He was very eager to explore the topic, light, in Science class. He described one of his experiences at home.

> Oh, man, wow, like I got zapped by a light when I exploded a light bulb with my dad's car battery and another time, well, I sure did *feel* it [laughs] because I got this really strong, you know, charge? Like when I put two wires like, you know, the red and the black one, right, are the one way, I, well, like I put 'em the other way around and got this jolt and there were sparkles all around and in my eyes, boy! I really like to study science. It's my best subject. We did some stuff with light in second grade I think. I remember I showed the teacher some ways to work with electricity. I had this book and I showed her what to do and all. I'd like to know more about light.

Martin's natural inclination to tinker gave him a sense of confidence in science that other students did not express.

ORGANIZATION OF MARTIN'S CASE REPORT USING
PERSONAL CONSTRUCT THEMES

Martin's Personal Constructs

Martin's personal constructs regarding science learning are presented in Figure 6.3.

Theme 1. Self Expression Through Science

Martin's Self-Characterization: I like expressing my own ideas and creating new ways to do things.

My Image/Impression: Science is a vehicle for personal expression and creativity for Martin. He enjoys talking with others about ideas and working with others to do the activities. Martin likes to stand out and is original in his ideas and thinking.

This theme reflected Martin's intense interest in the science learning experience as a form of personal expression. Throughout the term, he showed very little interest in considering ideas he had not discovered himself, or that he did not believe were true. The following example presents an instance where he spoke of his strategy of "just forgetting" an idea that did not make sense immediately. He talked about "throwing away" an entire lesson sequence when he did not instantly understand what he was supposed

1. Working with other kids to find out.	1. Mr. Ryan is just telling you.
2. Getting or giving help.	2. Just doing your work yourself.
3. Thinking up what to do on your own.	3. Being told what to do.
4. Working.	4. Goofing around.
5. Showing what you think and feel.	5. Just correcting the worksheet.
6. Creating new ways to do things.	6. Just writing down the answer.
7. Going ahead and trying.	7. Stuck. Having trouble understanding.
8. You know what you're doing and can do it.	8. You don't know what you're doing.
9. Playing around, experimenting around with the equipment.	9. Working on your worksheet.
10. Easy work.	10. Hard work.
11. Having a good time in my work.	11. I'm bored and I don't want to do it.
12. Really interesting new ideas.	12. Boring, repetitious stuff.
13. Confronting new ideas.	13. Just sitting there doing nothing.
14. You get it figured out.	14. You're trying to find a way to figure it out. You're working on it.
15. Just listening to the teacher.	15. Talking to find out what to do to figure things out.

Figure 6.3 Martin's science learning constructs

to do. We reviewed the videotape of Mr. Ryan's unusual statement to the class, "The reason that I see Martin is because light is coming from him into my eyes."

> Martin: Well I really didn't get that. So I just forgot about it.
> Ms. Shapiro: Do you think that he was right? What do you mean?
> Martin: Probably he was. What the teacher says, goes, right? But I don't think so. It doesn't make sense to me. Not to me. So . . . if it doesn't make sense, I just don't worry about it, I go on, just go on. If I can't see it, how can I think that? Sooo . . . just have to go on.
> Ms. Shapiro: Oh, I'd be bothered by that I think.
> Martin: Nope. Not me. I just forget it and do something else.

In a review of another segment of the videotape, Martin watched himself struggle to read the instructions on the worksheet. He grappled with the idea of light bending as it passed through a beaker of water. He turned to me as we reviewed the tape, "I threw this whole lesson away. I didn't even want to be there."

> Ms. Shapiro: You aren't enjoying the light unit?
> Martin: I was. *I was.* You know, like before. But not now. 'Cause, Mr. Ryan, like he's showed us all of this stuff already! I want something different. It's getting boring, just the same stuff as before. So, I wasn't even there. I threw the whole lesson away in my head. The light goes through the beaker and crosses. So? We saw that before. So I want something new. New, new, new. More technical.
> Ms. Shapiro: What do you mean by more technical?
> Martin: Well, like something else happening, man. Some new ideas to think about. You know? Different. More about light. Not review stuff, man.

In fact, the lesson was not a review, but introduced a new idea that Martin was not grasping. Though he had described what he observed, the crossing of the light beams, he was not grasping the main idea of the lesson, that the light rays were bending as they passed through the water. The bending of the rays was the reason they eventually crossed.

In his description of the activity, Martin echoed his personal construct, "boring, repetitive stuff" to explain his willingness to carry on with the activity. He was interested only in what represented the promise of some new visual experience or manipulation. This determined whether or not he was willing to become involved in an activity. By contrast, Martin used the opposite pole of the construct, "Really interesting new ideas," to describe a situation when his involvement was intense and he was readily expressing new ideas with others. We viewed many video segments showing Martin's struggle to read the directions on the worksheet. He was obviously frustrated when this kept him from participating fully in the experiences he valued so highly in science—doing the experiments!

The Grasp of Lesson Ideas

I asked Martin to describe the ideas he believed were presented in the light beam lesson. I wanted to know what he was understanding and what he found boring. He told me that he believed that the main idea of the lesson was that the beams of light passing through the beaker bend or refract. When they do this, he said, the beams cross at a point beyond the beaker. But he believed that he had learned this before.

> Well, the beams bend down at this point. That's refraction. The bending, when they bend down. Right there, and then, see, this is where they bend up. So? We did that already.

Martin observed and described what was happening, but he did not understand the reason behind the bending of the beams of light. He focused on the result only, the fact that the beams crossed. He therefore equated the point of crossing with the bending of beams. Although it was true that he had seen light rays cross before, those examples were explained by the reflection, not the bending, of light rays. Martin had made an error similar to Donnie's by seeing refraction or bending occurring only at the convergence point. Because he had not used the term "convergence," I asked him to show me where the convergence point was. He answered, "Oh, that's where the beams go on and on forever. If you could see that far, they'd go on forever."

Of course, the convergence point is just the opposite. It is the point where the beams come together. What Martin considered his "boredom" with the lesson was not so much rooted in the fact that he had "done everything before," as in the fact that he was clearly not understanding the main ideas of the lesson. He was not really interested in the development of the ideas in the lesson. He was interested in active, dynamic involvement with the materials, with expressing his own thoughts about this involvement, and in "coming up with new ideas." Therefore, Martin was focused on his own interests and agenda. He had seen this or that effect before. He was not interested in seeing it again.

The agenda of the curriculum maker, however, was to provide examples illustrating two different concepts. In this particular curriculum package, the distinction between reflection and refraction was not clearly made for the student. It certainly did not take into account the orientation of a student such as Martin, whose real interest in the materials was as a vehicle for an exciting time of creating new effects and expressing his ideas about them. Martin wanted to *do* things with the materials. He would benefit from being guided to make the attempt to look at the materials from the point of view of the intent of its authors, and to ask, for example, "What is the main idea of this lesson?"

Despite his serious academic problems Martin often went out of his way to appear nonchalant in class. He seemed unconcerned with whether or not he was grasping ideas. On reflection, this could well be because of the intense frustration that he had often experienced in his attempts to understand. He expressed annoyance as we talked about Mr. Ryan's discussion of refraction from a previous lesson.

> Martin: Oh. I don't remember refraction. I don't remember what it means. I really don't care.
> Ms. Shapiro: You aren't interested in knowing about it, I take it.
> Martin: No. 'Cause what good is it? The words are all hard and they don't help you, like, you can't do anything with them.
> Ms. Shapiro: I wonder, did you notice the comments that Mr. Ryan made here on your sheet about your answer?
> Martin: No [laughs]. I never read them. I figure, you get it wrong, you tried, right? But you got it wrong. You get it wrong, so you get it wrong. With this stuff, sometimes I just want to do it, get it done, finished, goodbye, go on. I want some new stuff now. New stuff.

The second intertwining theme of Martin's personal orientation to science study refers to the enormous value he placed on physical involvement in the activities.

Theme 2. The Great Tinkerer—The Joy of Physical Involvement in the Activity

> *Martin's Self-Characterization:* I usually think up all the things to *do* in the group. I do them and the other kids just write it all down, all my answers.
>
> *My Image/Impression:* Martin enjoys physical involvement with the materials, the doing of activities. In his joy in manipulating materials, taking things apart and putting them back together, Martin is the consummate tinkerer.

The Interplay Between Personal Expression and Doing

What was of continuing interest to Martin was the actual firsthand experience of manipulating equipment and materials. He wanted not only new ideas to think about, he wanted adventures that were action packed! Martin showed good ability to deal with new ideas, when interested. On occasion, his discussion of ideas was spontaneous, exuberant, and punctuated by sudden excited flashes of insight. On one occasion Martin and I were reviewing a videotape together in the interview room in the school. The room was glassed in on the side facing the hallway, allowing us to see the comings and goings of persons in the office area. As we watched the videotape, we noticed that Mr. Ryan pointed out how light can be both reflected and bent at the same time. Martin watched, then very suddenly commented, "Hey, look at the light reflecting off of this side of the window!" He stood up and looked up at the glassed-in side of the room and exclaimed,

> Look! Hey lookit! The light! The light! You can see it, like bouncing off the window this way *and* you can see it going right through the glass! Wow! That's cool, man! I never saw that before!

Martin had noticed the reflection of light from the glass. At the same time, he observed that there were beams of sunlight passing *through* the glass to the hallway. He was thrilled with this discovery. About a week later, he attempted to bring this insight to class during a large group discussion on prisms. Mr. Ryan was explaining that the rainbow colors were produced by both the reflection and the bending of light. Martin waved his hand exuberantly.

Mr. Ryan: Yes, Martin?

Martin: That's just like when I was talking with Ms. Shapiro the other day . . . we saw that the light in the office room was bouncing off the glass window and it was passing through the window. Is that like a prism?

Mr. Ryan: Not quite, Martin, there has to be an angle that the light bends at for us to see color. It must have been sort of shiny so you saw that, you noticed that.

Martin: Well, the light was sort of bright. Hey, is a prism then, sort of like a diamond? Is that the same thing as a diamond? The way it makes the light go?

Mr. Ryan: Well, it does work the same way, Martin, but this is just glass, a diamond is a special piece of a mineral. But, yeah, and that's why girls like diamonds so much, Martin, because they're sparkly and pretty.

Although Martin's spontaneous insight provided an opportunity to reemphasize the main point of discussion, it was unfortunately misunderstood by Mr. Ryan and the idea itself was diverted by Mr. Ryan's remark. Martin did continue to pursue the connection between his experience and the lesson. This example demonstrates his interest in making connections between his own firsthand experience and the concepts that were being presented.

In another example, Mr. Ryan had been speaking to the class about light movement and the density of liquids. He described how light beams were bent differently through liquids of different density. Due to lack of time, the students did not perform any of the activities in the unit to demonstrate this phenomenon. Mr. Ryan only discussed the idea with the class. He felt that the actual experience was not crucial to the development of the ideas in the lessons. Several days later, in preparation for the next lesson, Mr. Ryan reminded the students of the ways that light passes through various liquids. Martin waved his hand wildly.

> Martin: I, you know what you were saying about different liquids and stuff? Well, at breakfast I tried all kinds of stuff. I shined two flashlights through water and then through orange juice.
>
> Mr. Ryan: Orange juice?
>
> Martin: Yeah [excited]. Yeah, and then I put milk. Like a few drops of milk in the water, in a glass of water. And they were different. And then . . . I got out some cooking oil and shined it through that, too, and it was about the same as the orange juice.
>
> Mr. Ryan: Well, good, Martin, good. I'm glad that you tried that and told us about that. Orange juice surprises me. I've never tried that. Good, good.

Martin was excited to share his home laboratory findings. He had the complete attention of the class, and seemed happiest when he was able to discover on his own and share with others.

On reviewing the tape, Martin reiterated his interest in working things out, figuring things out for himself. During Lesson 9, "Believe It Or Not," the students looked through a beaker of water at the word "light" written on a piece of paper. The paper was first to be held up against the beaker, then gradually moved, 10 cm at a time, away from the beaker. As the paper was moved away from the beaker in this manner, the word was to have appeared reversed when viewed through the beaker of water. But to most of the children it appeared only as a blur. The children were instructed to move the paper gradually away along a meter stick, then to watch to see at which point the word actually changed.

Martin was one of a very few students who saw the word and its reversed image clearly through the beaker. Mr. Ryan visited Martin's group early in the session. He showed the students how to hold the paper and adjust the angle to look through the beaker. Although Martin did not understand the reason for the reversal of the image in terms of the explanation that Mr. Ryan had given, he was very successful in the *actual manipulation* of the equipment. Although he achieved the correct response on his worksheet, he did not possess the understanding that should have accompanied it.

Martin's View of Teacher Guidance

As we watched a videotape, Martin remarked on how he appreciated the teacher's guidance in helping him to achieve success in the activity.

> Martin: You don't learn anything by just putting up your hand and giv- ing the answer to the questions. Like Mr. Ryan usually gives a clue . . . usually not the answer. Because if the teachers don't make you challenged to do something, you're going to get lazy, and you're al- ways going to want . . . help. That's what the teachers are trying to get away from. My dad used to be a teacher. So that on your *own will*, you'll try to work out the problem by yourself without much help. If you always ask the teacher, the teacher always comes and gives you a better clue than actually giving you the answer. I don't think that is what a teacher *should* do.
>
> Ms. Shapiro: Mmhm. I've been trying to find out more about how stu- dents are thinking about this. So you believe that the teacher should not give the answer directly to the student?
>
> Martin: I think if you want to get your students to be one of the best students, to keep them *interested* in the thing . . . you don't just tell them the answers, you give them clues to build on. And when he builds on that, when it comes up, you'll go, yeah, I *remember* this, and you can just write it down.

Although Martin was considered one of the lowest academic achievers in the classroom, as well as one of the most impulsive and difficult students, he was one of the most expressive and verbal individuals, a very frequent and welcome contributor to classroom discussion. The first and second themes of Martin's personal orientation interweave as his personal, expressive needs in Science class depended on opportunities for physical involvement. Martin gave high value to activities in which he could become physically involved. He had a need to be guided by the teacher, but there was a stronger need to experience closure and a sense that *he* had done it, that *he* had discovered the answer, in his words, "by my own will." Although the other children generally valued the opportunity for physical involvement in science, it had a particularly important meaning for Martin.

Donnie's orientation was similar to Martin's, in that she sought to discover solutions to problems by her own efforts. But Donnie was more concerned that she actually *understand* the ideas that the lesson materials and Mr. Ryan were presenting. She became deeply entangled in the processes of reasoning and thinking that allowed her to come to understand the phenomena being discussed. Martin's chief interest was the experience of working with the materials, the solutions to problems was secondary. Donnie felt that she should be able to understand the scientific ideas presented through her own thinking efforts. She believed that if she concentrated hard enough and put forth sufficient effort, she should be able to figure things out. Martin believed that with the teacher's guidance, or "clues," as he called them, he should be able to figure things out as he manipulated the materials. But if not, Martin said, "well, then I just forget it." Donnie's mission was to understand in a deep and personal way. When she did not understand, she was very disturbed.

Who was the more fortunate student? Donnie, who knew she did not know and was disturbed by not knowing, or Martin, who learned what he could and chose not to be concerned with what he did not know. Donnie, who was so worried about deeply understanding the material was developing a low sense of confidence in her ability to do well in science. She believed she should be able to come up with the same ideas as the physicist who had created the explanation. Martin was very interested in these questions, but it did not seem to disturb nor affect his view of himself as a success in science when he could not answer all of the questions. Although Donnie was the more thoughtful and academically successful science student, Martin *considered* himself to be successful, whereas Donnie considered herself to be a very poor science learner.

Reflection on Science Learning

Martin had difficulty with all of the written aspects of the initial surveys. This made our conversation time all the more important. My usual practice of jotting down a note or comment during conversations with participants had to be completely dropped after one session with Martin. Martin was remarkably verbal. He spoke quickly, and was impatient with pauses or lapses in our conversations. Taking notes proved to be problematic, for he became quite distracted whenever I moved my focus away from him and onto the paper. My solution was to tape record every session with him and to make very few notes.

Martin was very interested in my research involvement with the class and had many questions about the purposes of the project. He often spontaneously offered his opinions and what he believed were the opinions of his family members on the quality of current educational practices. In all of our conversations, he worked hard to take a directing role in the conversation. He seemed aware of his need to discover his own way in learning. Martin contrasted his personal construct, "Thinking up what to do on your own" with "Being told what to do," and "Showing what you think and feel" with "Just correcting the worksheet." These contrasting constructs show his interest in the personally expressive nature of learning experiences. This is a person who likes to direct his own learning! Martin valued physical involvement—"working with the other kids to find things out" and frequently commented on the challenge of "getting it figured out, like how it all works."

Throughout our conversations, as we reviewed the videotapes of lessons, a pattern of tension emerged, underscoring his need for active, physical involvement. Martin spoke of quickly dismissing and rejecting ideas and experiences that he could not quickly respond to or grasp. When he was not able to immediately grasp the main concept of a lesson, or when he was not able to read the instruction sheet to find out how to carry on in the activity, he became extremely impatient with the lesson. Frequently he did not understand what he was supposed to do, and when this happened he very quickly became bored. Mr. Ryan remarked to me after one incident in which Martin appeared frustrated and was complaining loudly about not understanding what to do:

> I don't know exactly what the problem is with Martin. He seems to like science and he does well when he's interested. But sometimes he just can't seem to control himself. I wonder sometimes if he may be a bit hyperactive.

Martin shared with me some of his own views about his working habits and approaches to science in his description of an out of class project.

> Martin: You know, I'm making a bird cage out of a little piece of wood. For a little bird nest. And I thought maybe for a science project. I'm doing it at home in the garage. I like to do a lot of science stuff at home on my own because I don't like to get stuck on one thing for a very long time. Like when I'm doing something? I'd like to do something else, right away. Like, if I'm working on a, like, if

I finish a project, right? Then sometimes I might start screwing
around with something else even while I'm still working on the
other thing, or something, and I like, I don't like to stay at one thing
too long.

Ms. Shapiro: A lot of people are like that. They like to keep several
projects going at once. Is that true in school too?

Martin: Well, I don't like to stay on one thing too long. But in school,
not really. 'Cause as long as it isn't too hard. 'Cause, like if I know
what's going on and stuff, then I just am right there with it, I don't
move from it, you know? I'm just right there. But if I don't get it or,
say, like if we've done that before, man, let's get outa here [laughs]!

Through talking with Martin, I was continually amazed by the extent of
his awareness of his own approach and style of working. He possessed an
unusual facility in conveying this awareness to me. This attribute has been
found among more academically successful students (Rohrkemper, 1984;
Rohrkemper & Benson, 1983). I found that Martin and several of the other
children in the study demonstrated great insight into their own approaches.
These were often expressed in highly philosophical ways concerning how
they create their own meaning and what it means to them. I believe that this
ability can be used by educators to assist learners to take greater responsibility for learning.

Martin was a tinkerer. He was encouraged to pursue this interest by his
family. An important aspect of the special meaning of science learning for
Martin resided in the enormous pleasure he spoke of deriving from the physical manipulation of objects and the discovery of how things work. Each encounter with Martin was an exuberant reenactment of his most recent adventure in taking apart the family blender or vacuum cleaner, of fixing a radio or
toy. He gleefully detailed how he had blown up light bulbs using the family
car battery. After the description of a disastrous experiment with the kitchen
blender, Martin asked me not to mention the escapade to his family should
I happen to see them. Although his parents encouraged his tinkering interest,
which was now moving under the hood of the family car, Martin was aware
that he often took things apart beyond his ability to put them back together.
In these adventures, and throughout discussion of class activities, Martin
spontaneously described in detail the procedures he employed, the various
tests he used to find the answer to a question, which procedures worked, and
which failed. This continuing effort, the excitement of being involved in the
doing aspect of the experience of science, and his strong ability to clarify
what "worked" and what "did not work" were dominant and pervasive
themes in the ways that he lives out the experience of learning science in
and outside of the classroom.

A third theme of Martin's personal orientation to science learning involved the importance of social interaction. This theme illuminated his need for help from others and also showed his interest in demonstrating his abilities to others.

Theme 3. The Need For Social Interaction

Martin's Self-Characterization: I like expressing my own ideas with other kids, not keeping it to myself inside and all. I like trying out my own ideas and going ahead.

My Image/Impression: The need for social interaction. There is value for Martin in interactions with others who help him in important ways to pursue his own aspirations and interests and to gain self-esteem through such social interaction.

In Kelly's (1970) view, individuals behave in the ways they do because it is from this stance that their world has the greatest meaning. Martin developed the social skills that allowed him to secure the help that he needed to read the science worksheet instructions. He needed this help in order to *do* the activities—the source of his greatest pleasure in science learning.

During the lesson "Bounce Those Beams," for example, Martin explained:

Martin: In this lesson, like, I was trying lots of ways and the other kids were writing things down. That was great because I had some trouble figuring out what to do like. See, I'm saying to Steve, "What does that mean there on the worksheet?" I was starting to write. I made Steve read the whole thing and I wasn't even listening [laughs]. I was busy trying out some ways of bouncing the beams. I was trying to figure out how to do it as I went along.

Ms. Shapiro: You were working along there and didn't understand the question?

Martin: Yeah, I was working on it. I had just asked Yasmin. She's telling me what to do and once I got it straight I just went right on and tried all the different ways that I could think of. I had, well, I could understand it and I just had trouble reading it. Once Yasmin gave me those two words, I couldn't get, I just said, "Here I go, how about this way—try this." I was the one that figured this out, how to get the beam reflected around the book. Mr. Ryan said that nobody had figured it out by my way, and so the other kids, the people in my group, they put my ways down a lot because I always get things figured out.

This conversation again showed how aware Martin was of his own ability to "figure things out" and how important the esteem of his classmates and teacher was to him. Martin valued their admiration of his talent. He valued working with people with whom he could develop a rapport, people who would enhance his own orientation. Because he recognized Yasmin's strong reading ability and her task orientation, Martin often asked for her help to understand what was to be done in the lesson. Martin and Yasmin often compared thoughts and ideas as they worked toward a solution to a problem. They became aligned in the effort to carry out the mission of becoming involved in the science activities. In doing so both became involved in the experience to the fullest extent possible.

As productively as Martin aligned his efforts with those of Yasmin, he misaligned his efforts with Melody, also a participant in the research study (Chapter 7). She showed a strong interest in the aesthetic aspects and features of the light activities. This aspect was also shared, though less often, by the other students. But Melody had an overriding interest in the social interaction within the group and among members of the classroom. Because Melody's particular orientation to learning often ran counter to Martin's, the resulting consequence was that she often actually thwarted his movement toward physical involvement in the activities. Martin's interaction with Melody punctuated the differences in their orientations. He was at times hostile toward Melody when the group was engaged in an activity and both students were attempting to live out their anticipations and expectations for science learning. Martin's orientation to science learning caused him to align with classmates with whom he could form a productive association in his learning mission.

Martin's Personal Orientation and Small Group Interaction

During the lesson, "Lenses and Light Beams," the children were instructed to set up an arrangement of materials so that two beams from the light source passed, this time, through a magnifying glass. In the second portion of the activity, the children described the beams and compared the behavior of the light through the lens to the light through the beaker of water. Finally, they looked at the card with the word "light" printed on it, through a magnifying lens held at various distances from the card.

Karen: Oh, hey! Look at this! Look at the numbers!
Martin: Oh, did you see that! The light! Look at this! Wow! Neat! Look at this, Steven. Look, look, look at this, Steven. Move it. Look what happens when I move the light.

Steven: Neat. So now what do we do?

> *Martin experiments with the visible beams from the light source and magnifying lens. He is very excited about the results and wants to share the experience with Steven. The unusual behavior of the light beams through the magnifier appears to give him a great incentive to try to read the directions to find out what to do next.*

Martin: Okay [reads]. Set up an ar–ar–ange

Steven: Arrangement.

Martin: Okay, set up an arrangement so that the two beams from the light source pass through the magnifying glass. Place a sheet of paper on, er, under the arrange-ment.

Steven: Yeah. We did that.

Melody: Martin, Martin . . . let's double it. Look. Oh, pretty. Martin, Martin.

> *Again, Melody is trying to distract Martin. She asks to use his magnifier. She wants to place it on top of her own to see what the doubling effect will be. This is not one of the tasks the students were being asked to accomplish. Martin ignores her.*

Martin: [To Steven] I don't get that. What are you supposed to do?

Melody: Martin, Martin. Could I see your magnifying glass?

Steven: Look at the worksheet again.

Martin: Okay. Set up the arrangement without the water, right?

Steven: Okay, here I'm putting it. . . .

Martin: It goes straighter! It goes straighter!

Steven: Okay, you've got to have the two beams pass through the water. . . .

Martin: Hey look it crosses! Oh. [Denny has come over from his group to watch] Hey, Denny, get out of here! Hey! Hey! I know! I know! Maybe it gets brighter! Maybe that's what it does!

> *Martin is so excited by what he is seeing that he continually interrupts Steven and grabs the materials away from him. Denny joins Martin's group. He is also trying to find out what to do. Martin sees his approach as an interference and makes Denny go away. Martin is also very frustrated with Melody.*

He commented during the replay of the lesson that "All she ever wants to do is fool around. She never tries to figure things out. Just does what she wants to do. She's all over the classroom." We watch as Mr. Ryan comes over to the group.

Melody: Oh, Mr. Ryan, you know what we discovered? Lookit what we discovered!

Mr. Ryan: Okay. What did you discover about question one?

Melody begins to talk about the shapes inside the light source and Mr. Ryan repeats his question sternly. Martin is listening to their conversation.

Martin: *Well, like the light source, right, the light coming from it is really wide now, right? And it's not as bright. But when you do put the light here it gets closer, too.*

Yasmin: *And it gets bigger.*

Mr. Ryan: *Let's have a look. Let's see what happens. What does it do?*

Martin: *[excited] See, it gets bigger and then. It goes across. It crosses!*

Mr. Ryan: *Oh, that's right. So the two narrow light beams go through the magnifier and they. . . .*

Yasmin: *Cross. Neat.*

Mr. Ryan: *Do you see them crossing way back over there?*

Martin: *No. [Martin works with the magnifier and the light source] Oh, yeah, it does, yeah.*

Mr. Ryan: *[Stands up and addresses the class.] Okay. We've only got 10 minutes to carry this through.*

Martin: *Okay, Mr. Ryan. Mr. Ryan, what's this word?*

Mr. Ryan: *Evidence.*

Martin persisted in asking the students around him for help in reading the worksheet even as they were all preparing to leave. I watched as he continued to work by himself on the activity throughout the clean-up period and into recess, one of his "ace-favorite times." This persistence in light of the great difficulties Martin had in reading and writing, and the fact that it was recess, was further evidence of his great joy in doing science. Martin found some of the abstract concepts in science difficult, but his enthusiasm for participation in the activities and in physical involvement with the materials seemed to override these problems. With the help of others, Science was one of few school classes in which Martin experienced a sense of achievement and success and was able to express the excellent ideas he held.

CHAPTER 7

Melody: The Social Butterfly

An Aesthetic-Social Orientation to Science Learning

Melody was immediately friendly toward me and we spoke often in the classroom. Frequently, at recess, she held my arm and we talked as we walked around the playground. Like Martin, Melody received remedial instruction in reading and mathematics. She made a special point to explain this to me: "I'm in this group because I don't have the higher scores in math and reading that some of the other kids have. I need help in these subjects because sometimes I don't understand the math, sometimes I don't get it."

THOUGHTS AND FEELINGS ABOUT LEARNING SCHOOL SCIENCE

When asked, "How do you feel about learning science?" Melody checked the highest possible positive statement on the survey sheet, "I *really* like it!" On several occasions throughout our discussions, Melody spontaneously commented, "OOOoooh, I like coming here and doing this [discussing the videotapes with me]. I just love science. It's so much fun. You get to do so many neat things." Melody told me that Science was very similar to some of her other subjects, but that there were some differences.

Science is not so different from Language and it's sort of like Health. In Science and Health, like, the kind of health we're doing now, you're learning about how to do different stuff like we're studying on teeth with Mrs. Andrews and like you get to learn what teeth can do to you, how they can help you. And we learn in Science what light can do to you and how light can help you.

She contrasted school science with "the kind of science that I teach myself at home."

Melody: After school I see lots of interesting stuff. Sometimes I don't pick it up because it could make me sick. Last year, I used to live in the country and there's a pond near our house and it had sort of a forest all around it. And there was a big patch of raspberries and I seen a whole bunch of interesting bugs and flowers and we seen a lot of strange types of moss and that. Well, that kind of science doesn't help me in my life, like the kind of learning I do in school does. Like, the science that I teach myself at home just gets me interested and I've started liking certain things. I used to collect rocks and that was interesting to me. We used to have this long road in the country and there used to be a lot of pretty rocks.

Ms. Shapiro: So you feel that seeing these rocks and knowing a bit about these rocks does not really help you in your life?

Melody: Well, it gets me interested in them and I start collecting them. It just makes me happy to see all of the interesting things that are on rocks. The different colors and all the different shapes and sizes.

Ms. Shapiro: I see. It makes you happy to see all of these things.

Melody: Yes. It gets me interested. A lot of them are really pretty. It was really interesting. I miss our house there.

"These things make me happy," emerged as one of Melody's personal constructs in the repertory grid conversation regarding the activities of the light unit. It is the first theme described in Melody's orientation to science study, as it was apparent that enjoyment and happy experiences were important to her in her science learning.

Melody's Ideas About Ways of Learning Science

Melody's classification of Typical Science Activities grouped by preference appear as follows:

A. "Activities you like the very best"
    Watch demonstrations by my teacher
    Do experiments on my own
    Do science worksheets
    Do experiments with other kids
    Talk about science ideas with other people
    Go on field trips
    Make science diagrams and drawings
    Do Science Fair projects
B. "Activities you think are just okay"
    Read the textbook

Write reports on science topics
Read library books on science topics

Melody did not give any of the topics a "C" (dislike) rating. When we reviewed her activity groupings, she commented on the second group, "I don't like to read stuff very much, but it's not that bad, I don't mind it sometimes. I just have a little trouble sometimes. Sometimes I don't understand." Throughout our conversations, Melody frequently portrayed her experience with the phrase, "I just don't always understand." It was not only in Science class that Melody stated that she was not understanding, but in all subject areas. Despite these difficulties, she appeared to enjoy science. Melody stated that she did not like to read, even for pleasure, and regarded herself as a very poor reader. Although she stated that learning science in school "helps me with my life," she also reflected,

> Some of the things we learn are sort of hard to learn. Some things are hard . . . it's mainly because I can't understand [them]. Some of the questions that Mr. Ryan asks us and . . . some of the things we have to do. I just don't get it.

Her difficulty with reading may have contributed, as it did in Martin's case, to the difficulty that she was experiencing academically. But in contrast to Martin, Melody did not show real interest in understanding the ideas presented. Despite the difficulties she appeared to be experiencing, there was clearly a great deal of enjoyment for Melody in the science lesson. When I asked her why she had not placed activities in the category marked "The activities that you don't like" she commented:

> Oh, I really love Science. There's not very much about it that I really don't like. Will you be coming to the Science Fair? Katherine and I are going to do some kind of experiment with molds, and we, that's what we saw last year that a sixth grader had done, so that's how we got the idea there. We're gonna set our stuff up, our molds and stuff and everyone will come by and ask us things and stuff.

Throughout our conversations, Melody consistently expressed more interest in the social interactive experiences of school than in learning the ideas of science and other subjects.

MELODY'S IDEAS ABOUT THE NATURE OF LIGHT
PRIOR TO THE LIGHT UNIT

What Is Light?

Light comes from lightbulbs and makes things bright so we can see them. There is also light outside, like the sun and the streetlights sometimes at night.

Melody equated light with its source. She did not explore the idea beyond these statements.

Where Is the Light?

The light in this room is wherever there isn't darkness or shadows. Like over there in the corner over there, there isn't any light. There's some light here where we are, and over by the light up there (points up to the ceiling), there's a lot of light.

Again, Melody associated light with its source. She also gave the reasonable and commonsense view that light stays predominantly close to its source, rather than moving throughout the room.

Association of Light Phenomena with Everyday Objects

Melody checked several items on the list that most of the students in the class did not associate with light. I asked her how she associated light with the following objects: (1) A magnifying glass: "Because you can catch light rays with it sometimes and shine them around," (2) Clothing: Melody described a sequined blouse and a metallic-cloth dress that her mother owned that she recalled reflecting light, (3) Plants: Melody commented that plants required light in order to grow, and (4) A telescope: Melody recalled going to the Space Sciences Center and viewing sun spots through a telescope. She commented that because the sun is an important source of light, and a telescope is used to look at the sun, then there is a relationship between light and the telescope.

How Does Light Allow Us to See Objects?

Melody commented on the diagram: "The boy sees the light from the sun and that lets him see the house." I asked Melody if the boy actually needed to see the sun in order to see the house. She said, "No, because the

Figure 7.1 How does sunlight allow the boy
to see the house? Melody's response

light rays would shine on it anyway. But the boy would have to be able to
see the sun because if the sun were not there, he would not be able to see
the house."

Light Beam Interaction With Objects

Melody's drawings of light reflecting and passing through objects (Figure 7.2) show several different conceptions of light ray reflection. She was the only member of the study group to draw the light rays in the final example reflecting off the solid, a flat rock. However, she did not show light rays passing through the window glass. Her idea about light reflecting off the solid rock was based on her experience that "some rocks that I look at are shiny, and light reflects off them."

How Do We See Color?

In Melody's view, "Colors are all around in everything and we see all the different colors. Like the green leaves and the blue sky. We see it all. I don't know *how* we do that [laughs]." Like the other children, Melody held the view that colors are in the object that we are looking at and that our eyes "see" the colors in objects.

Feelings and Experiences Associated with Light and the Study of Light

Melody described some of her thoughts and feelings about light:

Light can be really pretty. You know like a really pretty candle. My
mom puts a candle in the bathroom and takes a bath and she turns out

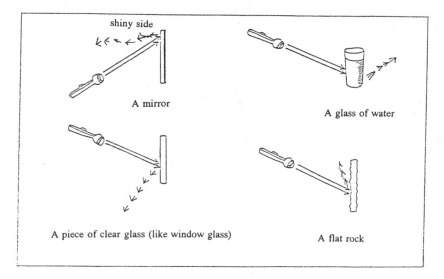

Figure 7.2 How do light beams interact with objects? Melody's response

the light to help her relax. The stars are pretty at night. I like colored lights. You know, like on the Christmas tree. And ours are still on the house. And I like it when it stays light later at night like in summer. Not like now when it gets dark so early.

Melody associated the study of light with the most recent science activity that the class was involved with, "Batteries and Bulbs." Although she recalled having some difficulty with "Batteries and Bulbs," she showed a very positive expectation for the light unit.

We studied a little about light with our last year's teacher and this year we did stuff with batteries and bulbs. And I liked to work with them, but they were hard to figure out. I didn't like that very much. It was too hard to figure out. I guess that light will be sort of interesting. We'll learn all about what it can do for you and to you and stuff.

ORGANIZATION OF MELODY'S CASE REPORT USING PERSONAL CONSTRUCT THEMES

Melody's Personal Constructs

Melody's personal constructs regarding science learning are presented in Figure 7.3.

1. Things we do on our own.	1. Things that we do with the whole class.
2. Talking about, asking about, hearing about things.	2. Just writing things down.
3. Talking about and writing out your worksheet questions.	3. Experimenting to get the answers to the questions.
4. Getting the answers from the teacher.	4. Mr. Ryan is asking you to give *him* answers.
5. Getting or giving help from the other kids.	5. Not getting help from anyone, having trouble getting it finished.
6. Things that are fun to do, easy.	6. Things that are hard to do sort of complicated.
7. Doing things that Mr. Ryan is telling us to do.	7. Doing things that get you into trouble.
8. Things that make me happy.	8. Things that upset me.
9. Paying attention.	9. Goofing around.
10. Mr. Ryan is telling us the right answers.	10. Talking with kids in your group. Getting answers from other kids.
11. Finding the activity interesting.	11. Would rather be doing something else.
12. Mr. Ryan is talking to us about things.	12. We get to look at things with the equipment.
13. You tell people what you think.	13. You just keep it inside. You don't tell anyone.
14. Talking about what you think *might* happen.	14. Trying to get the exact right answer.
15. You can't understand what you're supposed to do.	15. You know how to do it.

Figure 7.3 Melody's science learning constructs

As mentioned previously, the construct, "Things that make me happy," was a consistent phrase offered by Melody in the conversation. This construct, along with similar statements and viewpoints, are embodied in the first theme described in Melody's orientation to science learning. Her appreciation of the aesthetic qualities of phenomena also became a frequently appearing theme in both her orientation in the light unit and her approach to school life.

Theme 1. An Appreciation of the Beauty of Phenomena—An Aesthetic Orientation to Learning

Melody's Self-Characterization: It makes me happy to learn about all the things in Science. They're all so neat. I like to look at the pretty rocks and flowers around our house. It all gets me interested in science. I like to learn about things that are interesting like that.

My Image/Impression: An aesthetic orientation. Melody enjoys and appreciates the beauty in natural phenomena.

Throughout our discussions and my observations of Melody learning science, I noticed that she would often move away from the focus of a lesson to whatever she found attractive. When Melody worked with other children, however, the strength of this orientation in its full expression often created conflict with others. In the following video interaction segment, Melody, Martin, and Yasmin are working on activity 6, "Bend that Beam":

> *Melody has reached over to move the light source around.*
> *Martin: Get outa here, Melody!*
> *Melody: I was trying to fix it. Martin, let me use your magnifier.*
> *Martin: No. Get outa here. We're trying to do the* activity.
> *Melody: I just want to use it for a minute. You're supposed to share. [Melody moves the beaker around to create a new effect]*
> *Martin: Hey don't! Hey, that's not what we're supposed to do, Melody. Get outa here.*
> *Melody: I was just fixing it. Oh, oh, look Yasmin, look inside the light source. OOooooh! Neat! Wow, look!*
> *Yasmin: Neat eh? [All of the group members now gather around the light source]*
> *Melody: It looks likes a pretty little house in there. And looks just like grass down there.*
> *Yasmin: Hey, look. It looks like you can see a little school in there.*
> *Steven: It looks like peat moss.*
> *Martin: Oh, it's weird. It's all sorts of little silver things. [Reaches down into the light source] Oh, ouch! Hey! Oh, ouch! Hey! There, boy, is that hot! Man, I burned my finger.*
> *Yasmin: Yeah. My hand is way out here and it's hot.*
> *Martin: [Returns to the worksheet] Okay, Steven. Let's draw this. There. I drew mine. [Manipulates the light source] Hey! Look what it does when you move the light beams!*
> > *Despite the movement of the group back to the task at hand, Melody continues to look down into the light source. Martin covers part of the top to alter the angle of the beams passing through, one of the required lesson tasks, then moves the light box away from her.*
> *Melody: Don't! Oh, Oooooh. It looks like a bug.*
> *Martin: Whaaaat? [loudly] Who cares? Go away, Melody. Get outa here. Do what you're supposed to do. Okay, okay what's this word, Steve?*
> *Yasmin: [Interrupts] "Particular," dummo. You're supposed to see where it crosses and put it on the sheet.*

Melody succeeded in pulling the others away from the task to follow a line of inquiry that she spontaneously chose. Although she took them off the track, observations about the light phenomena that were shared by everyone in the group. This prompted discussion about the heat felt from the shining light source. This important association of heat with light was actually not mentioned at any point in the teaching objectives of the light unit. Despite this useful discovery, Melody moved the group even away from the unit goals.

Melody's interest in the aesthetic and her attempt to draw the other students in the group into thinking about the attractive aspects of the materials was of particular annoyance to Martin, who valued accomplishing the tasks set by the curriculum. Melody was also effective in pulling Yasmin away. Yasmin was usually more dominantly task oriented, but she also was drawn to the beauty and intrigue in the light source that Melody pointed out.

The casual observer watching this transcript segment might see it simply as an example of a student "goofing around," "off task," or "wasting time." I have attempted to observe the behaviors of students very differently by assuming that all behavior is part of an attempt to make sense of the learning experience. By being interested in how students are constructing meaning in their experiences in science, we can see how each person lives out and practices his or her own personal orientation to science learning. Given the freedom to do so, although in this case, it was simply taken, the students made discoveries about light and shared them with one another. Behavior like Melody's is often misinterpreted or not valued by the teacher. It is usually punished in the classroom because it conflicts with the tasks and goals stated by the curriculum and set by the teacher.

Mr. Ryan remarked candidly to me that throughout the year he had difficulty understanding Melody. He observed some of the videotape test sequences at the beginning of my visit with the class. In one lesson that we watched, Melody was seen sitting near the teacher as he explained a mathematics problem. As Mr. Ryan spoke, she fondled a "Care Bear" and communicated nonverbally with a student at the next table. Mr. Ryan remarked to me as we watched the tape:

> I spoke to Melody there about listening. She's a hard person to understand. I don't know what it is that she does, but I don't know, I find what she does very annoying, somehow.

The elements of Melody's personal orientation to learning in the classroom and her orientation to the science lesson were unknown to Mr. Ryan. He found her to be constantly off track, which annoyed him greatly. When I first began to talk with Melody, I also experienced some of the same annoyance with her actions. I wondered why she would so frequently change the subject in response to a direct question, move away from the task at hand, change the direction of our conversation, or hop around from subject to subject. My attempt to understand the children's orientations to science learning required a great deal of conversation with them in addition to observation

and reflection. But when I finally began to understand some of the anticipations and expectations that Melody held for Science class, it became clear
how her personal orientation guides her to consider and pursue what was
most meaningful in the study of science. The value of developing an awareness of students' personal orientation to science learning was very evident in
Melody's case. Not only would her teacher benefit from understanding how
Melody viewed science learning, but Melody herself would benefit greatly
by becoming more aware of the patterns in her approach to learning. This
could help her to take greater responsibility for her own learning.

I also came to appreciate Melody's great insight into the social dynamics
of the classroom setting. This skill actually helped her to grasp some of the
scientific ideas about the nature of light being presented in the classroom.
But Melody had very little knowledge of her own skills and talents. She repeatedly demonstrated a view of herself as never quite understanding what
she was "supposed to be doing," and a subsequent lack of confidence in her
science learning.

Theme 2. Lack of Confidence in Self as a Science Learner

> *Melody's Self-Characterization:* It's better when you can work with
> the other kids in your group and go to them to get help and answers.
> It's better than working alone because I don't always understand what
> Mr. Ryan wants.
> *My Image/Impression:* Melody believes that she usually does not un-
> derstand science concepts nor what she is "supposed to do" in science.
> She holds the view that she cannot understand science on her own
> and that she needs help from others. Melody believes that it is the
> teacher's responsibility "to make sure that I understand."

Melody and I watched the videotapes of her pervasive and persistent
"off-task" behavior as she worked in the small group. As she watched herself
on the videotape, she appeared unconcerned with her distracting behavior. I
began to wonder if she, herself, noticed this behavior. We watched together
as Mr. Ryan reprimanded her on several occasions for not pursuing the task
required. Not once did she appear embarrassed about her behavior, either on
tape or in conversation. As I reviewed our conversations, I found that her
comments about the incidents could be placed in one of three categories: (1)
References to the fact that she was not understanding what she was "supposed to" do during the lesson, (2) Statements about what she found to be
aesthetically interesting in the lesson, and (3) Comments about what another
person in the class was doing. Melody seemed unaffected by Mr. Ryan's insis-
tence to return to task. His remarks momentarily redirected her to the task,

but had no real lasting effect on her "delinquencies." A consistent complaint was, however, that she was not understanding what she was supposed to do in her lessons was that the teacher wouldn't make the effort to tell her. She did not consider it her responsibility to find out what she was supposed to do in the lessons, but rather, it seemed that she believed it was the teacher's responsibility to be sure she understood. Melody's difficulties and behavior appeared to be a mystery to her teachers throughout the unit. I was also baffled by her behavior at first. I tried to observe and understand the pattern in thought and action of this student who was so very bright and articulate, and yet, who performed so poorly in nearly all of her academic work. Melody was a mystery to her teachers, to me, and it seemed, in many important ways, to herself.

Melody consistently approached her studies with the view the she was poorly informed about what she was supposed to do. During the activity "Hit the Target," the students were given the task of discovering several different ways to reflect light beams around a book. We reviewed a videotape of the lesson sequence together. I asked her before we reviewed the lesson if she would be able to tell me what she thought was the main purpose of the lesson.

> Melody: Well, it was sort of an okay activity. It was sort of fun to see how you could make the light do what you wanted it to do and all. But I couldn't figure out what he meant by this mark that he made here [part of the diagram on the worksheet]. I didn't know what he meant by that. I didn't know if you draw it in or what. And he explained it, but I didn't understand it.
>
> Ms. Shapiro: I see. So before you even started on the lesson you didn't understand what to do?
>
> Melody: No. In this part he is coming over.
>
> *Melody's group is attempting to determine how to perform the tasks on the worksheet.*
>
> *Melody: [Peeling the backing off of the mirror] Oh, this looks neat.*
>
> *Yasmin: [To Melody] You shouldn't do that. You're not supposed to do that. Melody is sitting away from the others who are working on the activity. Mr. Ryan comes over to the group. He says nothing, but looks directly at Melody, who is still peeling the backing off of her mirror. He is obviously annoyed with Melody, but she does not seem aware that she is doing anything "wrong."*
>
> *Melody: [Smiles at Mr. Ryan] Look, Mr. Ryan, lookit the back of this mirror.*
>
> *Mr. Ryan: Now is that what you're supposed to be doing?*
>
> *Melody: [Defensively] Well, I'm working with them. We're doing . . . this . . . I'm getting this. . . .*

Mr. Ryan: *[Points to Melody] Do what you're* supposed *to be doing . . .* NOW!
    [He walks away]

Ms. Shapiro: Did Mr. Ryan help you to get back on track there?

Melody: Not really. He came over and just sort of looked at me. He
    just sort of looked at me and everybody and we [were] wondering
    what we were supposed to be doing.

Ms. Shapiro: So that didn't help you understand a little bit more of
    what you were to do as you worked?

Melody: No, I didn't even know what to do. Yasmin and Steven
    helped me, they showed me like they did the experiment thing, like
    Yasmin *especially* on what to do and we were supposed to try and that
    . . . we were supposed to put a book here and then put a mirror, and
    we were supposed to draw in where we put the mirror here and
    show where it went. But I could just . . . I got it figured out because
    I could just watch what the other people make, put the book in
    place, like that. I just put down then where I thought, there, about
    how the light went about where I *seen* the light go. They did it and
    so I could just watch and just write down where I seen it go.

Ms. Shapiro: I see, you didn't actually do this yourself?

Melody: No. I just did what I seen them do.

Ms. Shapiro: Can you show me how you understand how the light
    might be reflected around the book?

Melody showed me three arrangements of the light source and mirror
that would effectively move the beams around the book. Most of the students had been able to suggest one arrangement. She had employed two
mirrors in one of her sketches that had not been one of the suggestions made
by members of her group. This was quite an original use of the materials that
she had been given. Although Melody had not held the scientist's viewpoint
regarding the reflection of nonvisible light rays prior to the unit, she presented several ideas on the diagrams depicting light beam interaction with
translucent and opaque objects that contained elements of the scientists'
viewpoint.

Ms. Shapiro: These are very good ideas. Did you have some help with
    these?

Melody: Well, this one is the one we all had as a group, and this one is
    just like it, only turned around, sort of. I seen the group in the loft
    doing this one. They had it the other way than us. This one is one
    that I did with Yasmin.

Ms. Shapiro: But Yasmin didn't put this one on her sheet, did she?

Melody: No. It was sort of my idea. She didn't like it.

Ms. Shapiro: Did you finish the worksheet here?

Melody: I didn't have enough time. I liked experimenting with it. I began to understand when I seen them putting the book in place and . . . that's when I began to understand what I was supposed to do. But he confused me by where he put the little question marks, and here just a little line, I didn't understand what he meant, so I thought it was a pencil—doesn't that look like a pencil?

Ms. Shapiro: Yes, it does. You mean that Mr. Ryan confused you?

Melody: Yeah.

Ms. Shapiro: Didn't Mr. Ryan tell you what the symbols meant before the activity?

Melody: Oh, maybe. I don't remember.

Melody referred to the worksheet Mr. Ryan used to explain the use of symbols to the class. She remarked that she found "what Mr. Ryan had written and drawn on the worksheet" very confusing. Although she frequently pointed out that she did not understand what to do, I did not once see her ask Mr. Ryan for help or tell him that she did not understand what she was supposed to do. I asked Melody how she finally discovered what was to be done for the lesson, and how she believed that what she had discovered were the best approaches to reflecting the light beams around the book.

Melody: I seen what the other kids do. But only I seen the others use a book and I thought, it was, even then, I thought it was a pencil shadow.

During the previous lesson, symbols were presented for the students to use when reporting their results on the worksheet. Melody initially confused the pencil shadow symbol for the book symbol on the worksheet.

Ms. Shapiro: So, did you finally clarify these two symbols?

Melody: Well, it took a while. But, oh, yeah, finally. Because my friends are there to help me.

Ms. Shapiro: Was there anything else confusing to you? Were the directions easy to understand?

Melody: I don't really read them. I just work with the other kids and watch the other kids and we get the answers together. Sometimes I get the ideas from the other groups. But in this lesson, I liked working with Yasmin the best. She always gets the answers. She's in my group this time and we did this.

Melody held a view of herself as a person who usually did not understand the science lesson. She appeared to live out this expectation by watching the other students as they worked through the lesson, then copying from their worksheets. Several of the students complained about this to the teacher. The practice was not strictly prohibited by Mr. Ryan, as the children were encouraged to work together, but Melody's approach was not in the spirit of cooperative activity. Melody's habit of copying answers was an important major strategy that she employed in her effort to complete the required worksheets in science. As she herself stated, she copied from Yasmin most frequently. Yasmin objected. She complained to Melody, and quite often to me. What this practice kept hidden from Melody, her peers, and her teacher, was the fact that she possessed very creative ideas of her own and was able to grasp the intent of directions and pursue her own ideas about solutions to the activities.

Theme 3. Socially Precocious. Involved with Others' Activities and Ideas

Melody's Self-Characterization: Science is so much fun. There really isn't anything about it that I don't like. I like to work in groups best because your friends are there to help you and you get to work with things and talk to people in the other groups to see how they did it, how they do it.

My Image/Impression: Melody shows social interest and insight. She is an aware socialite. Melody is able to repeat many of the main ideas of the science lesson because she has discovered them from other children.

Evident throughout Melody's study was the value she gave to social interaction in the classroom, and the importance of the help she received from other students. She showed a keen awareness of what other students were doing during the lesson, frequently leaving her group to explore others' progress.

Both Martin and Melody valued social interaction during group work in science. Both students commented that they found that the help others gave to them was essential in carrying out their responsibilities and tasks as students of science. Melody's social interaction theme was similar to Martin's Theme 3, but also different in important ways. Melody was more dependent on others to provide her with *the answers* to questions. She rarely attempted to find out for herself what was to be done and she rarely completed the tasks required. Martin needed the help of other students to find out what to do, but he fully participated in the activity. He was keenly interested in finding out for himself what to do, and wrote his own ideas on the worksheet. In his interactions with the other students and the teacher, it seemed important to him that he constantly demonstrate his abilities. Melody was more interested in social engagement with her fellow students—understandings were secondary. Her approach to knowing in science was built on developing an awareness of what others were doing, what they were thinking, and what they were finding out. Melody possessed a remarkable awareness of the social life of the classroom. She was continually moving from group to group to find out what the various groups were doing. Although Melody did not seem to be aware that she disrupted regularly when she did not understand the nature of the task she was undertaking, she had a remarkable awareness of what others in the class were doing and how they were thinking about phenomena. Mr. Ryan did not know about Melody's insights and she did not inform him of them. Her pattern of thought and action conflicted with formal classroom instruction. But oddly, it was because of, not despite, this behavior that she appeared to be grasping some of the material presented.

Speaking With Melody About Her Approach to Science Learning

The class continued the light unit with an activity entitled, "Lenses and Lightbeams." Students were asked to predict what they would observe when looking at the word "light" through two types of lenses, 1) an empty beaker, and 2) a beaker filled with water. We watched the videotape together.

Melody: Whose desk am I sitting at?
Steven: [Reading] Test your prediction. . . .
Melody: [To group] Do you put that in the water? [No response] Do you put that in the water? [No response from group. Melody puts her pencil in the water] Yasmin look, this is neat! The pencil gets small. [Yasmin is writing. No response. Melody splashes Mark with water and laughs.]
Mark: Hey, cut it, hey stop it. [Leaves the table to complain to Mr. Ryan] Yasmin has taken her beaker to the sink. Melody turns Yasmin's worksheet around and copies down her answers. As she does, Mr. Ryan comes to her table, places both hands down in front of her and asks:
Mr. Ryan: Are you doing what you're supposed to be doing?
Yasmin: [Returning to her seat] I was.
Melody: I'm just getting some help from Yasmin.
Mr. Ryan: [To Melody] What has splashing around water got to do with what you're supposed to be doing? I want you to get down to what you're supposed to be doing right now. Do you understand?
Melody: Yes.

Ms. Shapiro: What were you supposed to be doing?
Melody: Well, it was too hard to figure out.

Ms. Shapiro: I see.

Melody: There was something that you were supposed to see in the beaker, but nobody understood [laughs]. I got Yasmin to help me. I didn't want to ask Mr. Ryan. He was mad. Donnie's group was doing it and I went over to them and seen what they were doing. But Mr. Ryan told me to sit down. We were supposed to take this word "light" and predict what you think will happen. That's what I did. I predicted. Then I didn't know if I was supposed to also put the pencil in the water or what, so nobody would tell me or anything, so I put it in the water.

Ms. Shapiro: And then you splashed Mark with it?

Melody: Yes [laughs].

Ms. Shapiro: Were you disrupting here, do you think?

Melody: No. Not really. Mark wasn't sure what to do either. We didn't understand what we were supposed to do. When we put the paper up to the beaker it was all blurry. Mark was asking Steven to help him. He went down to the front of the room . . . where kids were looking at the beaker through a beam of light. And he saw that the beams were doing something like twisting when they went through the water. Mr. Ryan was working there, on the floor with him. And I went up to the loft to see the other guys doing stuff, and they were using a measurer, and they found out that at one place on the meter stick the word was doing something like changing or something, but I don't think that's what Mr. Ryan wanted. I was looking and stuff, but he just gets mad sometimes . . . I didn't understand what it was, what I was supposed to do, and when we can't figure out what we're supposed to do . . . he just got mad. He didn't explain or anything.

Melody's third theme reflected her sincere interest in participating in some way in the science lesson, and in expressing her viewpoint. Melody expressed many creative ideas and explanations and liked to share these with members of her group. Although her comments sometimes were not relevant to the lesson tasks, she often had unique insights, but did not possess the confidence and interactive skills to pursue her ideas.

Melody did have some ideas about the ways she enjoyed learning science. Again, they reflect her social interest:

I like to talk about things with the other kids and with Mr. Ryan, like I like to listen to him tell us things. That really helps me to get a better understanding. I like to say the answers sometimes. He sometimes asks me to say the answers.

The Broken Pencil Problem

I asked Melody about her interpretation of the activity in which the pencil appeared broken in the beaker of water. We watched the videotape of the activity, and before we reviewed the discussion, I asked Melody for her explanation of the unusual look of the pencil in the beaker of water.

Melody: Well, I got to say that I thought it happened because the water makes things look bigger and also because of the angle of the beaker. It's round and it makes the water look larger.

Ms. Shapiro: How does the water make things look larger?

Melody: I'm not sure. It makes things look bigger.

Ms. Shapiro: There was some discussion about this after the lesson.

Melody: Mark had the right answer. Mr. Ryan said so.

Ms. Shapiro: Do you recall what that was?

Melody: He said that light rays come from the pencil and bend or something. I wrote that down.

Ms. Shapiro: Is that correct?

Melody: [Laughs] Yes! Mr. Ryan said so.

Ms. Shapiro: So you accept this as correct.

Melody: Well, no. It's sort of hard to understand that. It doesn't, well, I can't figure that one out very well. Other people had trouble too. Like Nathan, [laughs] he even yelled out from the loft, "Light rays come from pencils?"

Ms. Shapiro: Well, let's look at your worksheet before we look at what the other kids were saying. Let's be clear about what you were thinking. Can you tell me what you put there and what you were thinking? What was your answer to the question?

Melody: [Reads] When the pencil is closer to you it looks skinny. When it is close to the wall, it looks fat. That's what Yasmin and I put [laughs]. [Melody had actually copied from Yasmin's paper] But I don't know what the right answer was. I think that they say it on the videotape.

Ms. Shapiro: Shall we watch it?

Mr. Ryan: When you looked at the beaker what did you see? Hands up!

Melody: Oh, yeah, in this part, Pierre gave an answer and I was thinking that he had the same idea as me. If you're wondering about my lipstick, Diane's been putting lipstick on us and it's that Crayola stuff [laughs]. My lips look blue! Oh. Mr. Ryan is asking what was happening and everyone is talking about what was happening to the pencil. Then he asked for a reason why.

Ms. Shapiro: I see. Did anyone have an explanation?

Melody: I think they did, but I don't think anybody had the right answer. Just that the pencil looked broken and the water made it look broken, er, bigger. That's all I remember. Sam said the water acts as a magnifying glass and I, I thought that that was a good answer. And Donnie said that maybe it was the water and the glass together. I thought that was a good answer because the water and the glass, they work to make it look larger.

Ms. Shapiro: How do they do this?

Melody: It's in a circle. And it's coming forward, where the circle part comes forward does it. It leans this way and so it makes it look bigger, when you look at it. That's what I said there [points to videotape]. And I was saying that might be the reason why it looked bigger, I wasn't sure or anything. But it *could* have, could be why. So I said that. But I don't think [laughs], I don't think so. . . .

Ms. Shapiro: No? What do you think?

Melody: No. I don't know why it does that. But it could be this circle thing because me and Yasmin were talking about it and trying to figure it out and that's what it did. That's what we decided.

Ms. Shapiro: You don't think that your answer is as possible as any of the others?

Melody: No. Probably not. Well . . . but what I'm saying *could* be right. It's just an idea. I don't know or anything. It's just what I seen and what I think. So it could be. Could be.

Ms. Shapiro: How would you know for sure?

Melody: Wait till Mr. Ryan gives us the right answers.

Ms. Shapiro: Then you'd know for sure?

Melody: Well, usually I'm not right anyway.

Through her social interaction orientation, Melody had a heightened awareness of the other children in the group, what others in the classroom were doing, and the answers they are coming up with. It appeared that in this way, Melody gained a real grasp of the overall activity and how it was being understood by the classroom community. Viewed from this perspective, it was not *despite* her habit of playing with the equipment and socializing that she was grasping ideas, but *because* of these behaviors that she was able to put ideas together without ever reading the directions or trying to figure out on her own what was to be done. For, at the end of the unit, when I retested the students, Melody was one of the few students to show some grasp of the ideas presented. Melody was aware of the other students' contributions and thinking as they learned about light, but had very little understanding of her own great talent in being wide awake and attentive to these ideas.

Although Melody consistently showed that she was not aware that the pattern of her own approach and orientation to science learning often led to reprimand, neither was Mr. Ryan aware of what was most meaningful to Melody during the science lessons. For Melody the benefit of understanding this pattern would be that it would form the basis for encouraging her to take greater responsibility for her own learning. For Mr. Ryan, there would be considerable potential gain in understanding the variety of orientations that guide students in their science learning and in understanding what is meaningful to students as they work at the task of learning science.

CHAPTER 8
Yasmin: The Student
A Dedication to High Achievement

The children are involved in the activity portion of a lesson on prisms. Yasmin leans quietly over her worksheet amidst a background of cheerful chatter and bustling activity. She turns and carefully checks the angle of the light shining through the glass prism set in front of her, then looks behind her to a wall chart that shows the range of colors in the white light spectrum. She opens an immaculately organized pencil box and selects a colored felt pen. Again she leans forward close to her paper and painstakingly colors in the beams she has drawn, checking periodically to be sure that she has the same colors as those on the wall chart.

There is movement all around Yasmin. She works intensely, quietly, and in a concentrated manner. Louise bounces over, leans an elbow on the table. Looking at Yasmin's drawing she asks, "Can I borrow your ruler?" Without lifting her eyes, Yasmin responds, as if to her paper, "Pauline has it." Louise rushes off to find Pauline.

Melody sits down at the desk next to Yasmin. Yasmin continues working quietly and methodically, coloring in each beam in the spectrum. Using a black pen now, she outlines each color individually. Yasmin asks Melody, "Those guys have the same as us?" Melody nods and begins to color her own worksheet.

This snapshot scene of Yasmin working during science class is typical of her style and involvement throughout the science unit. My initial impression of Yasmin was that of a person with an unusually strong commitment to task. Yasmin's involvement in science is marked by consistently diligent efforts to determine the task required in a lesson, then a move to command all of the resources needed to accomplish what is required of her.

THOUGHTS AND FEELINGS ABOUT LEARNING SCHOOL SCIENCE

Science was not Yasmin's favorite subject. Despite this, she commented that in some ways she did like it. Yasmin told me that she often found that "some of the ideas in science are very difficult to learn," but, she went on, "in many ways science is very fun, particularly when you get to do things with the materials."

I asked Yasmin if she liked to do science activities at home or read about science. She said, "No, not at all. It's not something I'm really interested in outside of school." Although Yasmin had lived in Canada since her family's arrival from India when she was 4 years old, English was not the language spoken in her home. When we discussed her family life, Yasmin told me about the many responsibilities that made demands on her time. She explained, "I take care of my sisters at home and that takes a lot of time, so I don't do a lot of extra things right now."

I asked Mr. Ryan what he knew about Yasmin's background. He said that he realized that he was aware of very little beyond Yasmin's in-class performance. He did not know that Punjabi was the language spoken in her home, nor was he aware of her extensive home commitments. Mr. Ryan regarded Yasmin as one of "the top students, perhaps the highest achieving student in the class." He referred to her as "a very together lady, a pleasure to work with."

Yasmin's Ideas About the Ways of Learning Science

Yasmin's classification of Typical Science Activities, grouped by preference were as follows:

A. "Activities you like the very best"
   Do experiments with other kids
   Go on field trips
   Make science diagrams and drawings
   Do Science Fair projects
B. "Activities you think are just okay"
   Do experiments on my own
   Do science worksheets
   Talk about science ideas with other people
C. "Activities you don't like"
   Read the textbook
   Watch demonstrations by the teacher
   Write reports on science topics

I reviewed the groupings with Yasmin and asked if she believed there was any sort of pattern in her groupings.

Yasmin: Well, I really hate the part there where you just read the textbook and write boring reports. I like doing neat projects with things, though.

Ms. Shapiro: You've placed "Watch demonstrations by the teacher" in the "don't like" category.

Yasmin: Oh, when he goes over things like before we do the activity? I find it hard to listen. I just start thinking of other things, like, what to do and things.

Ms. Shapiro: So you don't find that particularly interesting?

Yasmin: It's really boring. And when, like at the end of the activity, like when we go over the worksheet, and you have to go over everything, describing everything to the whole class, well, it's really boring.

Ms. Shapiro: Is it the listening that you don't like, or. . . .

Yasmin: I just usually figure out what to do, so it's just repetition.

Ms. Shapiro: You place working with other kids in a higher preference category than working alone here.

Yasmin: Yeah. It's much more fun to talk to other kids to find things out and do things like try to find out the answers with other kids helping. I like that better than just doing things alone. Alone there's no one to talk to, to find things out.

Yasmin rated science as "fairly easy" on the survey form given to all members of the class. She remarked, "Sometimes there is too much to learn. I just don't like it when you have all these little details to memorize and stuff." Despite the fact that Yasmin spoke of disliking the memorization of "all of the little details," it was very clear through working with and talking with her that she took the responsibility for learning details very seriously. Her conversation and personal constructs focused on the tasks of learning and the logistics of completing the tasks at hand. She did not refer to the science content of lessons as of particular interest, but was more concerned with the *accomplishment* of tasks.

Through discussion with her, and during attempts to explore how she put ideas together, it appeared that Yasmin made no spontaneous effort to connect ideas from previous lessons in the ways that I had observed Mark, Martin, and Donnie striving to do. She worked systematically, taking each task one at a time, doing each question as it was set before her.

YASMIN'S IDEAS ABOUT THE NATURE OF LIGHT
PRIOR TO THE LIGHT UNIT

What is Light?

Yasmin, like Mark, said that she did not know exactly what light was. In responding to the question, she offered reasons why she believed the topic should be studied in school.

I really don't know. It helps you see. It's from bulbs and the stars and
the sun. I think it's important to study because we use it at school and,
like, in our homes.

Where is the Light?

Yasmin stated that she believed that light was "in" its source, the overhead lights, a commonly offered commonsense viewpoint. She stated that in
the dark areas of the room there is no light present.

Association of Light Phenomena with Everyday Objects

Yasmin's profile of association of light with everyday objects was fairly
typical of the responses put forward by other class members. She mentioned,
as did several other students, that she had never seen a firefly, and therefore
did not associate it with light.

How Does Light Allow Us to See Objects?

Yasmin considered the light and the house entirely from the perspective
of the boy in the drawing (Figure 8.1). The arrows that she drew reflected
this view. She remarked, "Light falls on the boy and shines on the house.
Here the boy is looking at the house."

Light Beam Interaction with Objects

In each diagram (Figure 8.2), Yasmin showed light reflecting off all the
objects. Light beams were not shown passing through the clear glass nor

Figure 8.1 How does sunlight allow the boy
to see the house? Yasmin's response

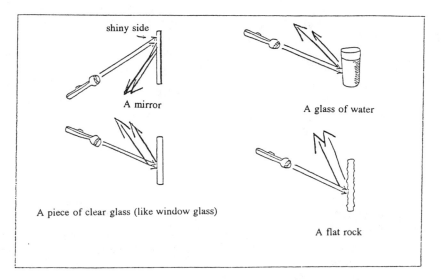

Figure 8.2 How do light beams interact with objects? Yasmin's response

through the glass of water. Her portrayal of light rays reflecting off the flat rock appeared consistent with the scientists' view of light beam reflection. However, in conversation with Yasmin regarding this diagram, she commented that "the light would only reflect if the rock were shiny enough. Light beams would not reflect from a non-shiny surface, like a hand or a person."

How Do We See Color?

> We see the color with our eyes. We see, like if something's been dyed red, we see the red dye in it, or we see the bits of yellow like in your sweater.

Yasmin stated that the dye color present in an object is what is seen by the observer. This had been the most frequently mentioned viewpoint by Yasmin's fellow class members, but as indicated previously, is not the scientific conception view.

Feelings and Experiences Associated with Light and Study of Light

> Well, I guess I'd say that I like it. It lets you see. I hate the darkness, the dark, so I guess I do like light [laughs]. I never really thought about it, though. Some light can be too bright and I don't like that I guess. I've never read about it or studied light before. I don't know

anything about what we'll learn. I don't think that it sounds very interesting.

It appeared that Yasmin had no real interest in the study of light phenomena and did not anticipate that the topic would be a particularly interesting unit of study.

ORGANIZATION OF YASMIN'S CASE REPORT USING PERSONAL CONSTRUCT THEMES

Yasmin's Personal Constructs

Yasmin's personal constructs regarding science learning are presented in Figure 8.3. Below is a description of her personal orientation themes.

Theme I. The Responsible Learner: A Task Orientation to Science Learning

Yasmin's Self-Characterization: My job in Science is to figure out what to do. When you do it, you have a better chance of it being interesting. If it's interesting to you, then you learn it better.

1. Experimenting with things.	1. Writing things down and answering questions.
2. You get it. You understand it.	2. You don't understand anything.
3. You're trying to get the answers. You're working to figure things out.	3. You're just correcting your work.
4. You're speaking up in class, giving *your* answers.	4. You're listening to others' ideas.
5. Paying attention.	5. Goofing around.
6. You're doing it.	6. Someone else is doing it for you.
7. Doing something fun.	7. Doing something boring.
8. Working hard to learn.	8. Working in a fun way to learn.
9. Just talking about ideas.	9. *Doing* something.
10. Getting ideas from listening to other people.	10. Asking questions of your own.
11. You need to get some help.	11. You're able to help someone else.
12. You're talking to others to find things out.	12. You're alone and not understanding.
13. Experimenting with other kids.	13. Spending the time getting the worksheet done.
14. Like the activity.	14. Hate it. I don't like working with it at all.
15. Learning big ideas.	15. Too many details to learn. Too many little things to learn.

Figure 8.3 Yasmin's science learning constructs

My Image/Impression: Yasmin has an interest in doing the job set before her and an interest in doing well in science and in school in general.

The responsibility to do well. Throughout our conversations, Yasmin spoke of a commitment to the responsibility of being a good student. She spoke of the importance of "the work we do to learn in school." She talked about her approach to learning science as one of "figuring out what needs to be done on the worksheet and then doing it." In small group work, she regularly directed the group to the task at hand. Students would often go to Yasmin to find out what was required on a worksheet, for she could be counted on to know what was needed to complete a lesson.

The importance to Yasmin of completing the task was the basis for her deep involvement with the activities. Often she became interested in considering the content of the lesson, but this always secondary to the primary commitment to task.

As we watched the videotape of the first activity of the light unit, "Beam Bouncing," Yasmin told me:

> At first a lot of kids didn't know really what they were supposed to do. Like it was hard drawing the diagrams. I had trouble deciding where to put the mirror and everything. It was hard at first, then when I figured it out, it became easier. Mr. Ryan came over and helped me figure it out. Like first I had the mirror right here and here and here and he suggested that if I hit the mirror right there, it reflected over here. So we tried it in my group again his way.

Yasmin said that she regularly asked Mr. Ryan for assistance:

> Before he came, like on the diagram we were setting up the equipment, like it was easy, then I was looking at the diagram from the side and I didn't know how to put the mirrors in and everything. So when I asked him to help me I was able to understand the rest and the rest became easy.

Yasmin, like Martin, worked to grasp the *procedural* aspects of science learning. They often had valuable exchanges of information about, in Martin's words, "what we're supposed to do on the worksheet." Whereas Martin valued doing the activity itself, Yasmin was interested in the successful completion of assigned tasks. Martin and Yasmin established a collaborative relationship. They usefully helped one another to understand the main task of the lesson.

Yasmin was very resourceful in her endeavor to figure out "how to do the worksheet." During the lesson, "Bend that Beam," for example, we watched as she would disappear from the video screen for periods of time. She spoke about her absences from the video screen:

> Yasmin: Here I was going over to Carly's group . . . to get some more ideas.
>
> Ms. Shapiro: Oh, what are you getting?
>
> Yasmin: Well, I wanted to know how Carly and Donnie and Mark were doing it. These guys [her own group] are just goofing around. They haven't done anything yet.
>
> Ms. Shapiro: It seems that you're always the one to be helping the others figure out what they are doing.
>
> Yasmin: Oh, well, I just like to be getting my work done and I like to finish my work. These guys [members of her group] are just goofing around and when we get to the end of the period, they'll just copy mine.
>
> Ms. Shapiro: You don't mind?
>
> Yasmin: Well I do. It sort of makes me mad. I get it done . . . and, well, Melody, she just *takes* my book and copies it.

After viewing the videotape I asked Yasmin if she would briefly summarize the main idea of the lesson. She responded, "Well, it was to learn. Learning about light was the main idea." In contrast, Donnie had responded to this question with specific ideas about light, attempting an articulation of some of the main light ideas of the lesson and the potential for application of the ideas, for example, "We learned that if something is in your way, and you need to get light onto something, then you can use mirrors and there's different ways more than one way you can get light onto a spot."

Yasmin was unusually resourceful in determining what was to be done. This talent was recognized by her teacher and her peers. It was notable, however, that despite her success Yasmin had little interest in the topic of study for its own sake. At the end of the unit, although she responded with correct answers on the worksheets, Yasmin emerged from the unit with little real understanding of light. The second theme reflects her greater interest in the ways of learning science.

Theme 2. An Interest in Ways of Learning Science

Yasmin's Self-Characterization: There are some very fun ways to learn. Some of the activities are interesting. I like to work with the other kids.

My Image/Impression: Yasmin has an interest in ways of learning science. She values enjoyable and efficient approaches to science learning.

More than any of the other children in the study group, Yasmin spoke of an interest in approaches to learning in school. She spoke about the ways that she saw activities being presented by Mr. Ryan and about the ways that tasks were best accomplished in school. Yasmin actually appeared to be more aware of the ways that tasks were best accomplished in school than of the actual content of the learning. Yasmin was very interested in performing well in science, and in school generally. She appeared to be very concerned with being seen to do well. On several occasions when Mr. Ryan came over to Yasmin's group to ask other members to return to their tasks, Yasmin made a noticeable effort to show him that she had been working all along, even though the others were not. The dominant theme that emerged for Yasmin was an interest and great resourcefulness in directing her attention to finding out what she must do to accomplish the tasks set before her.

Yasmin defined science as "an activity that is fun to learn." She made a distinction both in her personal constructs and in conversation between "working hard to learn" and "working in a fun way to learn." She made the distinction between activities in which one is "doing something boring" and "doing something fun," noting "I don't like a whole bunch of little details in science. There's sometimes just too many details to learn." She elaborated on this.

Yasmin: Well, science is all right. I like learning some of the stuff, but not all of it, because sometimes it's quite boring. Other times it's very fun.

Ms. Shapiro: What is it that you find boring?

Yasmin: Well, some things I don't like. Well, like electricity and light are very fun, but some things, like last year we learned about sound. I didn't really like that because you had to really learn a lot of things in just a few weeks, and then you had a test [makes a face]. You had to learn all about the eardrum. You had to watch films and do all sorts of memorizing. There was just too much to learn.

Ms. Shapiro: That made it boring.

Yasmin: Yeah, too many little things to remember all at once. I don't like that. It's more fun when you get to do things with it, like in electricity we made bulbs light. And in Science now we're making light go in different ways. It's more interesting because when you yourself get right into things.

Ms. Shapiro: Are you interested in knowing about light?

Yasmin: No. Not always really. It's not what I'd pick. But some of the things are really interesting that we get to do like the ways you can make light go.

Working With and Listening to Others

Following the discussion in which Mark had explained refraction, Yasmin described how group discussion was an interesting and enjoyable way of learning: "Listening to the other kids helps me to learn. It's easier, too, like when I have other discussions like this one. Listening to the other kids made ideas pop into my head so that I could give an answer.

Yasmin: I forgot what Mark said on Tuesday, so I just wrote what I thought before, that maybe it was because the beaker is round, and maybe because of the water.

Ms. Shapiro: Oh, I see, one or the other?

Yasmin: Maybe both. I don't remember what Mark said. But I know that he was right [laughs]. He wasn't speaking up too loudly. I couldn't hear. Mr. Ryan said the answer out loud. I got the right answer on the sheet after that. He put it on the overhead.

Ms. Shapiro: Are you saying that you don't recall whether that made sense at the time?

Yasmin: No. Mr. R. said, 'cause he said that, I remember a little bit— that because Mark took what, last week's problem, you know, the worksheet we did, and he then combined that . . . what he learned there, with this week's problem, that's how I think he did it. He sort of combined them together and that's how he came up with the right answer.

Ms. Shapiro: Can you tell me why the pencil appears bent in the water?

Yasmin: No! [laughs]

Ms. Shapiro: Do you think that it is important to know?

Yasmin: Well, yes. Like if we have a test on it, then yes, we have to know it and study it and learn it.

Ms. Shapiro: And if there is no test, do you think that it is important or valuable to know these things about light?

Yasmin: No. I don't think so. They're sort of fun, but I don't think that it is something I am going to use ever.

Yasmin recalled clearly *how* Mark came to the correct answer, but she could not tell me what his answer was nor could she relate any of the thought or ideas relevant to the development of the concept. It was clear that her interest in analyzing the *ways* of learning and achieving the correct answer had guided her to notice *how* the understanding was achieved in Mark's response. But she did not focus on the mystery or the content of the lesson, as Donnie had. Although she did not see any reason for knowing about light, she took her responsibility for learning about light very seriously.

Reflecting on Science Learning

During the review of the videotapes of lessons, Yasmin did not comment as often as other students in the group about the concepts that were presented in class that were in conflict with her own. It seemed that she was actually considering many of the content ideas for the first time during our interviews. Yasmin found reflecting with me on videotapes to be intriguing. She often asked to review a segment of the videotapes. As we reviewed the content of the lesson, Yasmin showed that she was very adept at reflecting on her own thinking. These instances showed her interest in and ability to become aware of and articulate her thoughts about content information during the classroom presentation, although she had not previously shown an interest in the specific content information. Early in the project, we discussed the difficulty of accepting the idea of the reflection of invisible light rays off all objects.

> *Mr. Ryan: So, I guess we've decided that light travels from the thing we see to our eyes. And we see it. Does anyone not agree with that? [No hands are raised]*
> Ms. Shapiro: Did you agree with Mr. Ryan?
> Yasmin: Well . . . I'm not sure. Yes, I think so. I agreed a little bit with some of the things about light. I wasn't sure about that answer, that the answer was right. I saw the other kids, but I thought that, like, light is something else, not the thing we see.
> Ms. Shapiro: What do you mean?
> Yasmin: Well, I think he was saying that the light and the thing, the light from the thing, is what we see, or something like that?

Yasmin and I replayed this section of the videotape. She became stronger in her disagreement with the ideas presented.

> *Mr. Ryan: And so the reason that I see Martin is because the light reflects from Martin into my eye.*
> Yasmin: I don't agree with that at all. Only some things have lights. Like the TV set. Like you don't really need lights to see the TV set.

Unless it's very bright. Like on this video recorder, you can see the little light here when it's on. And some kinds of toys. You can see these. And some stickers that glow in the dark. You can see those too.

Yasmin pointed out that listening to other students' comments about light pathways helped her to understand, but had also confused her.

Yasmin: Some people said that it [the light] went in circles. That made it clearer to me. But, I don't think he meant that.

We reviewed the videotape again and Yasmin was able to articulate her confusion.

Mr. Ryan: Do you have any idea as to what kind of path or pathway light would travel? For example, when you go home, you take a direction, you have a direction, you take a pathway home.
Yasmin: Here he said "when you go home, you take a pathway or directions," but he said "pathway" . . . I didn't get that because the thing is I'm not light! So I don't really see what he means.

Later on, Yasmin revealed another confusion concerning other aspects of the discussion about light pathways that she had not mentioned in class nor the first time through our viewing of the videotape.

Mr. Ryan: How does light get from there to there? Does it go in circles? Does it travel in zigzags?
Charles: It goes through wires?
Mr. Ryan: Well, there are lots of lights that get there without flowing through wires. Does it go through wires? There are no wires from the sun.
Yasmin: I couldn't figure out here if he meant how does it get to go there. But then I got the idea that it goes in a path. At first I thought that Mr. Ryan said it went in wires or tubes or things like that, but then when someone said it goes straight . . . I thought, like, I wasn't sure if he was asking how can you get it to go a certain way, or what makes it do that? Then someone here said, it was Chan, it goes in circles, and I said, "that can't be true" in my mind, "that can't be the right answer."

Although the predominating theme of Yasmin's thought and action during the light unit was her interest in tasks and ways of learning, it was apparent that these interests could guide her into new ways of thinking about light. It seemed that because of her interest in ways of learning, Yasmin would benefit from help to understand how lesson ideas built on and were connected to one another. This might create greater interest in the ideas within science learning for Yasmin, allowing her to deepen her understanding of subject matter *as well* as her talent in performing learning tasks successfully.

CHAPTER 9

Pierre: The Artist

Sheer Delight in the Details of Natural History

On the day of my first visit to the class, Mr. Ryan introduced me to the students and I explained what I hoped to accomplish in the classroom. I asked the class to consider the extent to which they would like to become involved in the study. Pierre was the first student to come over to speak to me as I stood by the side of the room. He asked, "Are you going to be here for the Science Fair, Miss? I did dinosaurs last year and I've got all the models on my desk. Do you want to come up and see?"

Pierre's desk was situated in a loft area in the classroom, a sort of balcony overlooking the classroom. He had set up a small display of model dinosaurs on the front edge of his desk. As he handled each one, he told me its scientific name and described its habits and environment in remarkable detail. He explained that he had used the models in last year's Science Fair project. Pierre spoke quickly and enthusiastically, sharing his collection with obvious delight. "Pretty neat, huh?" he said. "I had these in the Science Fair project last year and now I'm building a model world for them at home. For the Science Fair, I read a lot of books about dinosaurs and people asked me questions and stuff. This year I'm going to do models of outer space and rockets and read up on the planets and all of the space flights and maybe make a model rocket." Pierre rustled through his desk and pulled out several paperbacks on various science topics. He read the title as he showed me each book: "*Dinosaurs, Forces That Shaped the Earth, Rockets and Jets*, and *Space Travel Today.*" His science notebook, a three-holed folder, held photocopied worksheets from his most recent Science unit, "Batteries and Bulbs." He had spontaneously decorated the cover over the course of the term. I asked Pierre to tell me about the drawings on the cover of his notebook (Figure 9.1). "Oh!" he exclaimed, "This is a scientist's laboratory. It's got all the stuff that he's working on. There's his coat and there's his cat that lives there. And that's his picture."

I asked Pierre how he had known what to put in a science laboratory. He responded, "From books and things and movies, there's pictures that gives you an idea about what they look like."

Pierre was one of the quieter members of the class. He seemed very

Figure 9.1 Pierre's science notebook cover

serious about his work. I did not see him ask Mr. Ryan for help at any time. Although he frequently asked fellow students for help, Pierre almost always worked alone, observing the other children more often than he participated with them. He seemed interested but rarely contributed during small group discussions.

Despite our comfortable and friendly relationship, of all the children in the study, Pierre seemed to have the greatest difficulty reflecting on and articulating his experience verbally during our conversations following the lessons. Early in our meetings he surprised me by asking if I was a speech therapist. I explained the project in more detail and Pierre told me why he had questioned me. His brother, now in fourth grade, had worked with a speech therapist weekly since first grade. He wondered if we would be doing something similar. Pierre told me that his parents had asked that he be kept from progressing after his first year of preschool. I discovered that they had been concerned that he was not maturing physically and that he was not acquiring verbal skills quickly. Now in fifth grade, Pierre was an average, capable student. Mr. Ryan was not aware of his early school history. Although Pierre was physically smaller than the other children his age, he displayed unusual athletic skill on the playground. He told me that Physical Education, Art, and Science were his favorite subjects.

THOUGHTS AND FEELINGS ABOUT LEARNING SCHOOL SCIENCE

In all of our conversations, Pierre showed intense interest in learning science. The more I inquired about his interest in the topic, the more he exuded delight. He beamed, "Science is just great! I just love it. You get to learn all kinds of interesting things about the earth and about dinosaurs and about the human body, and you get to do experiments and things. . . . I don't really like learning about light, though."

At this point the class had not yet begun the study of light, so I asked Pierre how he had made this decision so soon and if he could tell me what it was about the topic that he did not like. He explained, "Well, like when we studied about it in 'Batteries and Bulbs.' There were these little batteries and bulbs and holders and stuff and wires. You had to light the bulbs and all. You had to get it to light and I just couldn't do it! I tried and tried and I just couldn't get it to work. It was just too hard. And then you had to get all the different ways. It was hard! It was sort of interesting in some ways, but it's sort of hard, you know?"

Like Donnie, Pierre equated the study of light with the unit most recently studied, "Batteries and Bulbs." In that unit, Pierre said, "We actually *made* light. This time we learn what it is and, sort of, how it works. It's a lot harder."

Pierre's Ideas About Ways of Learning Science

Pierre indicated that he did not like reading the textbook and enjoyed doing science worksheets the least of all the activities. His gave an "A" to all of the other activities on the list of choices and made an "A+" next to the activity, "Doing Science Fair projects." Overall, Pierre's regard for science was enthusiastically positive. His interest in pursuing science outside of the classroom was greater than that of any of the other children in the study group. He wrote on his survey form that outside of school "I like drawing things like models and dinosaurs and I like making things." I noticed that he drew constantly. He often gave me drawings after our conversations that illustrated or supported a point he had made during our discussion. With the same richness of detail as the drawings on his Science notebook cover, they conveyed better than words his love of science learning.

PIERRE'S IDEAS ABOUT THE NATURE OF LIGHT PRIOR TO THE LIGHT UNIT

What Is Light?

Light is rays, like rays of light. Like, there's light from the sun and from light bulbs and flashlights and lasers mostly. And lasers are magnified sunlight.

Pierre referred to light in terms of visible rays. In this example, he showed an awareness of at least one aspect of the basic principle governing the creation of laser light.

Where Is the Light?

The light is in the fluorescent lights up there and that makes it bright in the room, well, in some places in the room, anyway. There's no light right now because it's bright outside.

Pierre equated light with its source yet said also that it makes the entire room bright. He did not consider the light coming from outside to be the same as electric light.

Association of Light Phenomena with Everyday Objects

Most of the children who checked light in association with "eyes" stated that they did so because light is required to allow us to see with our eyes.

Pierre did not. When I mentioned this to him, he stated that we can see in the dark, so light is not important for vision.

How Does Light Allow Us to See Objects?

In an apparent contradiction, Pierre explained his drawing (Figure 9.2), saying "The light shines into the eyes of the boy. When the light shines into his eyes, that lets him see the house." In Pierre's view, light is required to allow the eye to "see" the house. Of course, this is in part the scientifically correct explanation and would be a good beginning point to build understanding of the scientifically correct conception.

Light Beam Interaction With Objects

Pierre's drawings (Figure 9.3) show light reflecting off every object except the rock. When I asked him about this, he stated that even though he had not drawn arrows in, light beams would have to go through the piece of window glass and the glass of water and that "only a little bit" would actually reflect off each of these objects.

How Do We See Color?

When asked this question, Pierre responded, "I see, like a blue pencil? [pause . . . audible sigh . . . Pierre dropped his eyes to the desk pausing again] That's a tough one. I don't know . . . with my eyes and my brain, I guess. If it's blue, my eyes see the blue and my brain tells me. I don't know *how*, though." Pierre's view was based on his understanding of vision. He was aware that he did not completely understand the mechanism of vision.

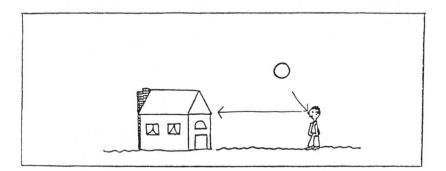

Figure 9.2 How does sunlight allow the boy to see the house? Pierre's response

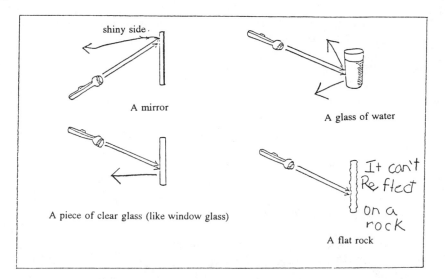

Figure 9.3 How do light beams interact with objects? Pierre's response

Feelings and Experiences Associated with Light and the Study of Light

Pierre talked about his feelings. "I like light. Sometimes not. At night I get under the covers and shine a flashlight through and on my face and hands and my brother gets real scared. [Shows me how he shines the flashlight] Oooh, when it's really dark, it's really cool. You can see the blood in your hand. We studied it last year and we opened a light bulb and it was really cool inside. This year we've done electricity with making light with batteries and wires. That was fun."

Again Pierre connected the study of batteries and bulbs to the study of light. Many of the children in the class commented on how interesting they had found it last year to observe the inside of a light bulb. In my own teaching, I found great interest in looking inside a light bulb, an activity that points to the great potential for interesting children in technological applications when studying light.

ORGANIZATION OF PIERRE'S CASE REPORT USING PERSONAL CONSTRUCT THEMES

Pierre's personal constructs regarding the study of science are presented in Figure 9.4. Below are his personal orientation themes.

1. Experimenting.	1. Mr. Ryan is just telling us things.
2. Just really enjoying the activity.	2. Correcting and copying down things.
3. You know exactly what to do.	3. You don't know what to do at all.
4. Helping someone else to answer.	4. Not giving away any of the answers.
5. Confusing to everyone.	5. He explains to us. He tells us what it means.
6. Group activity. You read questions and ask them to each other.	6. You do it all on your own.
7. Having trouble and have to ask the teacher for help.	7. Don't need any help at all.
8. You want to get going and do the work just *so* bad.	8. You're having trouble and no one will help.
9. You're thinking up on your own what you want to do.	9. The teacher is telling you what to do.
10. You're really worried about getting it right.	10. Not worried about getting it right or wrong, just enjoying the experimenting.
11. You really want to do it. You're working hard thinking of something.	11. Not doing anything at all. Goofing around.
12. Doing stuff you have to do.	12. Doing things you really enjoy doing.
13. You don't understand the question.	13. You're finding out from other kids what to do.
14. You're getting all your worksheet done.	14. You're stuck.
15. You're learning lots of interesting things.	15. You're sort of bored.

Figure 9.4 Pierre's science learning constructs

Theme I. The Natural Historian: An Interest in the Facts and Details of Science

> *Pierre's Self-Characterization:* Science is learning about all kinds of interesting things. It's about the dinosaurs, the earth, and the human body, and you find out how things work and the way that the world used to be.
>
> *My Image/Impression:* Pierre viewed science as an opportunity to learn all about the details of phenomena that delighted and fascinated him. He took particular interest in natural history, enjoying the many details of the story of science.

Despite the concern about science teaching that relates to the child as a "receptacle of information," and views the teacher as "transmitter" or "pourer of information" into the child, for Pierre a focus on detail is precisely what makes science interesting. Details and facts made Pierre wide awake to the learning he was exposed to. Pierre's personal orientation to science learning was based on his enjoyment of science as a set of facts concerning the nature of phenomena. During one of our videotape review sessions Pierre showed me some of his own ways of keeping track of terms and phrases during lessons.

Ms. Shapiro: What are you doing here?

Pierre: There I was writing down those words, you know, that tell about the light and which way it goes when you put it through the beaker of water?

Ms. Shapiro: Were you writing on a worksheet here?

Pierre: No. I just wrote them down so I could remember what they were here. I just like to keep a hold of them so I can remember them.

Ms. Shapiro: What were the words that you wrote down?

Pierre: AAaauuumm. Convergence and divra—or something.

Ms. Shapiro: Do you recall what they mean?

Pierre: Yeah. Convergence is when they come together and cross. Divra—um—gence is, when, oh, [laughs]. It's sort of hard to remember. That's why I wanted to write it down [laughs].

Pierre's natural interest in making notes and in keeping records was apparent throughout the light unit. He made notes on small pieces of paper that he placed in various places—in his Science notebook, his desk, or a pencil box. He would often write on the back of the worksheets in his Science notebook.

Like Mark, Pierre spoke of the enjoyment of hearing the "story" of science in class, as did several of the other children in the classroom. Interest was particularly evident during a session in which the children listened to the school nurse and their classroom teacher describe human growth and sexual development. A question and answer session followed. Melody had told me how interesting she found the questions from other students during these periods. Yasmin commented that listening during the question and answer periods helped her to "picture new ideas in my own mind. Somebody else's idea gets you to thinking in a new way sometimes."

I did not observe Pierre asking questions during these periods, but he did comment on how interesting he found listening to others. Pierre spoke of "the science lecture part" of a lesson, when Mr. Ryan answered student questions or gave the children specific information on the nature of phenomena. Pierre contrasted this with the preactivity discussion, which he called "the boring part of the lecture." Pierre said that during this time, "he's just telling you what you're supposed to do. You wish he'd stop. You just want to get to do it so bad." Pierre preferred those times when Mr. Ryan provided "all kinds of really interesting information." His delight in this process revealed an orientation to science learning as a view of an ongoing discovery of the way the world truly is, rather than a changing picture of the world described by Mark. I pursued Pierre's view of the purpose of science learning in elementary school.

Ms. Shapiro: Do you think that it is important to study science?

Pierre: Yeah, I do. You might want to continue studying in high school and at the university. In junior high school it gets harder so you have to get ready for that. Also, because you might want to become a science teacher or a scientist or something.

Ms. Shapiro: Do you feel that studying science helps you in your life at all?

Pierre: Well, yeah. It's sort of interesting. Light is important to know about because we use it all the time. We need to know how to fix light bulbs and things.

Ms. Shapiro: Can you tell me what we learned today?

Pierre: Well, sure, it was the light, like, which way light can go, like it went this way and then it went that way.

Ms. Shapiro: Is this valuable or is it important to know this?

Pierre: Well, it's interesting. It's fun to do when it's not too hard to understand what you're supposed to do.

Even though Pierre thought science study important for continued success in school, he also valued learning for its own sake. It became apparent however, that Pierre had difficulty with some of the science concepts. He often felt he was not performing well in the school science program. Despite his delight in the study of science, Pierre did not value classroom study as much as learning science through Science Fair projects and projects of his own design. He found the school experience of science learning to be a source of difficulty—a conflict to some extent, that led to anxiety.

Theme 2. Anxiety: Worry About Having the Right Ideas in Science

Pierre's Self-Characterization: Sometimes you just don't get the idea, you know. Well, science is, ah, a little more difficult than any other thing because you gotta look at it, test it, and try it, and stuff like that, but in math you just have to look at the question and then you have to do it. Sometimes I get really worried about getting the things right in science.

My Image/Impression: Pierre experiences *anxiety*. When Pierre does not understand what he is to do, or when he does not believe what Mr. Ryan is telling the class, he becomes troubled and tense.

Despite abundant evidence of his enormous enthusiasm for science, Pierre expressed anxiety in his participation in the school science program. He enjoyed hearing the story of science, but he was disturbed when he could not accept an idea. Being told a story is perhaps the nearest thing to direct personal experience of content, but when the story relates only the findings of science there is little opportunity for personal verification of information. During science lectures there is often little discussion about the tentative nature of findings, or of the variety of possible explanations forwarded by different thinkers to explain events. For Pierre, the information Mr. Ryan presented was either right, or if he could not verify it, perhaps wrong. Pierre took a strong stance on this position during our review of the discussion in which Mr. Ryan told the class that the reason objects are visible is because light reflecting off the objects shines into the eyes of the observer. I asked Pierre about the segment on the tape:

> Pierre: Yeah, he said that, but I didn't believe it!
> Ms. Shapiro: You didn't believe it. Do you think he was right?
> Pierre: No! He was wrong! That's silly.
> Ms. Shapiro: So, how is it that you see me?
> Pierre: It's the light. It makes me and you and him see everything. All the people in the class. Without light shining on things, you wouldn't see anything. [Pointing to the diagram on the worksheet] The light shines into his eyes from the sun and it lets him see things there.
> Ms. Shapiro: So, when Mr. Ryan asked if people thought [something] different [from what] he was saying, why didn't anyone put their hand up?
> Pierre: Well, I didn't because, well, the teacher said it was that one way, and I didn't want to say it wasn't the way that he said, so. . . .

Pierre had interpreted Mr. Ryan's comment as a suggestion that it would be wrong to believe in any other idea. Pierre would not contradict the teacher, even though on a number of occasions he told me that he did not believe what Mr. Ryan was saying. Pierre expressed considerable concern about getting the right answers on the worksheets. When Mr. Ryan noted that an answer on the worksheet was incorrect, Pierre's reaction was quite negative, and in many ways similar to the frustration that Martin expressed. I continued by asking Pierre about Mr. Ryan's responses on his worksheets.

> Ms. Shapiro: What did you think of this comment Mr. Ryan put in your book about the points where the beams cross? [Mr. Ryan had written that Pierre had given the incorrect term for the point of convergence]
> Pierre: Oh. I read that. Sometimes I go, "all right," and sometimes I go, "aw, bblbbkdfgfjdflkd." Sometimes they're not too helpful. I don't like them sometimes.

> Ms. Shapiro: What sort of comments do you find helpful?
> Pierre: Oh . . . comments? Well, if he just wrote a comment, but he says that this is right or not right and stuff. Sometimes he tells us to correct it and he shows it to you, you know, and that's sort of helpful. But I don't like doing the corrections. I just hate it.

Like Martin, Pierre found corrections on the worksheet to be exasperating. Somehow he found the experience of being corrected interfered with his enjoyment of science. Once Mr. Ryan made the comments or corrections, there was no requirement that the students correct their papers. Mr. Ryan did not discuss common errors in thinking with the class. He presented the correct answers on the overhead projector during the large group discussion following the activity period. Students were to copy down the correct answers. In Pierre's case, lack of understanding led to a frustration with the entire process. His frustration and lack of faith in some of Mr. Ryan's ideas also interfered with his taking the responsibility to reconsider the challenging ideas. His comment that he "just did not believe" what Mr. Ryan was saying was perhaps used to justify not listening further to the ideas Mr. Ryan presented, and showed that he chose to continue to believe his own ideas rather than feel confused.

Theme 3. Science for Its Own Sake—Learning Science on My Own

> *Pierre's Self-Characterization:* Learning science is learning about all kinds of interesting things. At home I have a special science place in my room where I do science projects and try out all kinds of things. I find out lots of things on my own sometimes.
> *My Image/Impression:* Pierre enjoys working and discovering on his own.

Pierre deeply enjoyed doing science activities in his own home. He talked about trying one of the activities from the light unit at home. He had built his own light source and described showing his younger cousin how it worked and what he was doing with it in school. When Pierre moved to the next school district, because of a family breakup, I visited him in his home. He showed me a special science area in his room where he had recreated all of the activities from Science class. Mr. Ryan was not aware that Pierre had worked this way on science at home, and commented that Pierre had never referred to such home experiences the way that Martin had. I wondered if some of my own students had worked in similar ways at home when I taught elementary school Science. I thought about the kinds of guidelines that teachers might provide to help children work on special projects at home to enhance and extend science learning.

Spontaneous Discoveries

Pierre often made spontaneous discoveries as he worked. We watched several examples recorded on videotape of spontaneous situations in which he had been working alone during the activity portion of a lesson and had made a special discovery. Pierre called that portion of the period, "the experimenting time—the time when you're doing it all on your own." In one such incident, Pierre was playing with shadows against the light source.

> Pierre: I was trying to figure out how to turn the light on over here and we were trying to plug it in. The light kept going on over there, so, every time I saw it, I put my hand close to the thing and I was going, ooooooh [laughs]. And I see my shadow over there and I was showing how, well, I don't really understand how every time your hand goes close to the light, it makes a big shadow.
>
> Ms. Shapiro: And so you. . . .
>
> Pierre: [Excited] And every time you go *really* forward, it, it makes a little small shadow! Pretty weird isn't it? I tried that with my flashlight there, and I thought there, you . . . how do you do that? How does it do that? Wow!

Although Pierre's experience was not part of the worksheet tasks assigned, he was completely engrossed in the activity. It seemed to make a significant impression on him and on his sense of self-confidence to be able to make such a discovery by himself. Later in the unit, Pierre used his observations to provide an explanation for the mysterious bent-pencil phenomenon.

This was an exciting segment to observe for several reasons. First, Pierre knew that his answer was not counted as correct by Mr. Ryan, yet, he was still able to pursue his *own* line of thought and reasoning and to give *his* explanation of the phenomenon based on his own understanding. Pierre showed the courage to follow his own line of thought and trust in his point of view. The second interesting aspect of the segment was that Pierre explained the phenomenon in terms of his observations of the behavior of light during the shadow sequence he was previously so engrossed in, and therefore recalled so well. He assumed that there were similarities from one system to the other. During our conversation, Pierre allowed himself the chance to explore his own line of thinking. Even though the answer was not "correct," we were able to understand why he believed that it was.

> *Mr. Ryan: Okay, what did you see?*
> *Pierre: The pencil looked like it was broken.*
> *Mr. Ryan: Absolutely right. Did you notice when the pencil hit the water line, it wasn't straight anymore? It looks like it's broken. And then, under water [drawing on the overhead] it looked like. . . . Pierre, since you noticed that, what is your explanation for the brokenness?*
> *Pierre: I think it is the roundness of the glass.*

Ms. Shapiro: You are the one here who said, "the pencil looked like it was broken," and then you were the first one asked to give an explanation. You said that it was the roundness of the glass. Was that answer accepted?

Pierre: [Laughs] No.

Ms. Shapiro: How do you know that? He didn't say it was wrong.

Pierre: He didn't put it up on the screen or anything, and then he asked somebody else for the answer. So then I thought, maybe it was wrong.

Ms. Shapiro: What would have happened if it were right?

Pierre: He would have put it up on the screen. Usually when something is right, he puts it up on the screen.

Ms. Shapiro: So, you say that you think it was wrong at the time, but you have still written on the sheet that I gave the class afterwards that it is the, you've written here, "I still think that it is the roundness of the glass."

Pierre: Yeah.

Ms. Shapiro: How do you know that?

Pierre: That's a tough question. Well, you know that it curves around that way. It's weird [laughs, looks at drawing]. Hmmm [Sighs]. Hmmm. Well, whenever there isn't any water in it, it's just straight, but when there is water in it, it just, huh! [Sighs, then laughs.] I think that it's the deepness of the water. Yeah. And whenever you put it [the pencil] to the back, it makes it fat and it moves. Now, I think that it's when you push it back, it makes it wide, the pencil. It works just like that, it's just like one of those things that when you walk up you're big and when you walk down you're smaller. One of those things.

Ms. Shapiro: Are you talking about trick mirrors?

Pierre: Yeah. Like those and like the shadow things.

Ms. Shapiro: What do you mean? I'm not sure what you mean.

Pierre: Well, there's this thing, it's a box, right, and it goes like that, right, and the floor's down like that and when you stand up like that, it's, you're big, and when you stand down, you're small. It's like that with the shadows and like [that] when you shine a flashlight. I didn't see these trick mirrors, but I've watched them on the show, "Three, Two, One, Contact." But this is really strange [points to the beaker]. I think there is something more that you gotta figure out [laughs]. Something more to it, but I can't quite get what it is. It's like a maze or something like that. Mr. Ryan told the answer, but I just all of a sudden forget stuff.

Ms. Shapiro: Did anyone have the idea in class?

Pierre: Well, a couple of kids. But most kids, they, Mr. Ryan explained the idea, but then everybody forgot about it.

Ms. Shapiro: Then everybody forgot about it? Do you mean that they actually did *have* it and you feel that you did understand it at one point?

Pierre: Yeah, I understood it pretty well, but then I forgot all about it. I'm just working very hard here, and then all of a sudden I keep on forgetting about it.

Ms. Shapiro: I see. So it seems not to stay in your memory? Stay with you?

Pierre: Yeah. Something just seems to push it out [laughs].

Ms. Shapiro: You don't recall, then, Mr. Ryan's explanation at the time, but you did believe it at the time?

Pierre: Yeah, I did, I guess. I didn't understand it very well, but I did think that he was right. But I don't now.

Like Donnie, Pierre believed that he did not have all of the information needed to answer the question. If he did have it, it would be like completing the "maze." All of the pieces would fit together and he would understand.

In this sequence, the value and importance of "doing it on your own" emerged as meaningful for Pierre. Whereas Martin pursued topics of his own interest outside of school in a fairly random and disjointed manner, Pierre made a more systematic effort to follow up on classroom activities and to find out more about the topic. Yasmin, in contrast, was interested only in what was being presented in class. She had no interest in light beyond successfully grasping the ideas presented in the classroom.

Pierre's case was particularly poignant to observe and portray. The more that I came to know him, the more I felt his sense of wonder and enthusiasm for science and his sincere interest in understanding the ideas of science. Would that enthusiasm blossom as he continued into junior high school and beyond? I wondered if the anxiety I was beginning to see would increase as he moved through the science program. Would his enormous talent in expressing ideas visually be recognized and developed in the coming years, or would the ways of science learning become more limited? For me, Pierre's case dramatically reemphasized the importance of providing science programs that recognize and value students' ideas as well as their approaches to science learning.

PART III

IMPLICATIONS: THE DEEPER MEANING OF LISTENING

CHAPTER 10

Personal Orientation to Science Learning: An Ecological Perspective on Knowledge Integration

Maxine Greene (1973) writes "no matter how the teacher conceives the human being, his primary task is to teach the young person to know" (p. 99). In practice, the traditional interpretation of teaching the young person to know science has meant an almost exclusive emphasis on the acquisition of a body of knowledge or a set of facts. This chapter revisits the case study reports to further challenge and extend this exclusive emphasis. The first section describes features of the construct used to reflect on the case reports, Personal Orientation to Science Learning (Figure 10.1). This construct places *the learning person* rather than the curriculum at the center of thinking about learning. It suggests that we consider learning ecologically by reflecting on the interrelationships among features in addition to the cognitive—such as social, cultural, and environmental factors—as important considerations in the integration of new knowledge. High status is given to the learner, including his or her thoughts, feelings, and actions. The learner is viewed as an important and responsible contributor in successful science learning.

THE IDEA OF A PERSONAL ORIENTATION TO SCIENCE LEARNING

Proposed features of a Personal Orientation to Science Learning appear in the outer section of the diagram presented in Figure 10.1. The diagram is also designed to portray an important view of the nature of the learner. At the heart of the diagram is the learning person. It is the learner, not the curriculum, that is the center of focus. The phrase "learning person," rather than student, is used because it allows us to think about learners beyond the context of children in classrooms. Teachers may be learners. And children may also be teachers to one another and their teachers. In the figure, arrows emanate from the learning person, who determines which of the aspects of science education will be "taken on" or "tried on." This suggests that the learner's thoughts and ideas influence actions and are guided by ideas about the nature of the learning environment. In planning experiences for the

Views and beliefs concerning:

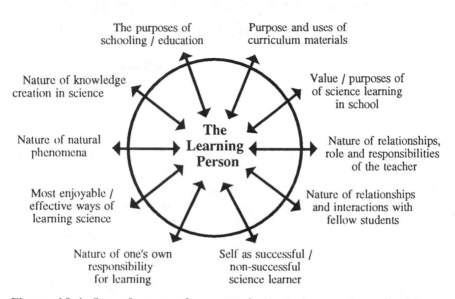

Figure 10.1 Some features of a personal orientation to science learning

learner, these ideas should be given a central position in our thinking. We attempt to help students to resolve the distance between their prior ideas about the nature of phenomena and scientists' views through the provision of counterexamples. We must also be aware that students take actions of their own guided by varied levels of acceptance of their roles as initiators of science learning and by views concerning features of the science learning experience that are multifaceted.

The learner has self-determination. Views and beliefs about science and science learning guide and direct the attention of the learning person. There may be similarities among individuals, but each person holds a highly personal set of beliefs that have a considerable effect on learning.

REVISITING THE CASE STUDIES WITH PERSONAL ORIENTATION THEMES

Revisiting the studies with themes built on features from the framework allows consideration of the interrelating influences contributing to each person's integration of science knowledge. Rather than as isolated aspects of learning, we can see these as constellations of interrelated aspects of learning.

This view is ecological, allowing insight into a more holistic view of the learning person.

The delineation of themes allows us to explore interweaving features of the construct, Personal Orientation to Science Learning. Some of the themes discussed in the sections that follow are:

1. View of Self as Science Learner
2. Views on the Nature of the Relationships, Role, and Responsibilities of the Teacher
3. The Meaning of "Getting Help"
4. Images of Science and Scientists
5. Ideas About the Nature of Phenomena

View of Self as a Science Learner

My conversations with Donnie yielded particularly good examples of how a student's development of a view of herself as science learner creates anticipations and expectations about participation in science and science learning. Donnie was aware that she was not grasping many of the ideas presented to the class. Still, she was intensely interested in fully participating in the lessons and in the class discussions. Donnie was disturbed when she could not answer questions. She did not realize that some of the questions were in many ways similar to those asked by physicists themselves in the search for fundamental understanding. She described a recurring sense in science that "I never quite get all of it." But in fact, Donnie did demonstrate a partial grasp of many difficult concepts.

Donnie's struggle as she attempted to understand was very apparent to Mr. Ryan. She had thought seriously and carefully about the problems presented in class. But Mr. Ryan commented that he found it "a bit frustrating" that Donnie was not putting ideas together for herself. He felt that he was asked to somehow do this for her and expressed frustration at doing so. There was no opportunity for Donnie or her teacher to recognize that through her personal approach to learning she was actually thinking at a very sophisticated level and was much closer to understanding than she realized.

The learning process is complex. Making connections among ideas is a gradual process requiring time, experience with materials, and a good deal of faith in science authority. Often, children make incomplete connections and have no opportunity for continuing discussion or extended experiences with materials. For many children like Donnie, the struggle to understand can lead to a feeling of incompleteness. Donnie's own efforts to put ideas together were not recognized and encouraged. She did not see her own struggle as beneficial nor did she find satisfaction in overcoming the challenge, for she never had a sense of understanding the problem. Her struggle led to a lowered sense of the possibility of being a successful science learner and on many occasions she spoke of science learning with discouragement and despair. Both Donnie and her teacher might find it beneficial to become more aware of the powerful negative, long-term effects of the gradual development of this view of herself as a science learner.

Mark held a very positive sense of himself as a science learner. It did not bother him when fellow students did not pay attention to some of the ideas and suggestions he posed as solutions. Mark was encouraged by his successes. They seemed to spur him on to even greater interest in what Mr. Ryan had to say and in how he approached the activities and the curriculum materials. He admired Mr. Ryan and valued his knowledge of science. He approached science activities confidently and seemed convinced that he could solve any of the problems presented to him. Mark was often able to help other students to grasp ideas and see problems in new ways.

The only difficulty for Mark was that the pace of the lessons was often too slow. When we referred to his personal construct, "Mr. Ryan is talking, but you're not really listening," Mark told me that he often found that he did not listen to procedural comments. Because of this, he was often anxious about moving on with the activities. Despite this, Mark's self-confidence was high and was matched by unusual success in his studies.

Martin spoke with confidence in his ability to do well in science. He expressed an almost grandiose view of his ability to find solutions to problems that had been difficult for other students. He told me that on one occasion during Science class he performed all of the activities and the other kids simply copied in their notebooks what *he* had written. From my observation, this, in fact, did happen often. But Martin had difficulties with other aspects of science learning. He was reluctant to listen to another person's idea or viewpoint regarding the manipulation of equipment. He struggled with the reading and writing required to complete the worksheets. These difficulties slowed him down and were at the root of several incidents in which he became frustrated with his inability to accomplish as much as he would have wanted. On these occasions, he would often reject the lesson and become disruptive.

Melody's sense of herself as a successful science learner was quite negative, even though she enjoyed Science class a great deal. She believed that she "never understood" what she was supposed to do in science. This attitude seemed to prevent her from trying to figure out the solutions to problems on her own. But because she sought so much assistance from others in science, Melody demonstrated the beginning of understanding of some of the more difficult ideas presented by Mr. Ryan in class. Despite a fairly negative sense of herself as a successful science learner, Melody told me that she looked forward to future studies in science.

Yasmin's sense of herself as a science learner was fairly positive. She knew that she was an effective student and that she was perceived as competent by Mr. Ryan. Yasmin almost always had the correct response on her paper, but frequently could not recall the main ideas of the science lesson. Yasmin told me she believed that she would continue to do well in her future work in science, but that it was not a topic of particular interest to her.

Pierre participated in two different worlds of science learning. The first world was his own. Here, he was "principal investigator" in the pursuit of studies about the natural world, which held a continuing and deep interest for him. In this world he was confident, informed, and in charge of his own learning. But in the second world, the world of school science learning, Pierre pursued topics that did not interest him. Here he saw himself as a less capable student, as one who rarely grasped concepts. He found his teacher presenting ideas he did not agree with and could not accept. Pierre was anxious about his performance and, though he wanted to do well very badly, he worked with the expectation that he would probably not do well in science. Pierre would sometimes give up on tasks he perceived as too difficult. I was left feeling deeply concerned that the great joy Pierre had expressed about learning science might be destroyed in future Science classes.

Views on the Nature of the Relationships, Role, and Responsibilities of the Teacher

How might the learner's views and beliefs about the role of the teacher influence the integration of ideas in science? The idea that light rays continually reflect from most surfaces was difficult for most students to grasp. Pierre insisted in conversation that the teacher was simply wrong in presenting this idea. In the end, he did not grasp the idea. Yasmin, Martin, and Melody suggested that the idea was "strange," "confusing," or "didn't make sense to them," but acknowledged that the teacher had the authority to present the idea. They expressed the view that Mr. Ryan had studied the topic, that *he was the teacher* and, therefore, must be correct. Yasmin, Martin, and Melody did not question the truth of the statement, but noted that it was difficult to accept. Mark said simply, "He knows because he's the teacher. He's taken light in college and he tells us what he knows." Mark was able to simply accept the idea based on his valuing of the teacher as authority.

Melody showed an interesting way of thinking whenever we discussed an idea that did not immediately make sense to her. She would say that the idea "probably wasn't true, but . . . it *could* be true." She suggested that she could consider the possibility of truth but that the idea seemed beyond her ever really knowing for certain. In her view, "we will never know for sure" whether or not the ideas in science are true. But at the same time, Melody put forward the view that Mr. Ryan's job as her teacher was to tell her what she was supposed to do and what she was supposed to know. She believed that it was Mr. Ryan's responsibility to be sure that she understood and that it was largely his fault when she did not.

Donnie's approach was quite different. She wavered at various points, at times acknowledging the truth of the teacher's statement, at other times questioning and challenging the concepts he presented. Mark, on the other hand, accepted Mr. Ryan's statements completely and immediately. He used them in the development of further ideas, as in the integration of ideas to understand refraction.

Martin's comment about the role of the teacher was edged with hostility, "Well, what the teacher says, goes, right?" Martin was experimenting with ideas about his own social and learning life in school. Sometimes, the notion of teacher authority was quite acceptable to him; at other times, he resented and challenged it.

Although Yasmin did not always agree with Mr. Ryan's viewpoint, she was able to remember what he said, at least long enough to place it on her worksheet. It was particularly significant to me, during talks with Yasmin, to observe her discovering some of her own ideas through the act of speaking with me. Yasmin had a very fine ability to think deeply about the ideas of the lesson, however, her greater interest in academic success overshadowed deeper thinking about the content. In the end, she did not grasp ideas about reflected and refracted light.

All of the children believed that their teacher had actually written the worksheet material they had been given and that he had created all of the activities they used. In fact, the materials were produced by the local school district. When I asked the students who they thought selected the topics they studied in science, all of the students said that they believed it was Mr. Ryan. Pierre added that "probably all the teachers at the school get together at some time so that they would not teach the same things."

The Meaning of "Getting Help"

"What are you supposed to do?" "What's this word?" "What do you write here?" "What's supposed to happen?" Procedural questions were the most numerous of the help requests made by the children in the study. However, if such questions are only to be categorized and counted, the important relationship between the child's personal orientation to science learning and his or her grasp of ideas might be missed. The theme "Getting Help" interweaves many of the personal orientation themes, such as the learner's sense of self as a science learner, ideas about responsibility for learning in science, views about the role of the instructor, and views of the goals of science learning. For some students, asking for help was an embarrassing, frustrating, and alienating experience. Some avoided asking for help, keeping concepts and ideas at the level of dilemma rather than risk a painful experience. Other children were able to ask for assistance in ways that facilitated and expedited the learning process.

For Martin, asking for help meant the admission to others that he was having difficulty. Students often called him "dummy" when he asked questions that appeared simple and obvious. Instead of asking for help with the worksheet, Martin would often continue working with the equipment and materials until he discovered a relationship or insight on his own. In one instance, because Martin persisted in pursuing his own experience with the materials, he waited so long before asking for help that he nearly missed the observation that light beams cross when viewed through a beaker filled with water. This observation was the basis of the development of the idea that light rays bend at different angles through different types of liquid. It was not until Yasmin insisted that Martin consider the observation, when Mr. Ryan came over to his group, that Martin appeared to feel comfortable asking for help. Mr. Ryan guided him through the activity and Martin asked him questions about the setup of equipment. Although Yasmin and Martin often teamed together to complete a task, Yasmin frequently belittled Martin for his impulsiveness and lack of attention to detail. At the same time, Yasmin benefitted from Martin's cleverness in finding the solutions to problems posed in the activities. Martin valued a special form of interaction with Mr. Ryan. He referred to this as "giving clues to the correct answer but not giving the answer." Martin valued "getting help" from Mr. Ryan because the nature of Mr. Ryan's guidance allowed him the satisfying experience of solving problems on his own.

Melody, in contrast, never hesitated to seek answers to questions on the worksheet directly from others. The significance of "getting help" for Melody appeared to be largely in the social experience of asking for answers, not necessarily in finding ways to understand ideas. Understanding the concept was secondary to the experience of engaging in talk with the other children. When Melody went to "get help," she usually spoke with fellow students about concerns irrelevant to science, often to the great annoyance of her fellow classmates, and always to the great annoyance of Mr. Ryan. Because finding out what she was supposed to do in science seemed secondary in Melody's search for "help," she did not appear to be concerned when she did not have the correct answers to questions. Melody told me that she particularly liked science and subjects where there were group activities because "I know my friends will help me." I did not observe Melody asking Mr. Ryan directly for help on a single occasion during the time I was in the classroom. She was often absent from her activity group when I went to work with her. Usually when I found her with another group and asked what she was doing, she explained that she was "getting help."

Although it was clear in conversation with Melody that she had no particular interest in light as a topic of study, it is noteworthy that she was one of the few students who, in the end, was able to provide an explanation of how it was that the pencil in a beaker of water appeared to be broken. Melody was able to grasp the ideas presented because of rather than despite her extensive social activity. Melody always seemed in need of help. In contrast with Yasmin, who rarely needed help, Melody showed some understanding of concepts that Yasmin had not grasped.

I observed Donnie asking Mr. Ryan for help on numerous occasions. She spoke very negatively about asking for help, saying that Mr. Ryan "usually gets mad" when she asked him a question and that she felt "embarrassed" when she "didn't know the answer to something." Mr. Ryan also expressed frustration with Donnie's requests for help. He had the sense that instead of doing her own thinking, she was asking him to do it for her.

Although the curriculum material did contain numerous terms and phrases that were very difficult for students, it seemed that the students' personal approaches and views about asking for help were significant and useful areas for reflection by both teachers and students. Mr. Ryan's practice of having the children correct their own worksheets at the end of each period did not allow him to gain insight into the types of errors the students were consistently making and the problems individuals were having over and over again with the material.

Some of the children in the study saw helping as something that they more consistently "gave" than received. This was the case for Yasmin, whom students approached regularly for help; however, in the end many children simply copied from her. This was upsetting to Yasmin and she complained about it often. Martin believed that at times he provided help to "everyone." He told me, "I do all of the activities and stuff and everyone else just writes down what I find out." Although this was true on several occasions that I observed, it seemed that Martin would also have benefitted from realizing that he quite often was working with materials without knowing what the task was that was to be accomplished.

"Getting and giving help" became a significant theme in the exploration of Pierre's experience. Pierre thought of himself as a science learner who usually required the assistance of others to read the worksheets and, in general, to understand what to do in science. The person who helped Pierre most often was Kim. Pierre told me that he liked working with Kim because "Kim is like working with a teacher. He knows what to do and always helps me with the answer." During the lesson on shadows and reflection, Pierre found himself working alone while his partner, Kim, ran an errand for Mr. Ryan. During Kim's absence, Pierre read the worksheet himself and began to experiment with the materials to determine the lengths of pencil shadows placed at different angles. Pierre worked quickly and had nearly completed the worksheet when Kim returned to the classroom. But on his return, Kim and many of the students in the groups near Pierre had difficulty with the activity. It was a very new experience for Pierre to be one of the few students in the classroom who was able to understand and perform the activity. Pierre enthusiastically commented to me as we reviewed the videotape, "This time *he* couldn't figure out what to do and *I could*. So *I* was like the *teacher* this time to him and I really knew by myself what he . . . what it was that he couldn't figure out. So I helped *him* this time." Pierre seemed delighted and surprised by this experience, which seemed to sharpen and highlight the content for him.

On another occasion, I had arranged for the videocamera to record Pierre without my being present so as not to distract him. On reviewing the tape, I observed a scene in which Pierre appeared surprised and even startled by his own discovery of light reflecting from a ruler with which he had been casually experimenting with on his own. Pierre was sitting by himself in front of the light box, using various objects in an attempt to try to reflect light rays. He spoke aloud to himself: "An eraser. Put it here. Hey. Light's going off it. What about the ruler? There. Hey. Light reflects off a ruler? Hey! *Light reflects off a ruler!*"

Pierre seemed very startled by this insight, as if he was not sure what to do with it or whether or not it was correct. He looked around for someone to share his discovery with but found no one. Through observing Pierre's videotape, I was reminded of the learner's need to share his or her competence and discoveries with others, and how significantly this contributes to joy in learning. It seemed that Pierre would also benefit from valuing his own wisdom, seeing the ways that he can be his own teacher. One of the greatest resources that we have for help in learning is ourselves—learning to trust our own insights, thoughts, ideas, and discoveries, and the value of our own questions in science learning—this is what Pierre experienced.

Images of Science and Scientists

Melody laughed when I asked her if she found herself working as a scientist does. "No, not hardly! They create the ideas and we learn what they found out." In fact, this idea was very consistent with Melody's approach in the classroom. When she pursued understanding in school science, it was for the purpose of finding out what "they" say (meaning scientists). She saw this as different from her pursuit of understanding outside of Science class, where in the natural world she believed that she was creating some of her own ideas about the world. Yasmin also believed, like Melody, that in Science class students did not act like scientists, but learned what scientists already know. Yasmin did not believe that she was involved in any type of science activity outside the classroom and, therefore, did not have an example of a situation where she pursued science like a scientist.

Martin commented that he usually preferred to create his own ideas in science. He told me, "Sometimes the teachers let you be creative." Mark remarked, "Sometimes we act like scientists and other times, we don't. The times when we do are when we are experimenting with materials and equipment." Pierre also said that he felt that he was working just like a scientist when he was experimenting (doing activities). He felt that science activities were often like a maze or puzzle and that scientists often solved puzzles and mysteries. Donnie stated that she did not believe that she was working like a scientist "because they already know all of the stuff that we are doing and we are just learning what they know."

Interest in Science Outside of the Classroom

Martin, Pierre, Melody, and Mark spoke of an interest in pursuing experiences with natural phenomena outside of school. Donnie and Yasmin indicated little interest in science activities outside of school.

Within the classroom, Martin, Mark, and Pierre spoke of the enjoyment of pursuing a line of thought or experimentation going beyond or deviating from the classroom lesson, and through which they discovered new ideas and insights. They often demonstrated this interest by pursuing their own line of thought with the materials in the classroom.

Martin, Mark, and Pierre also told of their out of classroom interests in science activities. Martin and Pierre consistently replicated class activities at home. Martin would often share his results with other members of the class in large group discussion. Pierre tended not to share his experiences or findings, or the fact that he had a science learning center in his room at home. Mark did not make reference to science activities outside of class, but spoke about "thinking about ideas" outside of the classroom and of casually exploring the different aspects of science that interested him through magazines, television programs, and films.

Melody shared stories with me depicting her great delight in exploring a variety of objects in the natural world. The stories demonstrated her very keen observational abilities. However, the considerable skills, talents, and abilities she appeared to possess seemed hidden from her, her teacher, and her classmates by her view that she rarely knew what she was supposed to do or discover in Science class.

Many children have the desire to replicate and pursue classroom science activities at home. Teachers who are aware of this interest can offer guidance through suggesting activities and other experiences, recommending books, or loaning equipment. This kind of support for interest that already exists among children should also be provided in curriculum documents. Students would be inspired to engage in creative and independent exploration thereby increasing their delight and interest in the topic being studied in the classroom.

Ideas About the Nature of Phenomena

As mentioned, learner ideas about the nature of phenomena have been the primary focus of research studies on student conceptions in science. But viewed from the perspective of features of a personal orientation to science learning, views and beliefs about the nature of phenomena are presented as but one of many interweaving features of learning science that affect learning outcomes. The ideas commonly held about the nature of light are outlined in Chapter 2 and individual views are presented in the case studies. In this theme area, some of the more pervasive difficulties students experienced in learning about light are outlined.

Basing thinking wholly on perceptual cues. Many students tended to base ideas and reasoning about light phenomena wholly on *perceptual* cues (Driver, Guesne, & Tiberghien, 1985). Light was thought to exist only when its effects were visible. A student following this line of reasoning understandably has difficulty grasping the idea of nonperceptible light rays pervading our environment, which is the basis for understanding the concept of refraction. The light box used in the children's study may have reinforced some perceptual confusion. When using the boxes, the children were engaged in a series of activities that showed visible light coming through slits in the box from the bulb inside the box. No reference was made in the curriculum materials to relate the visible beams to the existence or behavior of the non-visible light rays that normally pervade the environment. Because this bridge was never made, students were confused when the discussion turned to phenomena such as refraction, which did not involve visible beams but built on understandings of non-perceptible light beam behaviors.

Understanding color: Personally experiencing ideas versus accepting them. For most of the children, *color* was understood as a substance within an object—despite the fact that Mr. Ryan provided the class with the scientific explanation of color vision. Beginning with ideas about the white light spectrum, he described how objects appear to us differently colored because they "push out" or "absorb" light rays from different areas of the light spectrum. These ideas were intriguing to students, but also proved confusing. In one of our conversations about color, Donnie pushed her finger against my sweater, complaining, "I don't see anything pushing out." As this kind of pushing is not observable, once again we are attempting to build on a concept of nonperceptible reflecting and absorbing light rays that students cannot experience and must simply accept on faith. What also seemed confusing to students is that "pushing" usually implies an observable act and this term was being used in a far more specialized way than had been explained to them. Another difficulty emerging and not reported in the research literature was the confusion students had when asked to provide an *explanation* for an event. When asked to explain why a rainbow is observed when light is passed through a prism, for example, many students *described* what they saw rather than providing an explanation of the event.

Trouble with terms. Many students in the study also had difficulty using terms when referring to scientific notions about light phenomena that have different commonly accepted and real-world meanings. Saying that light "bends" is an example. Light "bends" is interpreted by most students to mean bending as a coat hanger might be bent, at a distinct angle. Many children said that bending occurred when light beams hit and reflected at an angle from a mirror. The scientific meaning of light ray bending relates to movement of light beams at a gradually changing angle, as through a lens.

Another example is the use of the simple term "reflection," thought by most students to mean that which is seen when one looks in the mirror. During lessons on light, "reflection" was consistently defined and reviewed for students in precisely this way, further confounding the development of the idea that nonvisible beams of light reflect off all objects. In class discussion, however, many children demonstrated that they had "learned" that the moon reflects light from the sun, thereby allowing us to see the moon. This idea was presented on the program "Sesame Street," and several children commented that they had originally become aware of the idea when it was presented in a poem in the popular book, "Free to Be You and Me."

THE SUN AND THE MOON

The Sun is filled with shining light
It blazes far and wide
The Moon reflects the sunlight back
But has no light inside.
I think I'd rather be the Sun
That shines so bold and bright
Than be the moon, that only glows
With someone else's light

(Thomas & Hart, 1974, p. 136)

As a result, many students stated that light reflects from the moon rather than being produced by it. Despite this, it was clear in subsequent conversations that the idea of light rays reflecting from light source to object and then to Earth was not extended to other objects in the environment.

Categories of Idea Changes in Science

Two weeks following the conclusion of the study, I spoke with the class and asked everyone to complete a survey that tested the ideas developed in the unit. I spoke with Donnie, Mark, Martin, Melody, Yasmin, and Pierre to understand the changes in their ideas from the beginning of the light unit. Several of these ideas are presented in Figures 10.2 to 10.5.

Gilbert, Osborne, and Fensham's (1982) suggestion that learning outcomes can be classified into at least five patterns of outcomes was useful in analyzing changes in the ideas of the children in the study group. The categories are as follows:

1. *The Undisturbed Children's Science Outcome*
   Some science language is incorporated to describe a viewpoint, but the child's original viewpoint is essentially unaltered (Pierre).
2. *The Two Perspectives Outcome*
   The teacher's presentation of the curriculum content is retained for class worksheet or examination purposes, but the student maintains the view that the world does not really work in this way in other settings (Yasmin, Martin, Donnie, and Melody).
3. *The Reinforced Outcome*
   The student's original viewpoint is reinforced. The child emerges from the learning experience more convinced of his or her own original viewpoint (Pierre).
4. *The Mixed Outcome*
   Scientific ideas are learned, understood, and appreciated, but the interrelationships among ideas are often not integrated and are held in contradictory ways. The learner's views become an amalgam of children's views and teacher's views (Melody, Donnie, and Martin).
5. *The Unified Science Outcome*
   A coherent scientific perspective is understood and is related to the workings of the child's environment. Gilbert, Osborne, and Fensham describe this outcome as "typical of the coherent scientist's perspective," and comment that it is "the outcome that all teachers wish to arise from their interaction with students" (Mark).

Overlap in the categories occurred in several instances. Pierre, for example, became adamant in his view that certain of the ideas presented by Mr. Ryan are simply "wrong." This idea also served to strengthen his pre-instructional position about the behavior of light. Melody at times exemplified the Two

(Text continues on page 178)

In these examples from one of the final evaluations of student ideas, the children were asked to draw arrows to show how the light from the sun allows the girl to see the tree. The second drawing checks for a deeper understanding of the concept. Here the student must apply his or her understanding.

	I don't know	*Donnie* is able to reproduce the scientist's conception, but he is not able to transfer her understanding to a new situation.
		Mark is able to draw in and discuss the scientist's conception in these and in all of the examples which are given to him.
		Martin's diagram is confusing. In conversation he shows some grasp of the concept, but is not able to demonstrate understanding in these examples.
		Melody draws and speaks of the scientist's conception in both examples, but in the discussion with her, I find that she does not always use the scientist's conception.
		Despite their arrows pointing from the sun to the tree, both *Amy* and *Pierre* hold to their original views that the girl sees the tree because the light is falling on her.

Figure 10.2 Summary of student ideas about light at the conclusion of the study

<u>Question:</u> What is your explanation for the unusual
appearance of the pencil in a beaker of water?

<u>DONNIE</u> _____
_____

    Donnie tells me that she has not answered this
question because she still feels that she does not
have "all the ideas about it right."

<u>MARK</u>

*The water is bending the light from
the pencil so it looks broken*

    Mark has demonstrated a grasp of the concept in this
and in many other examples which I have given to him.

<u>MARTIN</u>

*The water axs Like a
mag nifigher*

<u>MELODY</u>

*The water makes the bottom
half bigger*

<u>AMY</u>

The water acts like a Magnifier.

    Martin, Melody and Amy continue to put forward a
correct, but more descriptive response, rather than an
explanation.

<u>PIERRE</u> *The roundness of the glass*

    Pierre continues to insist that his original view is
correct.

Figure 10.3 Summary of student explanations of refraction

Question: Everyone saw rainbows when we looked through the
          prisms. How are rainbows formed?

Colors are inside the prism, the light shines on the prism and the colors are brought out, you need light for the rainbow to form.	Despite her incorrect response, *Donnie* has made the attempt to provide a fairly sophisticated explanation.
The prism bends and slow down the light so much that it splits the light into it colors.	*Mark* has grasped and conveys some of the scientist's view put forward by Mr. Ryan.
Threw the prisom	*Martin* provides a partial description rather than an explanation.
Im not sure but I think light gose in to the prisom and the angel of the glass makes a rainbow.	Some elements of *Melody's* response show potential for her understanding of the scientist's view, yet she includes a statement about her own sense of inadequacy in providing the answer.
4 dont know how they are formed I don't know.	Despite Mr. Ryan's explanation, *Amy* and *Pierre* say that they do not know how rainbows are formed and do not offer even a tentative explanation.

Figure 10.4 Summary of student ideas about the formation of rainbows

The personal orientations of students presented in the case study reports continue to be reflected in their comments about which experiences they most enjoyed, what they continue to wonder about, and what they found most difficult to understand.

<u>Question 1:</u>   What I liked most about the light unit was...

DONNIE

the reet
and different object, drawing and experimenting.

MARK

I liked
experamenting.

MARTIN

expe-
rement

MELODY

I got
to experament with things like light

AMY

doing
experiments and I used to use the equiment especially the colored cards.

PIERRE

I liked
almost everything. It is great

Figure 10.5 Summary of student reflections on the light unit

<u>Question 2:</u>   I am still wondering...

DONNIE	_how the prism makes rainbows and how it makes things up when it down and down when its up._
MARK	_how white light is made_
MARTIN	_The Light meater_
MELODY	_I am not wondering about anything else._
AMY	_what makes rainbows come out of the prism._
PIERRE	_Why the pencil gets fat in the becker of water._

Figure 10.5 Continued

Perspectives Outcome. This was particularly noticeable when she copied answers from others' papers without apparent interest in what she was writing down. She stated that she believed that the teacher was correct because being the teacher, he must know the correct answer. However, in other conversations with Melody, it was clear that she did not "really believe" that the world functioned in the ways that Mr. Ryan suggested. At other times, Melody demonstrated that she had grasped some of the ideas presented by Mr.

<u>Question 3:</u>   What I found difficult to understand was...

DONNIE   _how_ the beaker of water makes the light beams cross.
MARK
MARTIN   prisim
MELODY   light bends   _how_
AMY   _some of_ the questions on the sheet.
PIERRE   _how_ the prisim made rainbows when you shine the light through it.

Figure 10.5 Continued

Ryan and used them to explain phenomena. Scientific ideas were mixed with her own ideas about the nature of light.

Mark was one of several students in the class who showed a tendency to value the potential of others' viewpoints to enhance his own understandings in science. Mark exemplified the characteristics of the category, the Unified Science Outcome, and was not only very successful in grasping ideas, but held a deep interest in the ideas of scientists.

Some Key Ideas of Personal Orientation to Science Learning

Students approach science learning with different expectations. They listen, interact with one another, and participate in the activities of science learning based on the various ideas they have about subject matter, the meaning and purposes of schooling, and the social and cultural rules governing their activities in school. They have differing views of themselves as successful science learners. They have different views about the nature of science knowledge, their understanding of what their teacher is trying to accomplish with them, and how much responsibility they should be taking for their own learning. They differ in their range of previous science learning experiences and in their ideas about what they will do in the future. Various aspects of science lessons interest some individuals and not others. Finally, they have differing reasons for studying the topics assigned.

If change in student thinking is desired in any one of these areas, educators must be sensitive to the impact of many features of learners' experience. It is not only classroom students who make changes in their views and beliefs. The learning person can be anyone. Teachers are learning persons and need support to help them in their own learning. If change in individual personal constructs is desirable at any level, the complexity of learners' personal construct systems must be understood. It must be recognized that when change occurs, it is the learning persons themselves who are altering their personal constructs. Personal Orientation to Science Learning suggests that we take an ecological perspective that emphasizes the integration of classroom and scientific knowledge. This perspective also invites a rethinking of the aims of science teaching. This foundation leads us to Chapter 11 to reconsider these aims and how educators might work to help learners construct and reconstruct personal meaning in science.

CHAPTER 11

Developing Teaching Approaches That Build on Learners' Ideas and Actions in Science

This book, a study of children's knowledge construction in science, has been written to help the reader build an understanding of the wide range of factors that influence the integration of knowledge in science learning. The case reports of children's learning not only present "what children understand," but also attempt to build our knowledge of "how they understand." I have attempted to guide the reader through my own journey of research into the complex interweaving of these features. The first path took us through the historical basis for constructivist thinking about knowledge acquisition. We moved on along the road to an exploration of children's learning in classrooms and the nature of current research on children's learning in science. We stopped to reflect and select a topic of study, light, that would be useful in understanding learner ideas and knowledge construction. Case studies of student learning, the heart of the project, were presented based on themes in children's experiences of science learning. The idea of a Personal Orientation to Science Learning was developed as a framework for discussing important interweaving features of an ecology of science learning.

In the first section of this chapter, some of the key assumptions and characteristics of a knowledge construction perspective on learning science are summarized. In the second half of the chapter, a number of suggestions are made to help develop experiences that build on the learner's own efforts to construct ideas. Educators interested in these ideas will undoubtedly add many more to the list presented here. In the spirit of the constructivist perspective, these ideas are presented as points of departure for the reader to consider further.

KEY ASSUMPTIONS OF A KNOWLEDGE CONSTRUCTION PERSPECTIVE ON SCIENCE LEARNING

1. The picture of learners' understandings in science is far more complex than has been previously portrayed. Learners not only hold specific ideas about the *way the world is*, but each person has a *way of understanding* the world that influences his or her integration of knowledge.

2. Students cannot be simply *told* what to understand or believe. If new understandings are to be grasped, they must be reasonable and meaningful to the learner, who must be convinced that it makes sense to move to new explanations. The learner must actively and personally participate in the integration of new knowledge.

3. Learners are already making efforts to give meaning to the world long before coming to school. The nature and character of these efforts can be seen in patterns of thinking and behavior that give insight into how they organize their world.

4. There is a range of intellectual, personal, social, emotional, and cultural factors embedded in the classroom context that influence and are integral to not separate from cognitive development. Teachers must be aware of the effects of these features as they influence students' sense-making.

5. In practice, the goals of science learning have been based primarily on a sole focus on idea acquisition and concept change. Planning to help learners understand science should also take into account the learner's views and actions in the construction of knowledge. Learning experiences that are personally meaningful encourage and inspire learners to continue with and enjoy science learning.

6. By understanding the pattern of learners' thoughts, feelings, and approaches to science learning we may organize learning experiences that encourage students to consider scientific ideas and ways of thinking.

7. Teachers are also learning persons who need support in both their efforts to understand the complexity of student knowledge in science and to develop approaches to enhance learners' efforts to construct meaning in science.

   a) Teachers can build insight into learner knowledge and approaches to science learning by becoming familiar with research studies in the field and through organizing profiles of knowledge in their own classrooms.

   b) Learning experiences can be planned to enhance the active engagement of the learner in the construction of meaning.

   c) Activities can be organized to help learners develop knowledge organization approaches to take greater responsibility for their own learning.

LEARNING TO USE WHAT WE KNOW ABOUT CHILDREN AND SCIENCE LEARNING

Ritchie (1982) reminds us that a constructivist view of learning "should be used not as an endpoint from which to make generalizations, but as a beginning from which to achieve a deeper understanding of the individual's actions in social reality. Constructivism and constructivist theory examines the thoughts behind the actions of individuals" (p. 31).

The goal of this research has not been to develop a set of techniques that can be plugged in to the teaching "repertoire," but rather, it is to help educators make curriculum decisions based on a view of the student as an important, active, involved contributor in the learning conversation. Valuing the knowledge and approaches the learner brings to science learning will allow both the teacher and the learner to develop more engaging approaches in efforts to teach and learn. There are many ways to coerce students into producing correct answers on worksheets or tests, but it is far more useful to help a learner consider alternate ways of thinking about ideas.

The Importance of the Student's Active Participation in Learning

It has been demonstrated in numerous studies (Novak & Gowin, 1984) that learners more readily acquire new knowledge when they are able to relate new ideas to already existing ideas or to language structures already in place. In this way, it is argued, new ideas "make sense" in terms already familiar to learners. In Kelly's (1969) view, we straddle unknown worlds with our known world of knowledge. Contrary to this view, theoretical positions explain learning in terms of factors external to the person. That is, learning principles and approaches stress what must be done to *make the learner learn,* seeming to ignore the student's contribution in the construction of knowledge.

The assumptions presented here give high status to two aspects of knowledge: (1) the learner's ideas, thoughts and feelings; and (2) the learner's active effort to make sense of knowledge. When the child is viewed as active, rather than passive, it is recognized that he or she is naturally seeking to make sense of the world long before coming to school. Studies employing this conception of the learner focus on understanding how learners create meaning in their activities.

Helping Students Develop an Understanding of the Nature of Science

Of the students in the study group, only Mark explicitly understood science as an activity in which he personally participated to grasp the understandings of scientists. He accepted the ideas put forward as scientists' knowledge and realized that he was not personally responsible for creating all of the insights he gained during the study of science. Donnie, however, showed confusion in an apparent difficulty to distinguish her own thinking processes from scientists' explanations of phenomena. She did not see her task as science student as one of simply accepting the scientist's explanation, but saw it as her responsibility to figure things out for herself, a task she could not accomplish on her own. As a result, she regarded herself a failure in this task. Mark viewed scientific explanation as a creation of the scientific community, but also as an enterprise in which he was able to successfully participate. Donnie saw scientific explanation as a personal product, something she expected she should be able to "figure out" or create on her own. Mark acknowledged that scientific understanding was both a product of his own experience *and* the acceptance of the scientists' views and explanations. Donnie, and students like her, would benefit by being helped to value both the known world of ideas and the unknown world of scientific information and insight.

The potential of independent science projects in developing an understanding of the nature of science. One approach to inviting learners to appreciate the process of systematic data collection as part of the experience of creating new scientific insights is to involve students in research projects to gather data to solve a problem question of their own. This approach allows students to work as scientists do, to value what is learned through intensive study in one field. Two excellent resources for teachers who wish to begin work of this type are the book *Doing What Scientists Do*, by Doris (1991), and the Elementary Science Study (ESS) *Behavior of Mealworms: Teacher's Guide* (1976). Both resources offer guidance in involving children in the development of investigations to answer questions they pose themselves.

In the research study the children ranked participation in the Science Fair as the second most enjoyable activity in the science program, exceeded in popularity only by science field trips. Through participation in such projects, students are offered the opportunity to have direct experiences with natural phenomena and to organize their ideas about phenomena and share them with children and adults. It has not always been the case in practice, however, that learners have had positive experiences in the Science Fair. Overemphasizing the form and appearance of a project rather than focusing on the learner's involvement and understandings has delivered the wrong image of work in science to many students. Because students are typically asked to work on projects outside of class they often do not have help from the classroom instructor, and, in the end, many projects are not completed by students at all, but by parents.

A celebration of student science projects is an opportunity to organize ideas about phenomena and communicate these ideas with other learners and adults. This should be a basic aspect of the curriculum and not considered a "frill" experience. At the center of the project there should be a focus on students' personal interests in phenomena and idea creation. Students should be able to pursue a wide variety of types of projects, depending on their interests, from the construction of models, to in-depth reporting to formal experiments. A key feature of the project should be its capacity to allow students the joy of sharing findings with peers and other members of the community.

Using biographical and autobiographical literature. Roger Payne is an acoustical biologist whose studies of whale songs and the migration pattern of the humpback whale are now world famous. At a very early stage in his career, he wrote a small booklet for children, entitled *How Barn Owls Hunt* (1968). The booklet provides much more than information about how barn owls hunt. Payne tells the story of his own developing interest in barn owls, how he first learned about barn owls, and how he devised new ways to gain insight into barn owl hunting habits. Biographical and autobiographical stories such as these allow students to learn about science as a story of human interest and consider the effort required to pull together bits and pieces of information in the attempt to create explanations and new insights. Through biographical literature, learners can see that they, too, might participate in considering aspects of the problem. Science is portrayed as a human endeavor—as the ongoing search for answers as people approach problems with imagination, vigor, and joy, arising from the desire to understand.

Teaching Approaches That Address Children's Ideas in Science

In Chapter 2, the vast literature on children's alternate conceptions and research on the nature of light was presented. The research literature is helpful in understanding the kinds of difficulties typically encountered by learners at various age levels when they begin to learn about light. These studies also give insight into the nature of some of the processes learners engage in as they study the topic. Teachers and curriculum designers can use this literature to create diagnostic and preinstructional tasks similar to those given to the students in the study.

To show other ways that the research material can be of value, two ideas basic to an understanding of the nature of light presented below. The scientific conceptions about each idea are given, followed by a review of the views most typically held by learners and some suggestions for helping learners consider new perspectives on light behavior. At the end of each review summary are suggestions for engaging learners in communication and reflection on both light and their own learning processes. The two topic areas are: (1) How Light Travels, and (2) The Role of Light in Vision.

1. How Light Travels

The Scientist's Conception: Light travels from its source in straight lines.
Ideas Commonly Held by Students: Most learners, both children and adults, when asked about the nature of light and light movement hold the view that

light is a "given," that it simply "is." Rarely do students speak of light as an entity, a wave or particle, or as propagating through space. Younger students equate light with its source, saying for example, "light is in the light bulbs" or "I can see it around the streetlamp." Most students hold the view that light exists around and tends to remain around its source. Some describe light as moving or passing through translucent objects or bouncing off reflective surfaces. Although the ideas of light traveling is generally confusing, many children speak of light as traveling farther at night than it does during the day. The behavior of visible beams of light, such as those that come from a flashlight, are not directly associated with the kind of pervasive light we experience daily, such as sunlight and the light in a room. Because many activities designed to teach about light refer to visible beams only, it is confusing to children when reference is suddenly made to the behavior of pervasive light.

Approaches to Help Students Move Toward a Grasp of Scientific Conceptions: Because ideas about the nature of light and light travel are fundamental to later understandings of the nature of light, they are useful to address at the beginning of a study of light. Small and large group discussions based on the question "What is light?" will allow students to express some of their own ideas about the nature of light, and in many cases to begin thinking about a topic they may not have considered before. Organizing and categorizing learner ideas into a class learning profile can help the teacher understand the range of views in the class. This profile can be shared with learners to promote discussion and further thought about light behavior prior to the start of the unit. (Use of the classroom profile is discussed in more detail on pages 189–192.)

Learners can share their experiences with light and describe their feelings about light phenomena. A beam of light from a flashlight can be shone and students invited to describe how the visible beam of light is different from and/or similar to the light experienced from the sun or moon. Finally, students can be encouraged to discuss why it becomes dark at night and why it is that, at times, objects at night can be seen even though there is very little light in a room.

2. Light and Vision

The Scientist's Conception: Objects are seen because light traveling from its source to an object is reflected or absorbed, depending on the color of the object. The resulting scattering light goes into the eyes of the viewer. This information is transferred to the brain where it is interpreted as the seen object.

Ideas Commonly Held by Students: A large proportion of students have a view of vision that places the eyes in an active role. They believe that the eyes "do" the seeing with the aid of light. This view is often conveyed in diagrammatic form by showing a ray or arrow coming from the eye and going to the object. Other views were represented by other children in the study group, but this view was most common and is most frequent in the population as a whole.

Approaches to Help Students Move Toward a Grasp of Scientific Conceptions: These ideas are among the most confusing areas of understanding for students in science. Learning about light and vision is one of the first experiences in science learning when ideas of science cannot be easily experienced. Sometimes it is difficult for science teachers to recall how difficult it is to accept these ideas. We must understand that the idea of light reflecting from an object is counterintuitive. As noted in the case reports, many children comment that it simply does not make sense. Children are taught from an early age to confirm findings by using the senses—sight, hearing, touch, taste, smell. Suddenly they are asked to suspend or ignore this information and simply accept as true what they cannot see for themselves. It is important to understand the challenge this represents for students, and to realize that simply providing students with the scientific conception is not sufficient. The learner must be convinced that the scientific conception is a better idea if it is to be grasped by the learner.

It is useful to share the history of the development of ideas about the nature of light and vision. A good starting point might be to have students create as did the children in the study, a drawing to show how they believe light allows an individual to see an object. The teacher can group the range of ideas, showing some representative examples to the class. Student ideas can be compared to the ideas presented by Plato, who proposed a "visual stream theory" suggesting that rays actually leave the eye going to the object. This idea was prominent for centuries. Another prominent idea in the early 13th century was that vision required not only light radiation from the sun but also visual rays coming from the eye in order for vision to occur. These developments can be shared with students as they learn that scientists' current understanding of vision involves light reflecting from objects into the eye. The children will see their own ideas in the early explanations.

The Importance of Providing Students with More Direct Experience with Natural Phenomena

The "hands-on" emphasis of many curriculum programs in science provides opportunities for students to build concepts in science on a sound foundation of experience with equipment and materials. Despite research that verifies the effectiveness of hands-on instruction (Duckworth, 1987; Shymansky, 1989; Wilson and Chalmers-Neubauer, 1990) many Science classes at the elementary level are still conducted solely through having students copy notes from the board into a "science notebook" or by reading a textbook chapter and answering questions at the end (Tobin, Briscoe and Holman, 1990).

The curriculum program used by the children in the case reports involved engagement in an activity each day of the study of light. Highly structured activities were presented on worksheets, a kind of altered textbook format. Worksheet questions did not, however, encourage students to suggest original or creative ideas, to share new insights, to review material from previous lessons, or put together past experiences to create new ideas. The worksheets used in the lessons were self-corrected by the children at the end of each class period and were turned in to the teacher at the end of the class. Only one answer was regarded as the correct response to each question. This common classroom practice may promote the view that there is one single correct answer that must always be found in science. There is little interest in creative responses, but it is essential that the correct answer be indicated on the worksheet. Following this format might cause students to develop the notion that in science, "whether I understand an idea is not so important as having the correct idea written down."

I was amazed to discover that prior to the light unit, none of the children in the study group had ever looked through a microscope and only one had prior experience with prisms. The simple introduction of materials for free exploration is an important starting point for students to begin to feel comfortable with scientific experimentation. Providing opportunities for more preliminary experience with phenomena allows students to freely experiment with materials, giving them a basis of experience to use in considering scientists' ideas at a later time. This period of free exploration is an appropriate time to allow the teacher to determine the kinds of understandings and questions students have about materials before going into more structured studies. This might allow students to make exciting discoveries, to talk ideas over with one another, to relate new experiences to past experiences, to pose questions, and to make observations about phenomena with teachers.

In the case studies, a number of spontaneous discoveries were made and reported by the children that were not anticipated in curriculum materials, for example, the association of light with heat. The provision of opportunities to speak, write about, and draw to organize thinking about such discoveries gives rise to a view of science as an enterprise of invention that values curiosity and personally meaningful insight. By encouraging children to ask their own questions about phenomena before more formal studies begin we also portray science as something more than "a topic we learn in school *now* so that we'll be better able to study the harder science they give us in later years," as was suggested by one of the students in the study group.

Encouraging and Guiding Home Studies—
Ongoing Experiences with Light

Two students in the class showed me that when they went home, they not only thought about the science experiences undertaken in class, but also actually tried or practiced some of their class activities at home. This was very apparent in Pierre and Martin's cases. When I visited Pierre at home, I found that he had built his own light box and demonstrated its use with his younger brother and cousin. Martin told me about a range of follow-up tests of various dense liquids and light beams, for example, his breakfast orange juice.

The number of students who chose to remain after class to explore, to experiment with materials, and to discuss the activity long after the allotted time period was further evidence of the intense interest of students in the topic of study. Mr. Ryan was not aware that students were pursuing such activities so extensively outside of class. These experiences, prompted by the *children's own natural efforts to understand*, might be greatly enhanced and guided by the teacher and the curriculum. Students could be provided with suggestions for continuing investigations at home or for exploring new aspects of a problem given a new set of conditions to consider.

OPPORTUNITIES FOR COMMUNICATION AND REFLECTION
ON THE LEARNING PROCESS

A number of suggestions that also build on the learner's own efforts to understand are offered in the next section. It has been my experience as a classroom teacher and researcher that, in general, children have a strong interest in doing well in their studies and are eager to take the responsibility to do well in school. The suggestions below build on the natural predisposition learners have in communicating their ideas and in their intense interest in the thinking of peers.

The suggestions are presented to help develop reflexive awareness during science learning, that is, to help learners become more conscious of the learning process itself and to value and build on the students' own efforts and approaches to learning.

The Classroom Profile: Learning How Others
Are Thinking About Phenomena

During the study, I developed "The Classroom Profile," a device that has shown very good potential as a means of highlighting and emphasizing concepts found to have been very difficult for science learners to grasp. The

Table 11.1 The classroom profile: Students' ideas
about "The Broken Pencil Phenomenon"

Explanation (Ranked)	Name (For Teacher Reference)				Number of Students
1. "The water makes it look broken."	Phyllis Donald	Jessica Carlo	Lorene Monty	Di Ching	8
2. "Water bends the light rays."	Stella	*Mark	Sally	James	4
3. "The shape of the beaker makes it look broken."	*Pierre	Leslie	Rose		3
4. "The water and the beaker make it look bigger."	Kim	*Melody	Amy		3
5. "The water and the beaker act as magnifier."	Raini	Hyon Sin			2
6. "The water acts as a magnifier."	*Martin	Arnie			2
7. "Because we tilted the pencil."	Arcala				1
8. "The light rays and the glass make it look broken."	*Donnie				1
9. "The light rays do it."	Denise				1
10. Descriptive statements	Susan	Karin		Annie	3
11. Unusual water ideas	Rochelle Lewis	Danny Michael		Trellis	5
				TOTAL =	33

*Students in the study group.

Classroom Profile, shown in Table 11.1, allows the opportunity to share the thinking processes of a class of students as a way of (1) helping individuals to become aware of their own ideas about the nature of phenomena, and (2) comparing their ideas with the ways that other children in the classroom are thinking about phenomena. Several class profiles were shared with the children during the unit of study. In the preparation of each profile, students were asked to respond to a simple question or questions about current ideas they were studying. The first profile was built from students' written response to the question, "What is light?" The second was constructed based on responses to a question asked after the lesson on refraction. A diagram was placed on the top of the question sheet showing the broken appearance of a pencil in a beaker of water. The students answered the following question: "On Wednesday, you observed a pencil placed in a beaker of water. What is your explanation for the unusual look of the pencil in the beaker of water?"

I collected the students' answers and found that they could be placed into several groups. These groups were placed on the class profile chart and the names of the students providing explanations were listed next to each group. Student names either could be used for teacher reference or could be shared with the class, depending on the teacher's preference. I chose not to show students' names along with ideas. The number of students making similar statements was noted, allowing a rank ordering of the responses. This particular profile made it very clear to students that the most popular response (shown by the tabulation of statement groups on the chart) was not always the response most closely resembling the scientists' opinion. The Classroom Profile is useful in helping the teacher understand how individual children are thinking about the ideas presented. It also shows how groups of students are thinking along similar lines. Other information is also available. In this profile, three students made descriptive statements when they had actually been asked to provide an explanation. The distinction between an explanation and a description could have been made more clear to these students.

Sharing the general trends in the profiles with the class using an overhead projector was of great value to the students. They find it interesting to see the ideas of fellow students and enjoyed discussion and reconsideration of their own ideas. In the process of exploring the ideas with the students in the study group, the children noted that several categories could be combined further so that there were several basic ideas held by members of the class. Martin asked me which one was the correct idea. He recalled that Mark had been told by Mr. Ryan that he had the correct idea and wondered what Mark had written on his sheet. A discussion about the usefulness of the various ideas on the worksheet continued with the students in the study group. During this discussion with the class, several students remarked on the nonsensical nature of Mark's idea that water was bending light rays and that light rays were coming from the pencil. They challenged one another's viewpoints and reiterated their own experience of the activity. Melody asked me, "What would a scientist say? Would he say any of those?" Pierre asked me to explain how water could possibly bend light and would I please reiterate for him that point in the explanation that he showed me he was having difficulty grasping.

The Classroom Profile could be used at various points during the unit to both monitor learners' grasp of ideas and facilitate interest in and discussion of developing ideas.

Helping Learners Reflect on Small Group Interaction

The analysis of small group interaction in the case study reports shows the enormous untapped potential of small group discussion to provide more effective "sense-making" opportunities for science learners. All of the children participating in the study expressed enjoyment in working in small groups and placed high value on the opportunity to work together. All said that, given the choice of a chance to work with others or on their own, their preference was to work with other children. We can build on this natural interest of children to work together by helping them to make better use of small group discussions. They can reflect on small sample dialogues similar to those presented in the case reports to focus on improving group learning processes.

The children's efforts can be guided in the small group work by encouraging them to reflect on the dynamics of group work and how they might better listen to one another and consider the ideas that group members put forth—to everyone's benefit. Mark's group experience was an interesting case in point. When he very suddenly put together ideas to explain the appearance of the coin in the saucer, he voiced his idea several times to members of his group. Group members did not understand Mark's explanation and, ignoring his comments, continued to talk about the activity among themselves. If teachers are able to guide students to reflect on how often and how well they listen to the comments and suggestions of group members, they may become better listeners with one another. Students might be encouraged to consider the value of the special talents of others in the group as useful resources. Students might also be encouraged to consider that their own contributions are of value even when they do not seem to make sense to others at first. As demonstrated in the case studies, the children's various personal orientations to science learning were experienced through the interaction during these sessions. For Martin, for example, the group sessions offered an opportunity to receive assistance in reading the worksheet.

Students may become more aware of the value of the teaching role of the group itself and may consider ways that they might help one another to learn more effectively in the group. This seemed particularly important on a number of occasions when students expressed reluctance in or fear of asking the teacher questions. Donnie's experience was reflected in one of her personal constructs concerning her asking Mr. Ryan for help, "Being embarrassed, about to get into trouble."

There were instances, although more rare, when students did not want to give help to others, when they felt that other students wished only to reap the benefits of their hard work. Yasmin often expressed the sense of "being ripped off" by Melody. "She just copies my paper. She doesn't do anything!" Yasmin was far more willing to share ideas with Martin, who worked with her during the activity to come to some understanding.

Pierre's view of himself as a contributor to the small group discussion was originally quite negative. He saw himself as involved in a continual struggle with ideas—always needing help from others. On one occasion, Pierre realized that he was the only person in the group who had grasped the notion of the task to be accomplished in the group. He seemed surprised to find himself for the first time as the provider of information and as the helper in the group. When other members listened to Pierre, he seemed renewed with excitement in his sense of himself as a student of science.

The opportunity to work in groups allows children the opportunity to explore together in a natural way. The experience could be enhanced through encouraging students to become more conscious of the processes they are involved in together. Developing awareness of the various ways that children construe this experience will allow the teacher to suggest good working groups using learners' assistance to one another in the creation of meaning. Direct suggestions to the children concerning the value of the group activity for the experience of creating meaning would focus less on rules for keeping quiet and finishing worksheets and more on helping students observe how others are creating meaning in their work.

In addition to considering other students' interaction in the small group, students might be encouraged to reconsider their own individual approaches to learning in the small group setting. Here, we come up against one of the great barriers to the development of the type of student responsibility and reflexive awareness being suggested here. The pressures of an educational system valuing and rewarding the attainment of correct ideas only and encouraging a competition rewarding individual achievement often does so at the expense of the cooperation and the sharing that might beneficially occur within the group. When groups are working well, members are sharing insights and understanding and are teaching one another.

Videotapes hold great potential for building on the intense interest students show for one another's thoughts, ideas, and approaches to science learning. A series of videotapes presenting the strategies of different children learning science, perhaps of students not known to the class, could be developed and presented to students. Viewing these tapes would guide students to reconsider their own and others' approaches to learning, to become more conscious of their abilities, to take a more active part in their own learning, and to develop strategies that are effective and compatible with their own interests, style, and approach to content.

Helping Students Learn to Ask for Help Through Asking Questions

Joan Tough (1979) notes that it is often assumed that children enter classrooms already knowing how to formulate questions, as they frequently ask questions of teachers. The majority of questions asked in the classroom are procedural, asking for permission, directions, or instructions. Less often, children ask questions that seek further knowledge about a subject or request explanations. In Tough's view, children learn that they are not expected to ask such questions and that adult decisions, particularly those of teachers, should not be questioned (p. 125).

Students benefit from guidance in discovering the types of questions that best assist them to access information, and when or how they might best ask questions of themselves to uncover information through their own efforts. They might be encouraged to practice using specific types of questions in both large and small group settings. In fact, the students in Mr. Ryan's class were learning to ask a variety of questions as part of a reading program being used by several teachers in the school. Students were actually learning to ask questions using Bloom's Taxonomy as a framework. As they read and discussed stories, they systematically practiced writing questions about the stories that reflected the various cognitive levels—factual questions during one lesson and evaluative questions during another. The students asked one another the questions that they had developed.

During one of the light activities, the children *predicted* the results of reflecting a light beam from variously angled mirrors. Pierre commented to me after this lesson how similar the science task was to the language arts lesson that required the listing of prediction questions. The children can see how general learning skills apply from one subject to another. Helping students learn to ask questions will not only help learners clarify what is causing difficulty, but will help teachers see patterns in student views.

Another means of helping young children recognize the value of different types of questions is to discuss and practice interviewing people (advocated by Tough, 1979, p. 126). I have used this approach in the design of a unit on energy studies "The Energy Sleuth Kit" (Shapiro, 1986). In the activity "Calling Key Witnesses," students interview various witnesses who may have information about the use and possible waste of energy on the students' school site. The students prepare their questions in advance of the visit of the "key witness" and share them with other members of the class. The goal is to develop questions that will allow the students to achieve a maximum amount of insight and information through the types of questions they ask. Each individual in the class makes a unique contribution to this effort. In this way, the individual members of the class make a difference in contributing to the group's discovery of the types of information to be acquired through the use of good questions. Such an approach enables students to develop the skills needed to meaningfully question another person. These skills can be applied as students question one another or their teacher and as they participate in the class's large group discussions.

Helping Children Develop and Use Knowledge Organization Tools— Graphic Organizers

Keeping a diary, journal, or science notebook is a wonderful way to keep a personal record of results and observations, drawings and thoughts about class activities. Journal records reveal the development of ideas in a unit. They provide a record that allows children to connect new ideas with previous learning and give an interesting focus for discussion and review of key understandings.

Lesley Wing Jan (1993) suggests that as children learn to use language in science, they should also have opportunities to select some of their own ways of recording information and portraying ideas. Learners might design brochures on a topic of study. They might create posters or small booklets for younger children.

There are a variety of other means that children can use to organize ideas developed during a unit. Some of these may be modeled by the teacher such as outlines, concept maps, semantic webs, mobiles, and flow charts. Other devices can be invented by the children themselves.

During work on the light unit, I presented to the class an approach to help organize ideas about light, called "concept mapping." Concept mapping, a well-known knowledge organization tool, is a graphic organizer that students can use to visually arrange ideas to show the connections between and among concepts as they are being studied (Novak & Gowin, 1984).

In preliminary discussions, I spoke with students about their responsibility for learning. I told the class that I believed that "it is Mr. Ryan's responsibility to teach students and it is the student's responsibility to learn." I told them that I was going to show them one way they might organize their ideas to make learning easier and more effective. Here, I was greeted with great enthusiasm. They seemed very interested in learning and were anxious to begin. I told them that I had learned that their teacher, Mr. Ryan, was an avid astronomer and that I had asked him to give me an introductory lesson in astronomy. I took notes during his talk, and afterwards constructed a concept map to help me organize the ideas he had presented. On a large sheet of paper, I showed the class the concept map I had made linking the new ideas together. We looked at the map to see how concepts were linked with connecting ideas or propositions.

I showed the children examples of concept maps that children their own age and younger had produced (Figure 11.1). As they examined the concept maps, I demonstrated how the maps provide a type of visual road map (Novak & Gowin, 1984) that shows how meanings are connected by the learner.

Novak and Gowin refer to the connections between concepts linked by a word or phrase to form a proposition. They state that these links between concepts are intended to represent meaningful relationships between the concepts, and they contrast this with the all too typical rote memorization of terms and concepts common to science learning. The creation of concept maps was presented, then, as a search for meaningful relationships among the concepts presented. Mr. Ryan allowed me to spend a class session reviewing the concepts and ideas presented to date in the light unit.

The concept mapping session was a particularly valuable session for several pairs of students who chose to produce a map together. Not only did the children make connections among ideas that made the concepts more conscious to them, but they were also able to see one another's concept maps and how other individuals' unique views of content differed from their own. The teacher is also able to see where connections may be inaccurately or inappropriately made or where complete ideas might be missing altogether.

Using concept mapping or similar schematic representations such as outlines, diagrams, or flowcharts would require that the teacher have a clear understanding of the connections between the ideas presented in the lessons. The procedure also requires a teacher who is committed to encouraging students to take greater responsibility for their own learning. Learning to construct visual representations of learning requires both a preliminary period of learning to understand how to make these learning devices and time to regularly add connecting ideas to one's chart.

It is clear from the analyses of the case reports that individuals possess different talents and interests in their pursuit of understanding in science, as seen in their personal orientations to science study. Students should be given a range of options and encouraged to use creative approaches in the form and content of their representations. Britton (1972b) reiterates this viewpoint in his study of the teaching of students who are making plans for writing. What is an effective and valuable planning procedure for one individual, for example, the preparation and use of an outline, may be stultifying and obtrusive for another. The teacher interested in encouraging children toward self-organization might find these representational tools useful in helping children to become more conscious of their own learning. Careful use of ap-

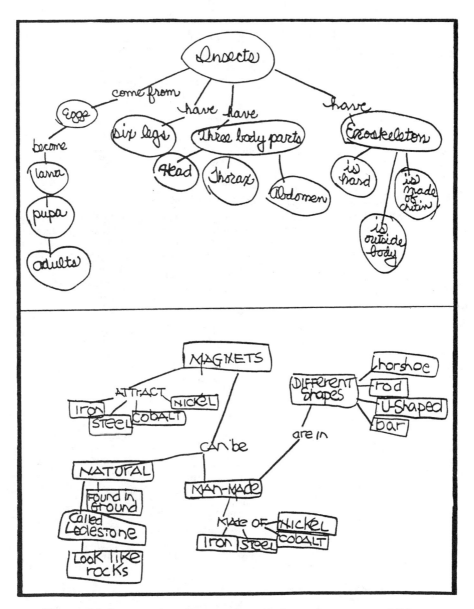

Figure 11.1 examples of concept maps drawn by younger children

Table 11.2 Toward a constructivist conception
of science learning and teaching

	Goals of Science Teaching	View of the Learner	View of the Teaching Task
Trend I	*Idea acquisition*	*"Tabula rasa"* The learner's mind is a blank slate.	*Transmission* Transmit scientists" ideas about natural phenomena to the learner.
Trend II	*Idea change*	*Misinformed* The learner has ideas about the nature of phenomena (misconceptions) that need correction.	*Correction* Replace learner's ideas with scientific ideas.
Trend III	*Knowledge construction* Development of the ability to grasp scientific explanations and approaches to understanding of events and phenomena.	*Active Participant in Learning* The learner has ideas about the nature of phenomena (alternate frameworks). Each individual also holds a personal view about the purpose and value of many features of the school science learning experience. Learners enter classrooms already seeking to make sense of the world. Each person has a personal approach to understanding. The meanings constructed by learners during science lessons may be very different from those intended by teachers and curriculum authors. In order to grasp new explanations, learners must become aware of the value of considering things in new ways: scientific explanations, and approaches to science learning. The learner must actively participate in this personal construction of new meaning.	*Construction* Assist the learner in the active consideration and construction of ideas by providing opportunities. Become familiar with pattern in students' current understandings and experiences with phenomena available in research literature. Become familiar with pattern of knowledge among one's own students. Provide opportunities to assist learners in their own active construction of meaning by using such approaches as assisting learners in the identification of meaningful problems, organizing learning experiences that emphasize extensive use of language in the creation of meaning, such as journal writing, large and small group discussion, the use of knowledge organization tools.

proaches like these will help learners find their own ways to take greater responsibility for learning.

Toward a Constructivist Conception of Science Teaching and Learning

I have attempted to show through examples and suggestions how a constructivist view of teaching and learning demands a rethinking of the goals of science teaching, the nature of the learner, and the nature of the teaching challenge. A summary of the implications of these views are shown in Table 11.2 (*previous page*).

Toward Science Learning with the Psyche Left In

> You have to find some other way through the philosophical maze,
> a way of leaving room for the individual to make his or her own de-
> cisions, inventions, constructions, a way to make a difference so
> that if this person or that one had not existed, something would
> not have happened the way it did. The individual matters.
> —Gruber, "Emotion and Cognition: Aesthetics and Science" (p. 136)

The individual's own efforts to learn matter. Each person has a unique approach to creating meaning in learning and this approach is reflected in patterns of thought and behavior. But if a child is to be successful in the educational system, he or she must adapt to curriculum goals and purposes that
often do not value the human experience of learning, that is, the intellectual
and emotional processes involved in the construction of meaning. When the
psyche is left out of our consideration of the learner, when the distance between what is personally meaningful and what is publicly sanctioned is too
great to be embraced, there is alienation, disinterest, and a desire to leave
the learning situation. Whitman sensitively portrays the effects of this gap in
the poem that introduces this book.

THE IMPORTANCE OF THE PERSONAL

In an effort to understand this gap, this work begins with a focus on
the personal. The meaning the individual gives to the world is a personal
construction. Meaning cannot be given or transmitted to the learner. It is a
result of the learner's integration of his or her own ideas with a wide range of
personal, emotional, cultural, social, and intellectual experiences. In school
settings, the experiences of the learner range from direct instruction and activities developed by teachers to interactions with other learners, texts, media
and other resources, parents, and even oneself. The ideas we eventually
adopt become our own as a result of experiences and interactions with the
events and people in the environment. Whether or not a person's concepts
will change depends on the willingness of the person to try new ways of

looking at the world. This view of learning applies to the learning person of any age; it may be a child or a teacher. But equally important is the knowledge and action of the teacher to understand not only the subject matter, but also the dynamic relationships in the teaching-learning dialogue that are essential in understanding student ideas and efforts to learn. This book is written as a resource for the educator who wishes to work toward building a science program that values the learner's contribution in the classroom experience—one that builds on learner knowledge and values the involvement of the learner in the process. It is not a how-to manual, for a constructivist view is not a technique but a philosophical position. Each reader will have his or her own ideas about how to best help the learner consider ideas in new ways.

New understanding and awareness is required to build curriculum and instructional programs to teach in ways that help learners build ideas in science. In order to do so, educators must have a deep understanding of the nature of science and the processes of knowledge creation. There must also be an awareness of student ideas about the nature of phenomena and the approaches students use to learn. As Smith (1973) points out, such an approach to teaching demands an entire series of changes in thinking about educational practice. It requires "a rejection of formulae, less reliance on tests, and more receptivity to the child. It demands a total rejection of the ethos of our day—that the answer to all of our problems lies in improved method and technology and of the emphasis on method that pervades almost all of teacher training" (p.46).

Changing the Image of the Science Learner

This work challenges us to consider the image we hold of the learner. Tillich (1952) wrote of the dilemma of striving to know and value the uniqueness of the individual, while simultaneously understanding the person as "part of the larger whole." He commented on the dual nature of the person's struggle "to be" as an important source of insight: "Each person is a unique representation of the universe, (and yet) is also a part of the larger whole of humanity" (p. 18).

It may be only partially useful to suggest that educators employ the first image of the learner, that is, keeping track of the different views of the nature of phenomena held by each child in the classroom. Likewise, sets of statements derived using an image of the "average student" may be valuable in showing trends in the reasoning of student populations as a whole, but do not allow insight into the range and variety of processes whereby the individual makes an effort to make sense of ideas. Both images of the science learner are needed to understand the construction of ideas.

The Importance of Giving High Status
to the Individual's Efforts to Create Meaning

The primary assumption of the study has been that students enter classrooms already seeking to make sense of life experience and that each person gives unique meaning to that experience. Frankl (1959) saw the individual's search for meaning as "a primary force in his life and not a secondary rationalization of instinctual drives. This meaning is unique and specific in that it must and can be fulfilled by him alone; only then does it achieve a significance that will satisfy his own will to meaning" (p. 154). We may not always agree with the way that a student does this, but by understanding the students' own purposes and developing approaches we can help learners consider new ways of thinking about ideas and perhaps also reconsider their own approaches to science learning.

The development of the six case study reports has been an attempt to understand the individual pursuit of meaning during the experience of learning science in the elementary school. A variety of approaches have been used in conducting conversations with six very different children whose unique orientations to science study are reflected in their thoughts and actions in the classroom. Key to the understanding of each student has been an attempt to convey the connection with what is referred to by Gruber (1978) as the "emotional substratum." Gruber suggests that understanding this powerfully influential set of factors begins with recognizing the significance of individual experience. This insight is missing in the majority of studies dealing solely with cognition.

Continuing to Talk with the Children

I have continued to talk with the children and observe them in their school settings even into the high school program. It is my hope that the research and the research journey that I have shared in this book allows the reader to consider science learning in a new way. I continue to visit Donnie, Mark, Martin, Yasmin, Melody, and Pierre. They live in a city 3 hours away, but I have visited all of them twice a year, frequently sitting with them in their classrooms since junior high school. Last year we had a reunion with parents and relatives. The children had not seen one another in 7 years.

They are 19, 20, and 21 years old at this writing. The names used in the study are, of course, not the real names of the participants. I have continued to document their changing ideas about the nature of light, their school science learning experiences, and their views on the meaning and value of science education in light of their movement into careers and adult relationships. While exploring the possibilities of a career in nursing, Donnie has embraced work in Rehabilitation Therapy and is currently pursuing a program of studies and part-time work in this field. Mark is completing an extra year of preparatory studies before entering a teacher preparation program. He has decided to become a science teacher. Martin is completing a year of work in automotive mechanics and is an active football player with professional aspirations. He works several part-time jobs. Melody left school at age 16 to have her first child. She aspires to complete the high school equivalency program and currently works part-time as a waitress. Yasmin is in the first year of a university program leading to a degree in Pharmacy. Pierre is completing an extra year of high school studies in art and hopes to become a professional graphic artist.

It is an ongoing goal to try to understand the meaning of science learning in the lives of these children, one that will not quickly end. During our last visit, Donnie joked with me, "Are we going to be still talking with you about science and light when we're, like, 45 years old?" I told her that I hoped so. Knowing all of the children has added enormously to my own life and my work with teachers in preparation. I have gained much in knowing them so well, and have been honored to have been invited into their personal lives and thoughts for 9 years now.

I have found through observing and conversing with the children that as I have learned to become a better listener, the children have become more responsive and shared more and more of their thoughts and feelings with me about their experience. As I continue to learn to become a better listener, the expectation develops within the children that what they have to say is important. As I become a better interpreter of their thoughts, feelings, and actions, I become more aware of appropriate suggestions to help address their understandings and views of science. As the children came to understand the purposes of my study, they are aware that what they have had to say was not only for me to hear, but also that their ideas will be shared with teachers, curriculum developers, researchers, and student teachers.

I have found, also, that the children have become interested in me, the listener, as a person. In the classroom, they would often ask me what I thought of an idea or an insight or if I would help them with some of their other school work. Now they ask me about my life, both personal and professional. Possibly the most important aspect of this approach to research and teaching is the demonstration that our sincere interest in what students have to say may create the expectation in them that their ideas, thoughts, and feelings are valued by us. With this expectation, students become more receptive to and place greater value on the learning that we attempt to guide them toward accomplishing.

In conclusion, I hope that this resource is an inviting starting point for the reader to engage in a fresh rethinking of teaching and learning, research and practice. We are all researchers in the classroom, students of the mystery of the processes of learning. Holt (1967) has written, "The human mind is a mystery. To a very large extent, it will probably always be so. We will never get very far in education until we realize this, and give up the delusion that we can know, measure, and control what goes on in children's minds. To know one's own mind is difficult enough" (p. 156). I hope, on the one hand, that reflection on the ideas presented here is a part of a journey of thought that helps to make the learner's mind less of a mystery. On the other hand, I hope that there will never be a loss of mystery in learning about learning— that the task of understanding what learners bring to science learning will be always fresh and challenging, and that the reader will never stop learning how to help make the process a more interesting, successful, personally meaningful, and fulfilling experience for children.

References

Anderson, C. W., & Smith, E. L. (1983a). Children's preconceptions and content area in textbooks. In G. Duffy, L. Roehler, & J. Mason (Eds.), *Comprehension instruction: Perspectives and suggestions* (pp. 73–91). New York: Longman.

Anderson, C. W., & Smith, E. L. (1983b, April). *Children's conceptions of light and color: Developing the concept of unseen rays.* Paper presented at the annual meeting of the American Educational Research Association, Montreal, Canada.

Andersson, B., & Karrqvist, C. (1982). *Ljuset och dess egenskaper,* EKNA projecektet, Institutionen for praktisk pedagogik, Molndal, Sverige. *Light and its properties.* (G. Thylander, Trans.).

Andersson, B., & Karrqvist, C. (1983). How Swedish pupils aged 12–25 years understand light and its properties. *European Journal of Science Education, 5*(4), 387–402.

Appelman, M., Colton, R., Flexer, A., & Hawkins, D. (1982). *Critical barriers to the learning and understanding of elementary science* (National Science Foundation Contract No. SED 80–08581). Boulder, CO: Mountain View Center.

Ault, C. (1980). *Children's concepts about time no barrier to understanding the geologic past.* Unpublished doctoral dissertation, Cornell University, Ithaca, New York.

Ault, C. (1984). Intelligently wrong: Some comments on children's misconceptions. *Science and Children, 5,* 22–24.

Bannister, D., & Fransella, P. (1971). *Inquiring man* (2nd ed.). London: Penguin.

Barnes, D. (1975). *From communication to curriculum.* New York: Penguin.

Bateson, G. (1972). *Steps to an ecology of mind.* Toronto: Random House of Canada.

Bateson, G. (1979). *Mind and nature: A necessary unity.* New York: Bantam.

Berger, P. L., & Luckman, T. (1966). *The social construction of reality: A treatise in the sociology of knowledge.* Garden City, NY: Doubleday.

Bertalanffy, L. (1975). *Perspectives on general systems theory.* New York: George Braziller.

Beveridge, M., & Brierley, C. (1982). Classroom constructs: An interpretive approach to young children's language. In M. Beveridge (Ed.), *Children thinking through language* (pp. 29–42). London: Edward Arnold.

Briggs, J., & Peat, D. (1984). *Looking glass universe: The emerging science of wholeness.* New York: Simon & Schuster.

Britton, J. (1972a). *Language and learning.* Middlesex, England: Pelican.

Britton, J. (1972b). *Writing to learn and learning to write.* Urbana, IL: National Council of Teachers of English.

Brook, A., Briggs, H., & Driver, R. (1984). *Aspects of secondary students' understanding of the particulate nature of matter.* Leeds, England: University of Leeds, Centre for Studies in Science and Mathematics Education, Department of Education and Science.

Brophy, J. E. (1982). Schooling as students experience it. *Elementary School Journal,* *82*(5), 519–529.

Brown, C., & Desforges, R. (1979). *Piaget's theory: A psychological critique.* London: Routledge & Kegan Paul.

Bruner, J. (1956). You are your constructs. *Contemporary Psychology, A Journal of Reviews,* I(12), 355–356.

Bruner, J. (1962). *On knowing: Essays for the left hand.* Cambridge, MA: Harvard University Press.

Buber, M. (1955). *I and thou* (2nd ed.). New York: Scribner's.

Callan, E. (1983). Interests and the curriculum. *British Journal of Educational Studies,* *31*(1), 41–51.

Capra, F. (1982). *The tao of physics.* New York: Bantam.

Cassirer, E. (1944). *An essay on man.* New Haven: Yale University Press.

Cicourel, A. V. (1974). *Language use and school performance.* New York: Academic Press.

Claxton, A. (1982). *School science: Falling on stony ground or choked by thorns?* In C. Sutton & L. West (Eds.), Investigating children's existing ideas about science: A research seminar (pp. 4–5). Leicester, England: University of Leicester, School of Education.

Cleminson, A. (1990). Establishing an epistemological base for science teaching in the light of comtemporary notions of the nature of science and how children learn science. *Journal of Research in Science Teaching, 27*(5), 429–445.

Crookes, J., & Goldby, G. (1984). *How we see things: An introduction to light.* Leicestershire, England: Science Process Curriculum Group, The Science Curriculum Review in Leicestershire.

Dewey, J. (1913). *Interest and effort in education.* New York: Houghton Mifflin.

Donaldson, M. (1978). *Children's minds.* New York: W. W. Norton and Company.

Doris, E. (1991). *Doing what scientists do: Children learn to investigate their world.* Portsmouth, NH: Heinemann.

Driver, R. (1983). *The pupil as scientist?* Milton Keynes, England: Open University Press.

Driver, R., & Easley, J. (1978). Pupils and paradigms: A review of the literature related to concept development in adolescent science students. *Studies in Science Education, 5,* 61–84.

Driver, R., & Erickson, G. (1983). Theories-in-action: Some theoretical and empirical issues in the study of students' conceptual frameworks. *Studies in Science Education, 10,* 37–60.

Driver, R., Guesne, E., and Tiberghien, A. (Eds.). (1985). *Children's ideas in science.* Milton Keynes, England: Open University Press.

Driver, R., & Oldham, V. (1985, August). *A constructivist approach to curriculum development in science.* Paper presented at the symposium, "Personal Construction of Meaning in Educational Settings," BERA Sheffield: England.

Duckworth, E. (1987). *The having of wonderful ideas.* New York: Teachers College Press.

Easley, J. A., Jr. (1982). Naturalistic case studies exploring social-cognitive mechanisms, and some methodological issues in research on the problems of teachers. *Journal of Research on Teaching, 19*(3), 191–203.

Eisner, E. (1981). On the differences between scientific and artistic approaches to qualitative research. *Educational Researcher, 10*(4), 5–9.

Elementary Science Study (ESS). (1976). *Behavior of mealworms: Teachers's guide.* New York: McGraw-Hill.

Erikson, E. (1975). *Childhood and society.* Bungay, Suffolk, England: Triad Granada.

Erikson, E. (1980). Children's viewpoints of heat: A second look. *Science Education, 64*(4), 323–336.

Feher, E. (1990). Interactive museum exhibits as tools for learning: Explorations with light. *International Journal of Science Education, 12,* 35–49.

Feher, E., & Meyer, K. (1992). Children's conceptions of color. *Journal of Research in Science Education, 29*(5), 503–520.

Feher, E., & Rice, K. (1988). Shadows and anti-images: Children's conceptions of light and vision II. *Science Education, 72,* 637–649.

Fensham, P. A. (1983). A research base for new objectives in science teaching. *Science Education, 67*(1), 103–112.

Fetherstonhaugh, T., & Treagust, D. F. (1990, April). *Students' understanding of light and its properties following a teaching strategy to engender conceptual change.* Paper presented at the annual meeting of the American Educational Research Association, Boston.

Fetherstonhaugh, T., & Treagust, D. F. (1992). Students' understanding of light and its properties: Teaching to engender conceptual change. *Science Education 76*(6), 653–672.

Fisher, D. V. (1992). *An introduction to constructivism for social workers.* New York: Praeger.

Frankl, V. (1959). *Man's search for meaning.* Scarborough, ON: Signet.

Freire, P. (1982). *Pedagogy of the oppressed.* New York: Continuum.

Gadamer, H. (1960). *Truth and method.* New York: Seabury Press.

Gadamer, H. (1975). Hermeneutics and social sciences. *Cultural Hermeneutics, 2,* 307–316.

Garfinkle, H. (1967). *Studies in ethnomethodology.* London: Basil Blackwell.

Gilbert, J. K., Osborne, R. J., & Fensham, P. J. (1982). Children's science and its consequences for teaching. *Science Education, 66*(4), 623–633.

Gilbert, J. K., & Pope, M. (1982). *School children discussing energy.* Surrey, England: University of Surrey, Institute of Educational Development.

Gilbert, J. K., & Watts, D. M. (1983). Concepts, misconceptions and alternative conceptions: Changing perspectives in science education. *Studies in Science Education, 10,* 61–98.

Glaser, B. G., & Strauss, A. L. (1967). *The discovery of grounded theory.* Chicago: Aldine.

Goldberg, F. M., & McDermott, L. C. (1986). Student difficulties in understanding image formation by a plane mirror. *Physics Teacher, 24*(8), 472–480.

Greene, M. (1973). *Teacher as stranger: Educational philosophy for the modern age.* Belmont, CA: Wadsworth.

Gregorc, A. (1982). Learning style/brain research: Harbinger of an emerging psychology. *Student learning styles and brain behavior.* Reston, VA: National Association of Secondary School Principals.

Gregorc, A., & Butler, K. (1983). Learning and teaching style—A status report. *NASSP Curriculum Report, 12*(4).

Gruber, H. (1978). Emotion and cognition: Aesthetics and science. In S. W. Madeja (Ed.), *The arts, cognition and basic skills: Second yearbook on research in arts and aesthetic education*. St. Louis, MO: CEMREL.

Guesne, E. (1978). Children's ideas about light. *New Trends in Physics Teaching, IV.* Paris: UNESCO.

Guesne, E. (1985). Light. In R. Driver, E. Guesne, & A. Tiberghien (Eds.), *Children's ideas in science* (pp. 10–32). Milton Keynes, England: Open University Press.

Helm, H., & Novak, J. (1983). *Proceedings of the International Conference on Misconceptions in Science and Mathematics.* Cornell University, Ithaca, New York.

Holt, J. (1967). *How children learn.* New York: Dell Publishing Company.

Hueftle, S. J., Rakow, S. J., & Welch, W. (1983). *Images in science: A summary of results from the 1981–82 National Assessment in Science.* Minneapolis, MN: Science Assessment and Research Project.

Hurd, P. D. (1984). Science education: The search for a new vision. *Educational Leadership, December–January,* 20–22.

Isaacs, N. (1974). Early scientific trends in children. In M. Hardeman (Ed.), *Children's ways of knowing: Nathan Isaacs on education, psychology and Piaget* (pp. 81–97). New York: Teachers College Press.

Isaacs, S. (1960). *Intellectual growth in young children.* London: Routledge & Kegan Paul.

Jan, L. W. (1993). Ways of writing science. In J. Scott (Ed.), *Science and language links: Classroom applications* (pp. 39–50). Portsmouth, NH: Heinemann.

Jantsch, E. (1980). *The self-organizing universe: Scientific and human implications of the emerging paradigm of evolution.* Toronto: Pergamon.

Jung, W. (1981). *Conceptual frameworks in elementary optics.* Paper presented at the Conference in Ludwigsburg, Wolfgang Goethe, Universitat Institute fur Didaktik der Phusik, Grafstrabe, Frankfurt.

Kargbo, D. B., Hobbs, E. D., & Erickson, G. L. (1980). Student beliefs about inherited characteristics. *Journal of Biological Education 14*(2), 137–146.

Karrqvist, C. (1983). How Swedish pupils, aged 12–25 years, understand light and its properties. In H. Helm & J. Novak (Eds.), *Proceedings of the International Seminar: Misconceptions in Science and Mathematics.* Cornell University, Ithaca, New York.

Kelly, G. A. (1955). *The psychology of personal constructs* (Vols. 1 & 2). New York: W. W. Norton.

Kelly, G. A. (1963). *A theory of personality: The psychology of personal constructs.* New York: W. W. Norton.

Kelly, G. A. (1969). The language of hypothesis: Man's psychological instrument. In B. A. Maher (Ed.), *Clinical psychology and personality: Selected papers of George Kelly* pp. 147–162. New York: John Wiley & Sons.

Kelly, G. A. (1969). The strategy of psychological research. In B. Maher (Ed.), *Clinical psychology and personality: The collected papers of George Kelly* (pp. 144–132). New York: John Wiley & Sons.

Kelly, G. A. (1970). Behavior as an experiment. In D. Bannister (Ed.), *Perspectives in personal construct theory* (pp. 255–269). New York: Academic Press.

Kuhn, T. (1970). *The structure of scientific revolutions.* Chicago: University of Chicago Press.

Kuhn, T. (1977). *The essential tension: Selected studies in scientific tradition and change.* Chicago: University of Chicago Press.

La Rosa, C., Mayer, M., Patrizi, P., & Vicenti, M. (1984). Common sense knowledge in optics: Preliminary results of an investigation on the properties of light. *European Journal of Science Education, 6*(4), 387–397.

Leinhardt, G. (1983a, April). *Routines in expert math teachers' thoughts and actions.* Paper presented at the annual meeting of the American Educational Research Association, Montreal.

Leinhardt, G. (1983b, April). *Student cognitions during instruction.* Paper presented at the annual meeting of the American Educational Research Association, Montreal.

Lincoln, Y. S., & Guba, E. (1981). *Effective evaluation: Improving evaluation through responsive and naturalistic inquiry.* San Francisco, CA: Jossey-Bass.

Lincoln, Y. S., & Guba, E. (1985). *Naturalistic inquiry.* New York: Sage.

Magoon, A. J. (1977). Constructivist approaches in educational research. *Review of Research in Education, 47*(4), 651–693.

Marton, F., & Saljo, R. (1976a). On qualitative differences in learning: 1. Outcome and process. *British Journal of Educational Psychology, 46*, 4–11.

Marton, F., & Saljo, R. (1976b). Symposium on learning processes and strategies: 2. Outcome as a function of the learner's conception of task. *British Journal of Education Psychology, 46*, 115–127.

Marton, F., & Svensson, L. (1979). Conceptions of research in student learning. *Higher Education, 8*, 471–486.

Maslow, A. H. (1966). *The psychology of science: A reconnaissance.* Southbend, IN: Gateway.

Matthews, G. (1980). *Philosophy and the young child.* Cambridge, MA: Harvard University Press.

Matthews, G. (1984). *Dialogues with children.* Cambridge, MA: Harvard University Press.

Minstrel, J. (1983). Getting the facts straight. *Science Teacher, 46*, 52–54.

Navarra, J. (1955). *The development of scientific concepts in a child.* New York: Teachers College Press.

Novak, J. D. (1987). *Proceedings of The Second International Seminar on Misconceptions and Educational Strategies in Science and Mathematics* (Vols. 1–3). Cornell University, Ithaca, New York.

Novak, J. D., & Gowin, D. B. (1984). *Learning how to learn.* New York: Cambridge University Press.

Nussbaum, J. (1976). An assessment of children's concepts of the earth utilizing structured interviews. *Science Education, 60*(4), 535–550.

Nyberg, D. (1971). *Tough and tender learning.* Palo Alto, CA: National Press Books.

Oldham, V. (1982). *Interpretations of difficulty in high school biology.* Unpublished master's degree thesis, Edmonton: The University of Alberta.

Osborne, J., Black, P., Smith, S., & Meadows, J. (1990). *Light research report.* Primary SPACE Project. Liverpool, England: Liverpool University Press.

Osborne, R. J. (1980). A method for investigating concept understanding in science. *European Journal of Science Education 2*(3), 311–321.

Osborne, R. J. (1981). *Force.* Learning in Science Project (Working Paper No. 16). Hamilton, New Zealand: University of Waikato.

Osborne, R., & Freyberg, P. (1985). *Learning in science: The implications of children's science.* Portsmouth, NH: Heinemann.

Parlett, M., & Simons, H. (1979). *Learning from learners: A study of the student's experience of academic life.* A case study prepared by the Group for Research and Innovation in Higher Education, London: The Nuffield Foundation.

Pask, G. (1976). Conversational techniques in the study and practice of education. *British Journal of Educational Psychology, 46,* 12–25.

Payne, R. (1968). *How barn owls hunt.* Cambridge, MA: Educational Development Center.

Piaget, J. (1929). *The child's conception of the world.* London: Routledge & Kegan Paul.

Piaget, J. (1974a). *The child's conception of physical causality.* London: Routledge & Kegan Paul.

Piaget, J. (1974b). *Understanding causality.* New York: W. W. Norton.

Pope, M. (1980). *Personal construct theory and current issues in education.* Paper presented at the University of Osnabruck, Germany.

Pope, M. (1981). *In true spirit: Constructive alternativism in educational research.* Paper presented at the Fourth International Congress on Personal Construct Psychology, Brock University, St. Catherines, Ontario.

Pope, M. (1982). Personal construction of formal knowledge. *Interchange, 13*(4), 3–14.

Pope, M. (1983). Personal experience and the construction of knowledge in science. *Learning and Experience in Formal Education.* Manchester Monographs, Sturminster Newton, Dorset, England.

Pope, M. (1985, August). *Constructivist goggles: Implications for process in teaching and learning.* Paper presented at BERA Conference, Sheffield, England.

Pope, M., & Gilbert, J. (1985a). Constructive science education. In F. Epting & A. W. Lanfield (Eds.), *Anticipating personal construct psychology* (pp. 111–127). Lincoln, NB: University of Nebraska Press.

Pope, M., & Gilbert, J. (1985b). Theories of learning: Kelly. In R. Osborne & J. Gilbert (Eds.), *Some issues of theory in science education* (pp. 17–41). Papers based on seminars at the Science Education Research Unit, University of Waikato, Hamilton, New Zealand.

Posner, G. J., Strike, K. A., Hewson, P., & Gertzog, W. (1982). Accommodation of a scientific conception: Toward a theory of conceptual change. *Science Education, 66* (2), 211–227.

Power, C. N. (1976). Competing paradigms in science education research. *Journal of Science Education, 12*(6), 579–587.

Prigogine, I., & Stengers, I. (1984). *Order out of chaos.* New York: Bantam.

Ramadas, J., & Driver, R. (1989). *Aspects of secondary students' ideas about light.* Children's Learning in Science Project, CSSME, University of Leeds, England.

Ritchie, T. J. (1982). In praise of idiosyncratic study. *Interchange, 13*(4), 31–38.

Rohrkemper, M. (1984). *The functions of inner speech in elementary school students' problem solving behavior: Self and others' perceptions* (Technical Report No. 9). Bryn Mawr, PA: Bryn Mawr College, Department of Education and Child Development.

Rohrkemper, M., & Benson, B. L. (1983). *Quality of student task engagement: elementary school students' reports of the causes and effects of problem difficulty* (Technical Report No. 4). Bryn Mawr, PA: Bryn Mawr College, Department of Education and Child Development.

Ronchi, V. (1970). *The nature of light.* London: Heinemann.

Schaefer, G. (1979). Concept formation in biology: The concept "growth." *European Journal of Science Education, 1*(1), 87–101.

Schmidt, W. H. O. (1973). *Child development: The human, cultural and emotional context.* New York: Harper & Row.

Schon, D. A. (1983). *The reflective practitioner.* New York: Basic Books.

Schon, D. A. (1987). *Educating the reflective practitioner: Towards a new design for teaching and learning in the professions.* San Francisco: Jossey-Bass.

Science Council of Canada. (1984). *Report 36: Science for every student.* Ottawa: Minister of Supply and Services.

Shapiro, B. (1986). *Energy sleuth: A grade six detective program.* Edmonton, Alberta: Department of Energy and Natural Resources, Conservation Branch.

Shapiro, B. (1989). What children bring to light: Giving high status to learners' views and actions in science. *Science Education, 73*(6), 711–733.

Shapiro, B. (1990). Changing the ways we listen to one another. *Alberta Science Education Journal, 2*(23), 39–46.

Shapiro, B. (1991a). The use of personal construct theory and the repertory grid in the development of case reports of children's science learning. *International Journal of Science Education, 13*(3), 217–226.

Shapiro, B. (1991b). A collaborative approach to help novice science teachers reflect on changes in their construction of the role of science teacher. *Alberta Journal of Educational Research, 37*(2), 119–132.

Shapiro, B. (1994). That's not true, it doesn't make sense: A qualitative study of one students' views of the worthiness of scientific ideas. *International Journal of Qualitative Research, 7*(1), 19–32.

Shymansky, J. A. (1989). What research says about ESS, SCIS, and SAPA. *Science and Children, 26*(7), 33–35.

Smith, F. (1973). Twelve easy ways to make learning to read difficult and one difficult way to make it easy. In F. Smith (Ed.), *Psycholinguistics and reading* (pp. 183–196). Toronto: Holt, Rinehart & Winston.

Smith, L. (1978). An evolving logic of participant observation, educational ethnography and other case studies. *Review of Research in Education, 6,* 316–377.

Sneider, C., & Pulos, S. (1983). Children's cosmographics: Understanding the earths's shape and gravity. *Science Education, 67*(2), 205–221.

Solomon, J. (1984). Prompts, cures and discrimination: The utilization of two separate knowledge systems. *European Journal of Science Education, 6*(3), 277–284.

Stake, B. F., & Easley, J. A., Jr. (1978). *Case studies in science education.* Washington, DC: U. S. Government Printing Office.

Stead, B., & Osborne, R. (1979). Exploring students' concepts of light. *Australian Science Teachers Journal, 26*(3), 84–90.

Stead, B., & Osborne, R. (1980). *Light.* Learning in Science Project (Working Paper No. 23). Hamilton, New Zealand: University of Waikato.

Stockdale, D. (1976). *An assessment of shyness in children by teachers.* Unpublished master's thesis, Iowa State University, Ames.

Sutton, C. R. (1980). The learner's prior knowledge: A critical review of techniques for probing its organization. *European Journal of Science Education, 2*(2), 107–120.

Sutton, C., & West, L. (1982). *Investigating children's existing ideas about science: A research seminar.* Leicester, England: Leicester School of Education.

Swift, D. J. (1984). *Against structuralism: Is genetic epistemology a "conservative-activist" theory of knowledge?* Paper presented at the Tenth Annual Conference of the British Educational Research Association, University of Lancaster, England.

Thomas, M., & Hart, C. (1974). *Free to be you and me.* New York: McGraw-Hill.

Tillich, P. (1952). *The courage to be.* Glasgow: Collin.

Tobin, K., Briscoe, C., & Holman J. (1990). Overcoming constraints to effective elementary science teaching. *Science Education, 74*(4), 409–420.

Tough, J. (1979). *Talk for teaching and learning.* Schools Communication Skills Project: 7–13. London: Ward Lock Educational in Association with Drake Educational Associates.

Toulmin, S. (1960). Ideal of natural order. *Foresight and understanding: An inquiry into the aims of science.* Bloomington, IN: Indiana University Press.

Varela, F. (1979). *Principles of biological autonomy.* The North Holland Series in General Systems Research, Vol. 2. New York: Elsevier.

Viennot, L. (1979). Spontaneous learning in elementary dynamics. *European Journal of Science Education, 1*(2), 205–221.

von Glasersfeld, E. (1986, October). *Knowledge from a constructivist point of view.* Paper presented at the Moscow Institute for Systems Studies, Moscow.

Vygotsky, L. S. (1962). *Thought and language.* Cambridge, MA: MIT Press.

Wade, B., & Wood, A. (1980). Assessing talk in science. *Educational Review, 32* (2).

Waterman, M. (1982). *College biology students' beliefs about scientific knowledge: Foundation for study of epistemological commitments in conceptual change.* Unpublished doctoral dissertation, Cornell University, Ithaca, New York.

Watts, D. M. (1984, July). Learners' alternative frameworks of light. In B. Bell, M. Watts, & K. Ellington (Eds.), *Learning, doing and understanding in science* (pp. 69–72). Proceedings of a conference, Woolley Hall, England. London, SCCR.

Watts, D. M. (1985). Student conceptions of light: A case study. *Physics Education, 20*(4), 183–187.

West, L. (1982). What is the value of these studies? *Investigating children's existing ideas about science: A research seminar.* Leicester, England: University of Leicester.

Wheeler, A. (1983). Misconceptions in elementary science—A Kellyian perspective. In H. Helm, & J. Novak (Eds.), *Proceedings of the International Seminar on Misconceptions in Science and Mathematics* (pp. 322–327). Cornell University, Ithaca, New York.

Whitman, W. (1965). *Leaves of grass.* New York: New York University Press.

Whitty, P. (1963). Pupil interest in the elementary grades. *Education, 83,* 451–455.

Wilson, J. T., & Chalmers-Neubauer, I. (1990). A comparison of teacher roles in three exemplary hands-on elementary science programs. *Science Education, 74*(1), 69–85.

Wilson, S. (1977). The use of ethnographic techniques in educational research. *Review of Educational Research, 47*(1), 245–265.

Wittrock, M. C. (1974). Learning as a generative process. *Educational Psychology, 11,* 87–95.

Ziman, J. M. (1978). *Reliable knowledge: An exploration of the grounds for belief in science.* New York: Cambridge University Press.

Zimbardo, P., & Radl, S. L. (1982). *The shy child.* New York: McGraw-Hill.

Zylbersztajn, A., & Watts, M. (1982). *Throwing some light on colour.* Unpublished manuscript, University of Surrey, England.

Index

Alternative frameworks literature, 19–22, 31
Anderson, C. W., 20, 22, 27, 28
Andersson, B., 30, 31
Appelman, M., 21, 30
Audiotaping, 15
Ault, C., 20, 21
Autobiographical stories, 185

Bacon, Francis, 4
Bannister, D., 40
Barnes, Douglas, 34
Barrier phenomena, 30
Bateson, G., 6
Behavior of Mealworms: Teacher's Guide
　(ESS), 184
Benson, B. L., 106
Bertalanffy, L., 6
Beveridge, M., 40
Biographical stories, 185
Black, P., 27
Bloom's Taxonomy, 194
Brierley, C., 40
Briggs, H., 22
Briggs, J., 6
Briscoe, C., 188
Britton, J., 10, 34–35, 196
Brook, A., 22
Brophy, J. E., xvii
Brown, C., 17
Bruner, J., 35
Buber, M., 37
Butler, K., 16

Capra, F., 6
Case reports, 17–18, 47–157
　classroom, described, 38–40
　Donnie, 39, 41, 43, 47–75, 104, 163–164,
　　166, 168, 170–173, 180–184, 192–193
　and follow-up contact, 202–204
　introduction to, 43–44
　Mark, 76–92, 164–166, 170, 173, 179, 183–
　　184, 191, 192

Martin, 93–110, 164–168, 170, 173, 193
Melody, 108, 111–129, 164–170, 173–174,
　178, 193
　Personal Orientation to Science Learning
　　in, 162–180
Pierre, 143–157, 165, 166, 168–170, 173,
　193
　selection of students for, 38–39
Yasmin, 108, 130–142, 165–168, 173, 193
Cassirer, E., 34
Chalmers-Neubauer, I., 188
Change
　personal, and constructivism, 10–11
　in student ideas of light, 173–179
Child's Conception of the World, The (Piaget), 10
Cicourel, A. V., 22
Classroom Profile, 189–192
Claxton, A., 20
Collaborative approach, repertory grid tech-
　nique in, 36, 40–43
Color, 29
　and experiencing versus accepting ideas,
　　171–172
　misconceptions concerning, 27, 55, 80, 95–
　　96, 115, 134, 147
Colored light experiment, 84–85
Colton, R., 21
Concept mapping, 195–197
Confidence, 87–92
Constructivism
　case study approach in, 17–18, 47–157
　conception of science learning and teach-
　　ing, 198, 199
　epistemological features of, 7–8
　foundations of, 10, 17, 19
　key assumptions of, 181–182
　and knowledge, 4–6, 7
　and language, 33–36
　objectivism versus, xiv, 3–4, 8–9, 32
　Personal Construct Theory in, xv, 10–11, 16,
　　35, 36–38
　personal focus of, 200–204

Constructivism (*continued*)
  and Personal Orientation to Science Learning, 161–180
  premises of, xiv–xv
  study of, methodology in, 11–18, 38–40
  teacher as researcher in, xv
  traditional approach versus, xiv, 3–4, 8–9, 32
  using what we know about children in, 182–189
Conversations. See also Listening
  importance of, xix–xx, 11, 37–38
  in Personal Construct Theory, 37–38
  repertory grid technique in, 36, 40–43
Crookes, J., 25
Curriculum, learner's ideas in design of, 66–67

Desforges, R., 17
Dewey, J., xiv
Diaries, 195
Difficulty, 12
Doing What Scientists Do (Doris), 184
Donaldson, M., 17
Donnie (case example), 39, 41, 43, 47–75, 104, 163–164, 166, 168, 170–173, 183–184, 192–193
Doris, E., 184
Driver, R., 7, 20, 21, 22, 25–27, 28, 171
Duckworth, E., 187

Easley, J. A., Jr., 21, 22
Einstein, Albert, 6
Eisner, E., 18
Elementary school
  science learning in, xvi, 13–15
  student ideas regarding light in, 13–15
Elementary Science Study (ESS), 184
Erickson, G. L., 20, 21
Erikson, E., 20, 37

Feher, E., 25, 27, 28
Fensham, P. A., 21, 31
Fensham, P. J., 20, 173
Fetherstonhaugh, T., 25, 27, 28
Fisher, D. V., 3
Flexer, A., 21
Frankl, V., 202
Fransella, F., 40
Freire, P., 33, 34
Freyberg, P., 7, 21

Gadamer, H., 37, 38
Galileo, 5
Garfinkle, H., 22
Gertzog, W., 8–9
Gilbert, J. K., xiv, 20, 173
Goldberg, F. M., 28
Goldby, G., 25
Gowin, D. B., 183, 195, 196
Graphic organizers, 195–199
Greek Skeptics, 3, 4
Greene, Maxine, 161
Gregorc, A., 16
Gruber, H., 200, 202
Guba, E., 22
Guesne, E., 7, 25, 28, 30, 171

Hands-on instruction, 187–188
Hart, C., 172
Hawkins, D., 21
Helm, H., 20
Help, meaning of getting, 166–169
Hewson, P., 8–9
High school, science learning in, xvi, 12
Hobbs, E. D., 20
Holman, J., 188
Holt, J., 204
Home studies, 105–106, 153–157, 189
How Barn Owls Hunt (Payne), 185
Hueftle, S. J., xvi
Hurd, P. D., xvi

Inadequacy, student feelings of, 50, 57–67, 163–164
Independent science projects, 146, 184–185
Intellectual Growth in Young Children (Isaacs), 28
Isaacs, Nathan, 28
Isaacs, Susan, 28

Jan, Leslie Wing, 195
Jantsch, E., 6
Journals, 195
Jung, W., 28, 29–30

Kargbo, D. B., 20
Karrqvist, C., 30, 31
Kelly, George A., xiv–xv, 10–11, 20, 35, 36, 37, 107, 183
Knowledge
  in constructivist approach, 4–6, 7

constructivist versus traditional approach to, xiv, 3–4, 8–9, 32
and degree of participation, 10
Kuhn, T., 6, 7

Language
in case examples, 70–74, 172–173
in constructivism, 33–36
terminology in, 20–21, 172–173
Language of hypothesis, 35
La Rosa, C., 25, 30
Learner
concept of self as, 16, 163–165
in constructivist approach, 8, 9
Personal Orientation to Science Learning, 161–180
reflective approach of, 104–107, 140–142, 145, 177–179, 189–199
Learning styles, 16. See also Personal constructs
Leaves of Grass (Whitman), xiii
Lens experiment, 108–110
Light
books on, student views of, 56–57
feelings and experiences in study of, 55–56, 80–81, 96, 115–116, 134–135, 148
research on children's ideas about, 22–31
student idea changes concerning, 173–179
student misconceptions concerning, 23–28, 51–57, 79–81, 94–96, 114–116, 132–135, 146–148, 171–173
as topic of study, xviii–xix, 13
Light meeting surfaces, misconceptions concerning, 27–28, 54–55, 79–80, 94–95, 115, 133–134, 147
Light transmission and vision
addressing children's ideas on, 186–187
misconceptions concerning, 23–27, 53–54, 80, 95, 114–115, 133, 147
Lincoln, Y. S., 22
Listening. See also Conversations
focus on, xix–xx
student use of, 139–140
and trust, 37
Literature review, 19–32
alternative frameworks, 19–22, 31, 185
on children's ideas about light, 22–31, 185–187
on context of child's interpretive framework, 28–31

research paradigms in, 21–22, 32
terminology in, 20–21

Magoon, A. J., xiv
Mark (case example), 76–92, 164–166, 170, 173, 179, 183–184, 191, 192
Martin (case example), 93–110, 164–168, 170, 173, 193
Maslow, A. H., 37
Matthews, G., 17
Mayer, M., 25
McDermott, L. C., 28
Meadows, J., 27
Meaning frames, 29–30
Melody (case example), 108, 111–129, 164, 165–170, 173–174, 178, 193
Meyer, K., 27, 28
Minstrel, J., 20, 31
Mirrors, misconceptions concerning, 27–28

National Assessment in Science Project, xvi
National Center for Educational Statistics, xvi
National Science Foundation, 30
Navarra, J., 28–29
Newton, Isaac, 6
Nonspontaneous ideas, 35
Novak, J. D., 17, 20, 183, 195, 196
Nussbaum, J., 20
Nyberg, D., 9

Objectivism, constructivism versus, xiv, 3–4, 8–9, 32
Oldham, V., 12, 21
Openness to new ideas, 82–86
Osborne, J., 27
Osborne, R. J., 7, 20, 21, 30–31, 173

Paradigms
research, 21–22, 32
scientific, 6, 32
Paradigm shifts, 6
Parlett, M., 22
Participant-observation techniques, 36
Pask, G., 37
Patrizi, P., 25
Payne, Roger, 185
Peat, D., 6
Pencil-in-beaker experiment, 61–66, 70–72, 87–91, 98–99, 125–129, 175, 190, 191
Perceptual cues, 171

Personal constructs
  aesthetic orientation to learning, 117–120
  anxiety, 151–153
  confidence, 87–92
  Donnie (case example), 57–75, 163–164
  enjoyment in expression of ideas, 69–75
  enjoyment in hearing story of science,
    82–86
  inadequacy, 50, 57–67, 163–164
  interest in facts and details of science,
    149–151
  interest in ways of learning science,
    137–142
  involvement with others' activities and
    ideas, 124–129
  joy of physical involvement in activity,
    100–107
  lack of confidence as science learner, 120–
    124, 164
  learning science on my own, 153–157
  Mark (case example), 82–92, 164
  Martin (case example), 97–110, 164
  Melody (case example), 116–129, 164
  need for social interaction, 107–110,
    124–129
  Pierre (case example), 148–157, 165
  self expression through science, 97–100
  self-sufficiency, 86–87, 153–157, 164
  social-aesthetic orientation, 67–69
  task orientation to science, 135–137
  Yasmin (case example), 135–142, 165
Personal Construct Theory (Kelly), xv, 10–11,
    16, 35, 36–38
  conversation in, 37–38
  self-characterization in, 36
  trust in, 37
Personal Orientation to Science Learning,
    161–180
  in case studies, 162–180
  categories of idea changes in science,
    173–179
  and "getting help," 166–169
  ideas about nature of phenomena, 171–173
  interest in science outside classroom, 105–
    106, 153–157, 170–171, 189
  key ideas of, 180
  student images of science and scientists,
    169–170
  view of self as science learner, 163–165
  views and beliefs concerning, 162

  views on teacher role in, 165–166
Philosophical development, 17
Piaget, Jean, 10, 17, 19, 23–25, 35–36
Pierre (case example), 143–157, 165, 166, 168–
    170, 173, 193
Plato, 187
Pope, M., xiv, xvii, 20
Posner, G. J., 8–9, 20
Power, C. N., 22, 32
Prigogine, I., 91
Prisms, 130, 176
Pulos, S., 20
Purpose of knowing, in constructivist ap-
    proach, 8

Questions, 28
  student, encouraging, 194–195

Rakow, S. J., xvi
Ramadas, J., 25–27, 28
Reality, in constructivist approach, 7
Reflection of light
  refraction versus, 99–100
  student conception of, 73–74, 85–86,
    121–123
  terminology of, 172–173
Reflective approach
  questions in, 28, 194–195
  on small group interaction, 108–110,
    192–194
  of students, 104–107, 140–142, 145, 177–
    179, 189–199
Refraction, 61–66, 70–72, 87–91, 98–100, 125–
    129, 175, 190, 191
Repertory grid technique, 36, 40–43
Research paradigms, 21–22, 32
Rice, K., 25
Ritchie, T. J., 182–183
Rohrkemper, M., 106
Ronchi, V., 55

Saucer experiment, 61, 87
Schaefer, G., 20
Science learning
  changing views of, 6–7
  constructivist epistemological perspective
    on, 7–8
  creation of new knowledge versus, 4–6, 58
  elementary school, xvi, 13–15
  enjoyment in expression of ideas in, 69–75

existential view, neglect of, xvi–xvii
high school, xvi, 12
light as topic of study in, xviii–xix, 13
outside classroom, 105–106, 153–157, 170–171, 189
social-aesthetic orientation in, 67–69
student images of science and scientists, 169–170
student thoughts and feelings about, 47–51, 55–56, 76–79, 93–94, 111–113, 130–132, 145–146, 163–165
Science projects, 146, 184–185
Scientific knowledge. See also Knowledge
paradigms of, 6, 32
science learning versus, 4–6
Self-characterization, 36
of Donnie (case example), 57–58, 67, 69
of Mark (case example), 82, 86, 92
of Martin (case example), 97, 100, 107
of Melody (case example), 117, 120, 124
of Pierre (case example), 149, 151, 153
of Yasmin (case example), 135, 137
Self-sufficient learning, 81–87, 153–157, 164
Shadows and darkness, misconceptions concerning, 27
Shapiro, B., 20, 36, 40, 194
Shymansky, J. A., 187–188
Simons, H., 22
Small group interaction, 108–110, 192–194
Smith, E. L., 20, 22, 27, 28
Smith, F., 201
Smith, S., 27
Sneider, C., 20
Social construction, knowledge as, 5–6
Solomon, J., 22, 30
Spontaneous discoveries, 154–156
Spontaneous ideas, 35
Stake, B. F., 22
Stead, B., 30–31
Stengers, I., 91
Strike, K. A., 8–9
Sutton, C. R., 19–20, 20
Swift, D. J., 10

Teachers
in constructivist approach, 8
as researchers, xv

student views of, 86–87, 103–104, 165–166
Teaching approaches, 181–199
Classroom Profile and, 189–192
constructivist, key assumptions of, 181–182
and graphic organizers, 195–199
and home studies, 105–106, 153–157, 189
and small group interaction, 108–110, 192–194
and student questions, 194–195
using what we know about children in, 182–189
Terminology
literature review of, 20–21
of reflection of light, 172–173
Thomas, M., 172
Tiberghien, A., 7, 171
Tillich, P., 201
Tobin, K., 188
Tough, J., 194
Toulmin, S., 5
Treagust, D. F., 25, 27, 28
Trust, and listening, 37

Varela, F., 6, 37–38
Vicenti, M., 25
Videotaping, 15, 36, 193–194
Viennot, L., 20
von Glasersfeld, E., xiv
Vygotsky, L. S., 17, 35–36

Wade, B., 34
Waterman, M., 58
Watts, D. M., xiv, 20, 25, 28
Watts, M., 27
Welch, W., xvi
West, L., 19–20, 21
Wheeler, A., 20
Whitman, Walt, xiii, 200
Wilson, J. T., 188
Wilson, S., 17, 22
Wittrock, M. C., 20
Wood, A., 34

Yasmin (case example), 108, 130–142, 165–168, 173, 193

Ziman, J. M., 5
Zylbersztajn, A., 20, 27

About the Author

Bonnie L. Shapiro is an associate professor at the University of Calgary holding joint appointments in the Department of Teacher Education and Supervision and the Department of Curriculum and Instruction. She has been an elementary and junior high school teacher in the United States and Canada and has written a wide range of articles on science teaching and learning, receiving in 1989 a *Science Education* Paper of the Year Merit Award for research in Learning Studies. Recently Dr. Shapiro was honored by the Alberta Science Teacher Association with an Achievement in Science Teaching Award for "contributions to science teaching in the Province of Alberta." Her work with graduate students and practicing teachers has resulted in numerous collaborative classroom projects focusing on the importance of teacher knowledge of learners' ideas and approaches to meaning construction in science.